THE PACKER WAY

THE PACKER WAY

NINE STEPPING STONES TO BUILDING A WINNING ORGANIZATION

Ron Wolf
AND PAUL ATTNER

ST. MARTIN'S GRIFFIN
NEW YORK

Library of Congress Cataloging-in-Publication Data

Wolf, Ron Michael.
 The Packer way : nine stepping stones to building a winning organization / by Ron Wolf and Paul Attner.
   p.   cm.
  ISBN 0-312-19312-2 (hc)
  ISBN 0-312-24320-0 (pbk)
    1. Green Bay Packers (Football team) 2. Football—Coaching—Philosophy.
3. Management. 4. Success in business.   I. Attner, Paul.   II. Green Bay Packers
(Football team)   III. Title.
GV956.G7W65   1998
796.332'64'0977561—dc21

                                                                98-8576
                                                                CIP

First St. Martin's Griffin Edition: September 1999

10 9 8 7 6 5 4 3 2 1

For Edie, the wind beneath my wings

—RON WOLF

For Lucy, Diane, and Douglas, for their understanding, commitment, and love

—PAUL ATTNER

And to everyone who has ever been a Packers fan

Contents

Acknowledgments ix

Prologue *1*
Introduction *7*

1 **STEPPING STONE NO. 1:** Identify What Needs to Be Fixed *15*

2 **STEPPING STONE NO. 2:** Hire the Best—Before Anyone Else Does *41*

3 **STEPPING STONE NO. 3:** Develop an Obsession with Winning Today *69*

4 **STEPPING STONE NO. 4:** Play to Your Strengths *95*

5 **STEPPING STONE NO. 5:** Use the Four C's to Measure Performance *119*

6 **STEPPING STONE NO. 6:** Making It Work *147*

7 **STEPPING STONE NO. 7:** Keeping It Going *177*

8 **STEPPING STONE NO. 8:** Handling the Unexpected *211*

9 **STEPPING STONE NO. 9:** Staying on Top *235*

Epilogue *261*

Acknowledgments

For their help in putting this book together, the authors wish to thank Bob Harlan, Mike Holmgren, Mike Reinfeldt, Jeanne Bruette, and the rest of the staff and players who are the Green Bay Packers organization, for their dedication and professionalism; John Rawlings and Mike Nahrstedt of The Sporting News, for their encouragement and understanding; David Black, for his vision in molding the concepts behind the book and guiding us through its completion; George Witte of St. Martin's Press, for understanding the project's potential and for his decision to give it life; Dave Kindred, for his wise counsel; Terry Oliva, Lisa Slagle, and Bridget Collins, for their hours of proofreading and caring; and especially our families, Edie, Jonathan, and Eliot, and Lucy, Diane, and Douglas, for giving us the time and support to make it all possible.

THE PACKER WAY

Prologue

Brett Favre wasn't the best college quarterback I've ever scouted, just the most intriguing. I first became enamored with his talents in the fall of 1990, when I was director of player personnel for the New York Jets and Brett was a senior at Southern Mississippi. During a scouting trip to the school, I studied him on game tapes. He was big and powerful and had a presence that was immediately impressive. I was finishing my research when Thamas Coleman, the coach who took care of scouts at Southern Mississippi, called me over.

"You should watch tapes of him when he was a junior and wasn't banged up," Coleman told me. The summer before his senior year, Brett had been in an automobile accident. He required surgery and had 30 inches of his intestine removed. As a scout, you're always receiving tips. Most of the time, you dismiss them. Still, the tapes I had just finished reviewing were from Favre's senior season, when he wasn't 100 percent. So I decided to take Coleman's advice and look at more games.

I already thought Brett could play. Sure, he was raw and took the darnedest chances. But something about him kept bringing you back for another look. He had a great arm that enabled him to make every kind of throw, and more important, he could scramble out of trouble. And he simply was a fearless competitor. You could sense that in the way he carried himself. He just had to win. Whenever he played, the field tilted in his team's favor. Few players possess that ability.

After reviewing his junior year, it became more apparent to me he deserved serious consideration in the upper echelon of the draft. In those tapes he was healthy, and he was dangerous. Okay, maybe he didn't have all the athletic skills of John Elway, but he was more than a prospect. I was watching a very good player. Favre stood 6-2, weighed about 215, and had nifty feet.

He never backed down from anyone. He already was a legend at his school, which fielded a second-tier Division I-A team. Because of Favre's fearless ways, the Golden Eagles pulled off a series of upsets during his career, topped by a triumph over mighty Alabama in his senior season. They weren't good enough to win those games, but they had Brett. And he was the difference. I felt he could make a difference for the Jets.

As a manager, you never can overemphasize the importance of identifying and hiring great leaders throughout your organization. You might be a truly unique leader, but to make your company No. 1, that's not enough. You must fill your business with others who can work with you to reach your mission of producing a winner. I'm amazed at how frequently companies botch this essential element of success. As the manager of a football organization, I can't play quarterback and I can't coach. If I don't have strong people in those positions, we'll never be on top. So I better make it my No. 1 priority to find the strong associates I need. Instead, I constantly see people in my profession overloading themselves with responsibilities rather than infusing their operation with better leadership talent. They don't spend the time and do the research necessary to identify the right people for the right spots.

That's why I was on the road, visiting schools like Southern Mississippi, searching for potential great leaders who could elevate the Jets. I wasn't sitting behind a desk, writing memos and isolating myself from the daily fluctuations of my business. To be an effective manager, you need to remain energized and excited about your vocation. Once you back off and become too comfortable with your success, you risk failure.

For the Jets to become dominant in our profession, we absolutely needed an elite quarterback. It would be the same if I was the president of a computer company and realized my director of sales was ineffective. If I failed to find a replacement, we'd have no chance of winning. The Jets weren't as strong as we had to be at quarterback—starter Ken O'Brien was nearing the end of his career—and we needed to rectify the situation quickly.

I didn't see Brett again until a few months before the draft, at the East-West Shrine game. I was sitting with Dick Steinberg, my boss and the Jets' general manager. Brett already had enjoyed stand-out practices prior to the game, and he played even better that day. When he touched the ball, something exciting almost inevitably happened. He certainly wasn't your ordinary quarterback. We kept looking at each other and smiling. This guy was special. Originally, I thought he was a second-round pick. By the time we left California, I told Dick that Favre was the best player in the 1991 draft. He agreed.

Problem was, the Jets didn't have a first-round draft choice. We had surrendered it in the 1990 supplemental draft for receiver Rob Moore. When we put together our draft board, we had Rocket Ismail first, even though he already had signed with the Canadian Football League, and we put Brett second. But we knew he wouldn't last until the second round.

Still, as the first round unfolded, no one selected him. We were astonished. We really didn't care if the rest of the league disagreed with our assessment of Brett. Other teams thought he was too undisciplined and too wild. We believed he was not only a future starter in the NFL, but a potential star. Yet, he was slipping, choice by choice.

Maybe in my younger days as a scout, I would have wondered what was happening. Maybe I would have questioned my judgment. But not this time. An effective manager has to rely on his instincts, and my instincts with Brett Favre were strong and sound.

By the middle of the first round, Dick started calling around the league. We didn't have a selection until the sixth pick of the second round. Maybe he could work a deal so we could move up in the draft and grab Favre before someone realized what a bargain he was. As the first round wound down, the tension in our draft room grew. Dick worked very quietly, and none of us were sure what he was concocting. Then he told us the Phoenix Cardinals were interested in a trade that would give us the fourth choice in the second round. We weren't sure, of course, but we guessed that would be high enough to secure him.

It was getting exciting. There's nothing more satisfying in my business than to put in long hours and find someone special like Brett who wasn't being rated as highly by other league teams. He wasn't a sleeper, but he certainly wasn't viewed as a hotshot prospect. If we could select him, I thought we'd have a great draft, even after just one pick.

But at the last moment, Phoenix backed out. The player they wanted was still available early in the second round, so they didn't want to move out of the fourth slot. As we sat there helplessly, they made their choice. Then the Atlanta Falcons, a team we knew had some interest in Favre, took Brett. One pick before our turn.

When you've been in this business for as long as I have—I began participating in the draft process in 1963 as a rookie scout for the Oakland Raiders—you learn to absorb your disappointments and move on. That's how I worked, and that's how Dick Steinberg worked. But I was unhappy. Whenever you just miss a great prospect, it hurts.

Once a draft is over, I never look back. You do the best you can. You make decisions based on experience and thoroughness, and hope you're happy with the final results. But Brett Favre was hard to forget. You don't see many quarterbacks like him who are out-and-out winners. He was a legitimate difference maker. Every successful business needs these difference makers. And the more you hire, the better everyone around them will be. In my profession, I know this for sure: if you don't have a big-time quarterback, don't make plans for the Super Bowl anytime soon. I also knew if I ever had a chance to run my own team, Favre was the guy I wanted at quarterback. I wouldn't need consultants or study committees to do my research. I wouldn't need to watch any more tape or examine any more résumés. I already had done my homework. I knew my conclusion was based on sound reasoning, not guesswork. Not that I really felt I'd be in a position to obtain his services.

Still, a guy can dream, can't he?

Introduction

I like to win. No, I have to win. You know the cliché that when you play a game, someone has to win and someone has to lose? I agree, but only if the other guy always loses.

Away from football, I'm not obsessed with finishing first. That isn't important to me. But when it comes to my job, there's nothing that drives me more than the thirst I have for reaching No. 1. There's no satisfaction being second-best. None at all.

I know. I've learned what it means to fail. It was a tough lesson to absorb, but I think it's made me a better manager and I know it's made me a stronger person.

See, I'm the guy who put together the original Tampa Bay Buccaneers. We lost our first 26 games, which is still a record for the most futile opening by any expansion club in NFL history. Every one of those losses cut deeply into my gut.

But I'm the same guy who helped resurrect the greatness of the Green Bay Packers. When I became the Packers' executive vice president and general manager in November of 1991, the word was out: no one could win in Green Bay. Certainly the Packers, a relic from NFL Past, couldn't begin to think they could thrive against the league's mega-metropolises like New York, Chicago, Dallas, and Los Angeles.

That couldn't have been more incorrect. Together with team president Bob Harlan, coach Mike Holmgren, and an extraordinary group of players and staff members, we've proved the Packers not only can compete in today's sports arena, but they also can win. And win big. In five years, we went from league doormat to Super Bowl champions. In year six, we again played in the NFL championship game. What an incredible journey it has been.

We didn't do it overnight, but we never thought we would. The resurrection of the Packers came about through a methodical, focused approach that measured progress not by touch-downs but by first downs. Or, if I can borrow from baseball, by singles, not home runs. I joined the Packers knowing we wouldn't win a championship my first year, but I darn well ex-pected to win one sooner rather than later. Still, common sense has to prevail over hollow promises. Before you can realize your dreams, you have to deal with the reality of your situation and change it. Step by step.

That is the Packer Way. To prosper in business or in private life, to ultimately see your dreams of winning turn into success, you need to follow a simple but effective blueprint. *The Packer Way* is based on Nine Stepping Stones to Building a Winning Organization. These steps are your guides to the top. Follow them, and I'm convinced you too can realize your goals, profes-sionally and personally. And once you're on top, these steps can help keep you there.

Through experience—through the horrible days in Tampa and the euphoric times in Green Bay—I have fine-tuned the principles of realistic management. Believe me, I know what works—and what doesn't. You can profit from my mistakes and learn from my successes. This is about management under fire. These are concepts that have evolved from the day-to-day world of business, not from the pages of a textbook.

I'm sure of one thing. Too often, whether at home or at our job, we aren't patient. We want to be greedy and take giant leaps, instead of settling for shorter, more well-conceived steps. We want to be Babe Ruth, we want to be Joe Namath; we don't want to be Ty Cobb or Pete Rose. We want to triple our sales in a year, when doubling them makes more sense. We want to alter the image of our business, make significant personnel moves, and increase our production dramatically—and we want to do it now. Those goals are terrific—but the target date isn't. I'm impatient and demanding too, maybe the most impatient and demanding person you'll ever meet. Yet, I'm also realistic enough to know I must temper my impatience to allow the Step-ping Stones to function. You can accomplish change quickly.

But the improvements will hold up over the long term only if they're based on a solid foundation, not some wild dream. Too often, we want the glory without putting in the hard work needed to secure lasting success, whether it's building personal financial security or obtaining a top position in an organization.

It's only human. The big hit creates the big thrill.

But what about all the strikeouts in between? I'm not always right, and I'll never say otherwise, but I'm convinced of one thing: if you want to strike it rich quick, you'll fail. If you follow the Nine Stepping Stones—if you mix patience with methodical progress—you've given yourself a great opportunity to win your own Super Bowl.

I know. Like I said, I've learned through both the bitterness of failure and the extraordinary excitement of winning. The losing taught me some difficult lessons, but I'm sure that if I hadn't endured the turmoil of Tampa Bay, I would never have felt the thrill associated with the success of the Packers.

I came to Tampa in 1975 after working my entire football life for Al Davis and the Oakland Raiders, a span that covered 12 years. It was time for me to be on my own, to show the whole football world that I had the right stuff to construct a winner. You know that feeling. You've been an assistant manager for years and now you have the opportunity to run your own division of the company. Or you're on your own, starting a home business. You can't wait to implement all your innovative ideas. You can't wait to dazzle your peers. You've never considered failing. I didn't. I was prepared for some rocky moments, but I never expected it to be as bad as it became in Tampa Bay.

By the time I was fired by owner Hugh Culverhouse in 1978, I was ready to leave. The team was losing, and the front office wasn't running effectively. I always thought if you put in long hours, worked extraordinarily hard, and maintained an unchallenged loyalty to your organization, you absolutely had to succeed. After all, isn't that the American way?

I was wrong.

I gave everything I had to my job in Tampa Bay, and it still wasn't enough. I hadn't been smart enough going in. I was placed in a position of responsibility without the necessary authority. As soon as Hugh Culverhouse decided on my title, I probably should have known I could be headed for trouble. Instead of naming me general manager with total control over football decisions, I was called vice president of operations.

"You can work your way into being a general manager," he told me.

I had to prove myself to him. I have no problem with that— every day, you're really proving your value by your performance— but when he hired me, he should have felt more confident about my abilities. I was so happy about the opportunity that I didn't recognize Culverhouse's concerns. I soon found out that was a mistake.

A friend of Culverhouse had recommended that we hire John McKay as our first coach. McKay was the incredibly successful coach for the University of Southern California, and I couldn't quarrel with the choice. He had a great reputation and obvious skills. If we could lure him to Florida, it would be a significant step for the organization. I thought we could win with McKay; I saw no reason to oppose the decision.

But it eventually became the catalyst that drove me from Tampa Bay. And it was the start of a valuable management lesson for me. Even if you work 20 hours a day, your success is not guaranteed—not when your performance is being judged by the success of someone you didn't hire.

With the Raiders, we were all geared to one thing: winning. It was our first and foremost thought, the goal that drove all of us. And because of that, we all worked together to make sure we never discovered what it felt like to lose. We simply all had the same agenda.

I thought every organization worked this way. I soon learned how wrong I was. John McKay and Hugh Culverhouse were contemporaries. They both had served in World War II. They both liked golf and each other's company. They socialized together. I wasn't comfortable doing any of that. I don't play golf.

I work. Either I'm on the road scouting, or when I'm in the office, I'm studying tapes and doing whatever else I can to make my team a winner.

Soon, it became clear what was happening. I might have had a title, but I had no control. And that became a huge problem. My work ethic suddenly didn't matter. As the months went by, John McKay's power within the organization grew and my authority diminished. He had Hugh Culverhouse's ear, and I didn't. Forget what the organizational chart said; John McKay slowly gained control over football operations. There clearly was a separation of church and state and I was on the wrong side of the power structure.

It got to the point where Culverhouse felt McKay knew more than I did about player personnel, my area of expertise. So the Bucs no longer needed me. And I was gone. Later, I was replaced by a guy named Dick Beam, who began with the Bucs as John McKay's driver. That really hurt.

As a manager, you simply must have the final call over your area of responsibility. If you can't eliminate interference, you'll be undercut constantly. You'll never be allowed to function properly or with great confidence. You just can't be the boss in name only. You need authority to hire those working for you and the power to fire those who mess up. We've all seen it in our job: someone has a title, but all the major decisions affecting his area are made by someone else. He has no real influence in the decision-making process. Soon, everyone else in the organization recognizes his weakness, and his credibility is shot.

I learned something else from my experiences in Tampa Bay. As a manager, you must recognize your strengths and concentrate on them. Then hire others to shore up your shortcomings. Culverhouse wanted me to run the business side of the operation as well as the personnel area, and it was just too much. I found myself giving too many speeches and worrying more than I wanted to about the ticket office. Micromanaging doesn't work. Surround yourself with competent people who complement your strengths, then concentrate on what you do best.

If the Packers' trainer comes into my office to talk about an order for athletic supporters, I ask him if he's happy with the supporters we currently use. Then I tell him to order what he thinks will work best. I'm not an expert in that area, he is. I rely on his judgment. Something else: if he makes bad decisions or misuses my trust, he's gone. Immediately. Still, you need to delegate and then allow your people to show they can execute their jobs properly. You can't be afraid to let others succeed—or fail. If I was in charge of a private business, I would never insist that every piece of paper pass by my desk for my approval. If you lack that much confidence in your organizational leaders, I'm willing to bet your business will never achieve its full potential. One of the worst mistakes you can make as a manager is to believe you're so vital to the company's success that nothing can function without your input.

When I left the Bucs in 1978, I figured I had botched my final shot at running a team. The next season, the Bucs made the NFC championship game. The franchise was only four years old; no team had ever reached the title contest faster. And they did it mostly with players I had obtained. So I knew my tenure in Tampa hadn't been a failure, even though it was perceived that way. I wondered if anyone would give me a chance to prove I could do better.

I felt I was a failure at 40. I had wanted this opportunity for so many years, and now I was washed up, looking at finishing out my career as a road scout.

But I still could dream. I told myself that if I ever got another opportunity, I would do things differently. I would handle all personnel decisions with unquestioned authority. I would hire and fire the coach. I would hire and train my own scouts. I would form my own scouting system. I would involve all coaches in the evaluation of players.

I returned to the Raiders' personnel department in 1978, then moved to the Jets in 1990 when General Manager Dick Steinberg offered me a great opportunity to run their personnel department. After working so long for the Raiders, I needed a change. I needed to see how another organization operated. I went to New York believing it would be my final NFL move. If it didn't work out, we would stay in New York until our children finished high school—even if I had to find a job outside of football.

Then, in late fall of 1991, Bob Harlan called. Four years earlier, I had talked to the Packers about taking over their football operations, but the job didn't seem a good fit. They weren't ready to give someone full control. Bob, who became president of the club in 1989 after 18 years in the organization, eventually decided the Packers needed a major overhaul. Instead of having authority shared, as it was then, by the coach and general manager, he wanted one man to direct the football operations. He wanted me.

He offered me what I sought: absolute control over football-related matters. I have the authority to hire and fire coaches, trainers, equipment men, scouts, videotape people, you name it. I run the draft and I pick and sign free agents. I don't sell tickets. I don't have my own television show. Bob has shown incredible faith in me by allowing me to function without interference. He's my boss, but he's also my counselor and my friend.

Al Davis understood what Harlan and the Packers had done. He told me, "With the power you have, you're like an owner." In Green Bay, I focus on winning. None of my duties distract me from that purpose.

This is where our journey toward success begins. Before you can tackle the first Stepping Stone, you must be given the appropriate tools for success. I have them with the Packers; you've got to insist on having them too.

To utilize these Stepping Stones, you certainly don't have to be a sports expert or a sports fan. You don't have to know the difference between Brett Favre and George Brett. Whether we like it or not, professional sports now is a big-time business, and if we don't operate our teams like you would your own business, we won't make it.

Employing the Nine Stepping Stones to Building a Winning

Organization will prove fascinating and, I'm convinced, will make you a success. Like I said, I don't have all the answers, but I do have confidence in my ability to teach you how to be a better manager.

The Nine Stepping Stones should serve as a guide in your trek to the top. Obviously, you have to remain flexible and be willing to adapt to individual situations. But if you don't have a formula for success, you'll never make it. You'll wind up floundering. You'll wind up questioning your own ability.

If you embrace a plan like the one I'm about to outline, you'll have both structure and direction. I can't guarantee you a Super Bowl ring when you finish, but these Nine Stepping Stones will give you a chance to realize your ultimate dream. To be No. 1.

CHAPTER ONE

Identify What Needs to Be Fixed

Funny how life works. People tell me all the time how much they love the Packers. They tell me what a great job I have. They tell me how their children and wives and husbands and friends schedule their lives around Packer games. They tell me how they collect Packer souvenirs and memorabilia until entire closets are full. They talk as if this love affair with the franchise has always existed. They act as if the years between 1968 and 1991, when it wasn't very much fun being a Packer fan, never took place.

They may not remember that nightmarish era. But I do. In those years, Packer-related items were not No. 1 in merchandise sales within the NFL, as they are now. In those years, the Packers were not perennial Super Bowl contenders, as they are now. In those years, the Packers didn't regularly fill Lambeau Field, as they do now. In those years, you could travel anywhere in the United States and never see anyone wearing a Packer item. Today, virtually everywhere I go, I run into someone sporting a Packer hat or jersey. In 1991, you couldn't even find Packer stuff in Green Bay. I know. I tried.

I may have a great job now—and I do, the best in football—but in 1991, when I was hired by the Packers, I remember my football friends telling me I was headed for the Pro Football Graveyard. And that truly was what Green Bay had become. It was a dead end, both for players and administrators. I know what my friends were thinking—that I would be buried with the Packers, that I would become just another piece of frozen tundra. I might as well have taken a job in the Arctic.

The negatives of failure were littered everywhere in Green

Bay. No Packer from the 1991 team I inherited made the Pro Bowl. That club limped to 4–12 record, the nineteenth time in 24 years the Packers had finished below .500 since Vince Lombardi's last league title in 1967. The Packers wound up eight games behind the Lions, seven behind the Bears, and four behind the Vikings—and that was just in the National Football Conference (NFC) Central division race. The gap between the league's elite squads and us was enormous. Under coach Lindy Infante, we had lost 17 of our last 21 games.

In 1991, the Packers ranked nineteenth in actual per-game attendance, and they had 25,000 no-shows their last two contests. I soon realized the situation had reached such a crisis point that both the city and the organization were convinced their team probably couldn't be much better. And they had accepted it.

When I walked through the doors of the administrative offices in late November of 1991 as the new executive vice president and general manager, the Green Bay Packers were in as much trouble and turmoil as any franchise in the league. We were like a company with a quarter-century of lagging stock prices. Or a small business that had seen sales fall steadily, with no relief in sight. Or a person with constant debt problems who had watched his credit-card bill grow steadily larger, without a clue of how to stop the increases.

I try not to live in the past. Indeed, I pride myself on my ability to deal quickly with both the good and the bad and move on, rarely looking back. But I'll never let myself forget what it was like in Green Bay during that winter of 1991–92. It makes me appreciate what has happened to us since. But it also serves as a sobering reminder of what can result when business matters, whether personal or corporate, are not managed properly and intelligently.

We got the Packers started toward the top the same way you can and should begin fixing your business and financial challenges. By doing nothing.

Nothing, that is, but watching and studying and talking and

analyzing. In my first days with Green Bay, I took no dramatic steps, made no telling decisions, delivered no memorable announcements. I was determined to help turn the Packers into champions, but I wasn't about to undertake this challenge without a carefully conceived plan.

That's why I had no "game plan" when I walked through those doors. I could have made a splash by telling the media I was determined to turn things around within four or five years, but I wasn't interested in creating headlines. If I formed preconceived notions about what had to be done, it would be unfair to both Packer employees and myself. "Something" obviously needed to be resolved—this much failure over so many years is symptomatic of major organizational difficulties that can't be fixed with Band-Aids—but I thought it would be counterproductive for me to already have a blueprint in mind before I thoroughly understood the current situation.

I'm not an advocate of the Big Splash Theory. As you will see, I sometimes will do things that are designed to have a dramatic effect on the organization. But when you want to make things right for your business, and keep them right, the best and most logical step to take is . . . backward. Back away, whether you've inherited the problem or already are in the midst of turmoil. Spend your time searching for understanding.

The Packers wouldn't be where they are today if this pause to reflect, analyze, and understand had not been implemented. We're in a society anxious for quick solutions and immediate answers. But an effective manager has to fight those urges. No doubt, you'll feel a lot of pressure to speed up the process, whether it comes from the chairman of the board, a division president, angry speakers in a stockholders meeting, or a credit-card company threatening legal action. And it's only natural to want to quickly demonstrate your managerial skills where others have failed.

Still, the philosophy behind the first Stepping Stone to Building a Winning Organization can't be ignored.

Before offering solutions, you must identify what needs to be fixed. Or you'll risk never locking in the right structure that will enhance your enterprise over the long haul. As you'll see, I put together my action plan only after a methodical analysis of the entire Packer football operation. Once I felt comfortable with my study and had a well-grounded feel for the people and the atmosphere, I formulated my next steps.

I may be in the business of football, but I can identify with many of the problems encountered in the private and public business sector. After all, as much as it saddens me, NFL teams no longer are low-key operations existing for the love of the game. We are multimillion-dollar enterprises with the same fiscal entanglements and employee problems that every business encounters daily. Because of the nature of our game, I may have more means available than you to speed up the process of obtaining success. But the fundamentals I applied to remolding the Packers are solid principles that can be used just as effectively even if you aren't overseeing an NFL franchise.

Of course, what may be a sufficient period of time to study the Packers—I spent a month before making my first major move, the firing of Lindy Infante—may be far too much, or too little, to meet your needs. You'll have to determine what suits your situation best. But it's crucial that when you're ready to finish Stepping Stone No. 1, you don't feel you've rushed through the process. You never want to look back and say, "I was hasty, I could have used more time." Resist the temptation—and it is only human nature—to become an instant hero by arriving quickly at glittery solutions. I'd rather make this a marathon than a sprint.

Let me use those first months with the Packers as an example of what I mean.

I was fortunate. I benefited from the wisdom of Bob Harlan, the president of the Packers and my boss. Bob decided midway through the 1991 season that he no longer was comfortable with the way the club ran its football operations. At that time, Infante and Tom Braatz, the executive vice president of football operations, split the decision making. Neither had authority over the other. It was not a situation conducive to success. I understand, for example, that before the 1989 draft, they disagreed on the Packers' first-round pick. One wanted Barry Sanders, the other Tony Mandarich. The hierarchy above Braatz and Infante voted for Mandarich, a move that ultimately affected the future of both executives.

Bob Harlan thought there was a better way to do things. So he dismissed Braatz in November of 1991. He figured if he could hire a replacement immediately, the new guy would have time to study the operation before the season ended. It was a brilliant concept.

I was the Jets' director of player personnel when Bob called General Manager Dick Steinberg to request permission to talk to me. The Packers had interviewed me in 1987 to take over their football operations. That's when I met Bob, who was then an executive vice president. I took myself out of consideration because I didn't think the position gave me a chance to succeed. I wouldn't have had the power, authority, and freedom to truly run things.

But this time, things were different. The job he outlined met my every expectation. I would be in charge, and there would be no interference from him or the Packers' Board of Directors, which represented the stockholders in the unique ownership of this franchise. I would have the authority to hire and fire every-one in the football operations, from the head coach to the trainer to the scouts. We would be first-class all the way, and if I agreed to come on board, I would have a good chunk of time to analyze the 1991 Packers before the regular schedule played out.

I didn't waste much time saying yes. Bob had presented me an excellent opportunity, not only with the job description but also by hiring me when he did. I didn't have to rush to make decisions. I couldn't salvage the dismal 1991 season—it was too late for that—so I could funnel my energy into figuring out what needed to be fixed. And that's what I did.

I discovered much of what I needed to know by asking ques-tions. Sounds simple, but I don't think managers and business owners use this methodology enough. Too often, we believe we already know the answers, so why ask the questions? This is the "full-of-myself" attitude that leads to failure or, at the least, the incomplete fulfillment of a task. It's an attitude that comes from success. As we're promoted or as we gain power, we start thinking we're pretty darn smart; otherwise, why would my boss or my new employer like me so much? Once your ego takes over, your mind shuts down.

Or, just as telling, we don't ask questions because we don't want to hear the answers, whether it's because others might disagree with our thinking or because they may be critical of something we've done. I see this approach far too often from businesspeople. Instead of listening, they're doing the talking, making sure you know how important they are. They set themselves above everyone else, proclaim their greatness, and ride a desk while others do their work for them.

I'm not being modest when I say the following: I understand I'm not the smartest guy in the world. I have shortcomings and I'm certainly not an expert on many subjects. But I want to *learn* everything I can possibly absorb.

If you don't ask, you can't learn. It's that simple. So I'm always probing for information. I'm not much for small talk, never have been. I love to joke around with my friends, but most of the time, I'd rather spend five minutes in a meaningful conversation, where I can discover something, than waste 15 minutes schmoozing.

I also don't mind being told I'm wrong. By asking questions, you won't always hear good news, but at least you give yourself an opportunity to have your mind opened to new information, new approaches, new avenues. And that can only make you a better businessperson.

I read all my mail. Somebody may have an idea that I haven't considered, and it makes no sense to cut off a chance to be exposed to it. Fans often see things far differently than we do. The same could be said for stockholders who speak up at stockholders' meetings or people who write letters to corporate offices, usually to complain about a service. As a boss, you should want to know what others are thinking. It prevents you from becoming too removed from the real world.

This practice can be applied to something as simple as the family budget. If you keep track of the budget and never ask your spouse what he or she thinks of the allocations because you're afraid of his or her input, you're inefficient. Ask questions and make it clear you want an honest answer, not something designed to impress you. I realize that can be a difficult hurdle, because so many of us are afraid of offending people, especially the boss. But if you can establish this kind of open, honest rapport within your organization, you've increased your chances of succeeding.

I conducted my study of the Packers on two levels. I had to evaluate the player and coaching talent. But I also had to examine and analyze the support staff and scouting operation. I was particularly interested in determining the leadership that existed under me; the work ethic of the players and staff, and everyone's spirit and attitude. Making roster changes without also cultivating the proper atmosphere with our staff would cut into our ability to improve.

By the time I finished, I wanted to understand the training room, the equipment room, the video room, the scouting department, the coaching staff, and the players. I wanted to know how they functioned and why they did what they did. I just couldn't concentrate on the key members of my operation. To improve, you must make sure the entire organization, starting from the lowest-level position, is fulfilling its mission.

It takes work and determination to obtain a complete picture, but it's worth the time. I don't care if you have two employees or twenty divisions; it's inexcusable if you don't understand how they all function. That doesn't mean you have to be an expert—we'll deal with that problem in a moment—but if you aren't familiar with all aspects of your business, how can you ever presume to have the knowledge to recognize what needs to be corrected?

It was crucial to me to see how everyone performed under pressure. Being called into my office for talks supplied some of that pressure—after all, I was new and everyone had to be concerned about their job security—but I took it further. I purposely turned things up a notch by being demanding—by demanding answers by a certain time, by demanding something be done a certain way. Again, I asked questions, probing to see what people knew and how they functioned. I gave them a chance to have their say. But this wasn't about fear; I don't believe in running an organization using fear tactics. Instead, it's simply a matter of production—can you produce, especially under pressure? I don't care if it's sharpening a pencil or ordering a paper clip. Can you do it correctly, every time, no matter the circumstances?

I call it "stirring the pot." It was an effective technique at this stage of my evaluation process, and as you'll see later, it remains an effective technique as you strive to maintain the quality of your product.

People tell me I have an intimidating personality. I'm not sure I agree, but I know I can be forceful. I use this strength to help me discover how a person will react when I deliberately challenge him. I'll walk around the office and stir things up a bit. I'll move from person to person and ask a question or two. I want to see what people really know without the luxury of being prepared, and I want to see how my approach affects them.

Will I hear what they think I should hear? Or will they be honest with their answer? In the process I'm determining who I can intimidate and who I can't. Because if I can intimidate you, I probably don't want you working with me. By stirring the pot, you give yourself an incredible opportunity to understand the people who help make your business work.

This also is one of the best ways to convince people their opinion counts. If you give them a chance to take part in the decision-making process and either they don't participate or aren't forceful enough with their views, you can later use that as an example to them and everyone else about how the company suffered from their lack of assertiveness. It happens all the time in scouting. We look at a prospect and I ask for opinions about his ability. Someone will really like him but won't sell him well enough to convince the rest of us he's worth drafting. And then later, that player will turn out to be very good. My question then becomes, why didn't you take a stronger stand when you had a chance? The company could have benefited from your knowledge, but you chose a safer route to avoid having your opinion tested in the draft.

Apply that to your situation when someone wants to develop a new product, a new client, a different method of production, a new advertising campaign or even a different sign on the door to your camera store. Encourage them to take a stand and make a statement by challenging their knowledge. Just as important, if they're convincing, adopt their recommendation. Show your faith in them; let them prove their worth. If they don't think you're listening, they'll stop airing their opinions—and that possibly could impede the growth of your enterprise.

You also shouldn't give more weight to views based on whether they come from old or new employees—people you inherited or people you hired. I didn't join the Packers assuming I could improve the situation only if I dismissed most of the current employees and replaced them with "my" people. I committed that mistake in Tampa Bay. We were creating a team from scratch in Tampa, so I didn't inherit employees. But I knew, and felt comfortable with, many people I hired for key roles. Most of them disappointed me terribly. They didn't function as I thought they would, and I realized that I had placed my comfort level—I wanted to be surrounded by familiar faces who wouldn't have to be trained—above what was best for the company.

I came to Green Bay determined not to create a comfort zone for myself. I believe these zones enhance laziness, not innovation and energy. You become far too reliant on others instead of taking the initiative yourself and doing what you've been hired to do, which is lead. It's human nature, I guess, to want to be around people you know and like. But it's not always best for business.

It's far better to follow Dick Steinberg's advice. When I worked for the Jets, he told me that he saw no reason to eliminate inherited employees unless they showed they couldn't perform adequately. He also told me not to allow personality conflicts to become the reason for a dismissal. With the Packers, I wanted to make personnel decisions based on production alone, not whether the person had a wonderful smile or told funny stories.

Yet you always have those inherited employees who believe they aren't "yours" because you didn't hire them. One Packer employee kept coming into my office and complaining that, because he wasn't "my guy," he wasn't faring as well as he had hoped. I patiently explained to him I didn't care if he came from Mars; if he showed he could do his job, that alone would make him "my guy." It got to a point where I told Bob Harlan if I heard his complaint one more time, I would be forced to replace him. The visits stopped, so I guess Bob passed along the message.

Obviously, if you show preference to the people you hire, it won't matter how much you tell current employees they're not held in a lesser light. It's only human nature to like some employees more than others, but an effective manager can't demonstrate job-related favoritism.

As Dick Steinberg told me, if I didn't judge everyone on a fair and equal basis, I could foolishly drive an inherited employee from the organization without cause. I wanted to give every Packer employee, old or new, a proper hearing and a reasonable chance to remain with us. You establish what you expect from each employee, and then see how they produce. Those who don't contribute to the improvement of our product won't last, whether they have 15 years of service or 15 weeks.

If you're a new boss, you'll encounter resistance from present employees who will protest, "That's how we've always done it." That's only natural and doesn't bother me, as long as there's good reason for their hesitation. Sometimes, I could misread a situation in a new environment, and I should be told how I might have arrived at a wrong conclusion. I'm willing to listen to anyone's thoughts. But after hearing what you have to say, I'll make a decision, and then I want you to abide by that choice, even if you disagree.

At the same time, a boss must never say, "I don't care how it's been, we're going to do it my way now." I go back to what I said earlier. You must keep an open mind in your analysis. In other words, you can't rule out how things have been accomplished previously in the company. As you'll see later, I have some strongly held operating principles that always govern how I manage. But I leave room for modification and expansion of how I want things done. My challenge is to examine the previous methodology, weeding out the bad and keeping the good.

As much as possible, I want to avoid situations where people excel somewhere else after not receiving enough time with us to demonstrate their abilities. If you begin your staff analysis with an attitude that you might be surrounded by excellent employees who can make your organization better, you'll execute much more intelligent, less hasty personnel decisions. Maybe some current employees aren't in positions best suited to their talents, or maybe they have too many superficial duties that don't allow them to function properly. It's your job to determine their strengths and how they can best serve the business.

That's what managing is all about—putting the right people in the right positions, where they can use their strengths and not be hindered by their weaknesses. I'm not asking anyone to be an Einstein. I just ask them, once they are in the correct spot, to strive to perform at their best. That's the least any business can and must require.

If you have a good detail person who doesn't have an engaging personality, why would you want that person in a job that deals constantly with the public? Or if you have a mechanic who's very strong in one aspect of auto repair, why would you ask him to handle repairs in another area where he is not as proficient? If I'm more adept with numbers and my wife is better with concepts, why would I think she should balance the checkbook?

Yet companies repeatedly reward overachievers with promotions to leadership positions even though they possess no leadership qualities. He's our best salesman? Make him sales manager, ignoring the fact he dislikes working with other employees. It's misguided thinking that leads to bad business.

Likewise, I can't emphasize the following enough. In the process of making changes—and even after your operating principles are established—never, ever stand up in front of your employees and say, "This is my operation and this is how we're going to do it. Period." If you do, you'll shut down the lines of communication. You'll send a message that what they think and say really doesn't matter because you'll do it your way no matter what. Your business will only be as strong as its ability to tap into the strength of its employees—and if you eliminate communications, you can never fully utilize their abilities.

Besides resistance, change also creates a sense of resentment. As the implementer of that change, I can't possibly be viewed in a loving light. I understand how terrible it can be to feel uncertain about the future, and a good manager tries to take this emotional roller coaster into consideration. To make it easier for everyone, be as decisive as possible with your decision-making. Figure out what you're going to do, and let everyone know as expeditiously as possible. Otherwise, you risk paralyzing progress.

I also would never use study committees or consultants to help me in my analysis. Employing either would have been a major mistake for the Packers, and it would also be a major mistake for your operation.

Study committees are a frivolous waste of time. They're a method used by managers who are afraid to make tough decisions. They convey a weak message: I don't want to shoulder the blame that will result when I sell off that division of our company or reduce the staff or close a store, so I'll lay it on the recommendation of my study committee. By relying on study committees, you're unnecessarily extending the decision-making period and you're cutting into your own credibility by letting others do your job for you. Besides, committees frequently present compromise proposals instead of what's exactly right for the company. Don't use them.

Same with consultants. All they ultimately do is substantiate what they're trying to sell you, which can be anything from a future service to a point of view. How do I know what they're recommending will work for me? It's somebody's opinion, based on what? This isn't their business. They really don't understand a doggone thing about it. Why should someone ask my employees questions and study my operations when I should be doing all that myself?

Let's say I wanted to strengthen the way we go about drafting. The last thing I would do is hire one of these so-called draft experts as a consultant. They write about these players and appear on television and talk about them, but how have they formed their opinion? Have they been there with NFL scouts during the year, using a stopwatch, measuring the players, studying tapes of eight or nine games on each athlete? Or did they more likely look at a few highlight tapes and become an expert? I don't want any part of that.

We ought to be able to improve our situation without the need to lean on a crutch, which is what study committees and consultants become. If we have a problem in an area of my expertise, I have confidence that I can solve it. If the problem involves something I'm not familiar with, I would educate myself quickly. My phone becomes my consultant. I ask someone I trust, someone who doesn't have an agenda. These are professional contacts I've established over the years. In my case, I know trainers and personnel guys and video guys and equipment guys who I can call for advice. If I don't, I know someone who can recommend a source for me. I would talk to people that I really respect and who've been in the business for a long time, and let them guide me.

Take the man who runs my equipment room, Red Batty. I needed someone for that position and Mike Holovak, who has been in pro football since the 1940s as a coach, scout, and front-office executive, told me Red was the best I could find. He also said Red wanted to work for me. I didn't need any more candidates. If anyone knows this business and what makes it work, it is Mike Holovak. And Mike was right. Red is a gem.

Funny, when I first came here, I didn't like what I saw in the equipment room. Things were messy, and that was unacceptable. Our players spend hours around that area, and it should be neat, well organized, and pleasant-looking. I let it be known I was unhappy. Now, the equipment room is as spotless as any place in our complex—because I hired a guy who keeps it that way.

In my evaluation of the Packers, I met frequently with Lindy Infante. I came away impressed with his sincerity and dedication. But his on-field results weren't as eye-catching. Other than one winning season in 1989, his four years with the Packers had produced mediocrity. The 1991 team was even worse than the poor 1990 squad. In talking to him and watching him work, it reminded me of what I learned when I headed operations for the Tampa Bay Bucs from 1975 to 1978. Because he put in so many long hours and gave so much of himself to his job, he thought that meant he was succeeding—that he was owed something because of his conscientiousness.

But long hours and caring about your job don't always result in success. It's far better to make sure you use your time wisely. Mike Holmgren purposely doesn't require from himself or his staff the 20-hour workdays that seem so prevalent these days around the NFL. This coaching staff has produced admirable results, yet they work sane hours. That's because Mike and his coaches utilize their time correctly. They manage their schedule well, they have a consistent routine, and they have a good grasp of knowing when they're thoroughly prepared. Then they go home. Infante worked longer hours, but accomplished a lot less on the field. He thought his devotion would produce victories; it didn't.

I turned up the pressure on him a bit. When I was hired, we had four games left on the 1991 schedule. I brought in some free agents for tryouts. They were good enough to help the team, but Lindy resisted. Despite the losing, he was comfortable with his current roster. I knew immediately we would have trouble working together, since he didn't embrace my style of aggressive management.

I'm not saying my way has to be right, but it's a style I believe in. And it's the style I would use to improve the Packers. So my key leaders had to buy into it or we could never straighten things out. To be a top-notch manager, you must have a style that's both effective and consistent, not one that changes on whim. And you'd better surround yourself with employees who can understand and flourish under your management philosophies. Lindy and I were not a good fit and I knew I had to replace him.

That was one of the first major conclusions I had reached about the Packer organization. A few weeks into my study, I also realized we didn't function in an atmosphere conducive to realize our potential. In fact, we were bogged down by an atmosphere that almost guaranteed a continuation of failure.

To say I was astounded by what I saw is an understatement. My entire previous work experience had taught me that winning was the only thing that mattered, yet the Packers were finishing off a horrible 4–12 season and the prevailing atmosphere was, inconceivably, as pleasant as could be. No one really seemed concerned, no one reflected a sense of urgency. Having spent most of my career with the Raiders, I had learned that anything less than winning was failure. But not with the Packers. Losing had become acceptable.

I wanted to see angry people. I wanted to see people upset with the situation. I wanted to see people appalled that the Packers weren't more competitive.

Instead, I saw people who were content to be working for an NFL team, and a city content that it had a franchise, even if it wasn't among the league's elite.

This was an organization encased in the Malaise of Excuses. Nothing should anger a manager more than having a business where excuses, not performance, become dominant. You've heard the alibis. We can't grow because others have more advantages than we have. We can't produce the best widgets because other companies have more money or more employees. We can't be the best because we're located in the wrong part of the country. We can never overcome our No. 1 competitor because they have more power and influence than we have. We can't make proper investments because we can't afford a financial adviser. We can't start our own business because no one will loan us the money.

Talk about these reasons enough and they become a company's mantra. They guarantee failure because they convince an entire organization that, no matter how hard we try, we're going to flop anyway.

It's the business version of a self-fulfilling prophecy. It's a malaise that infects every element of the operation, affects every employee, and casts a spell over the present and the future of the enterprise.

To accommodate the Malaise of Excuses, companies become comfortable with where they've evolved instead of being angry with their failures. Otherwise, they couldn't function amid all the alibis. I'm not saying you have to be No. 1 to consider yourself a success, but the moment a business and a boss stop trying to improve and stop striving to reach the top, the organization is destined to wallow short of its potential.

The Packers certainly didn't lack for excuses. Even before I arrived, I had heard some big ones. The rotten climate was to blame. The out-of-the-way location was to blame. I soon uncovered others. The inability to compete financially with the big-city franchises. The lack of media exposure. The uninviting racial makeup of Green Bay and its suburbs, which was predominantly white. The handicap of being a second-tier franchise in a small town that was unattractive to the league's stars. So it doesn't matter how hard we work and how much we care, the result usually will be the same. Maybe an occasional winning season, but to come close to duplicating what Lombardi pulled off in the 1960s, well, it isn't worth dreaming such foolishness.

The result was a lack of urgency. The fact they were the Packers was enough for both the community and the organization. This was a team headed for a 4–12 record, but it didn't seem to matter. Mediocrity had become acceptable. In 1987, when I was preparing to talk to the organization about running its football operation, I evaluated the players. The best one was tackle Ken Ruettgers. When I was flying into Green Bay in 1991, I took a yellow pad and drew columns. I had one for all-pro, another for star, another for starter, another for backup, another for can't-do-it, and so forth. I wanted to find out how much I knew about the current team. I put too many players in both the can't-do-it and need-information columns. They had too many athletes whom I hadn't considered seriously as draft possibilities for either the Raiders or the Jets. My evaluation of the current roster produced another startling result. The best players were Sterling Sharpe and Ruettgers. In four years, they had added only one more star.

Yet the coaching staff thought it had a good team that was just a few bad breaks from excelling. There was no fear of failure haunting anyone. Instead, when you visited the practice field, you felt you had entered a country club. Mistakes were tolerated. No one demanded a high level of performance. Wherever I looked, the mediocrity had become as routine as eating macaroni and cheese once a week for dinner. Everyone was polite and nice. The staff did their jobs—and then they went home every night promptly at five-thirty.

Oh, we lost? Well, too bad. We'll try to do better next week.

I found that to be revolting. This wasn't about macaroni and cheese and happiness, this was about success. The Packers didn't really have any long-range goals requiring excellence. I remember a game early into my tenure in Green Bay. We were ahead something like 35–0 when our tight end, Jackie Harris, dropped a touchdown pass. I really got upset. The people sitting around me didn't know how to react to my anger. They obviously thought I was crazy to become agitated with a 35-point lead. But I'd been involved in games before where teams have rallied from similar deficits, so I'm convinced no advantage can ever be large enough. You can't let down your standards and accept mistakes, no matter the circumstances.

The people within the organization were terrific individuals. They were genuinely good people and they cared about the team and the community. You liked being around them. But so much of what I'm talking about is how you perceive your job and profession. What they wanted from the Packers and what I wanted—and was determined to have—were different.

In the first game after I took over, the Packers were leading Atlanta by 14 points. But we made two huge mistakes in the fourth quarter and handed the game to the Falcons. That loss followed a pattern similar to most of the other defeats that season. I arrived early in my office the next day, anxious to see the reaction. I didn't observe any great sadness, either from employees or in the newspapers. The stories reflected a common theme: the team would be okay if it weren't for those darn errors. No one wanted to deal with the harsh reality that unless losing became repulsive to everyone, the winning would never start. Someone had to stand up and say, "Mistakes no longer will be tolerated. No exceptions. And if you keep making them, you're gone."

Look around your situation. Examine your operation for complacency, for a sense of satisfaction, for a lack of determination. The mind-set should be one of ambition, of striving to be better, of desiring to excel. The elements of failure can be everywhere— employees flaunting rules, reporting late for work, leaving early, spending too much time complaining and gossiping. I'm not advocating an emotionless, unfriendly atmosphere. Just the opposite. I cultivate a relaxed operation with a minimum of rules. But we don't tolerate country-club situations. We don't find errors acceptable. There has to be a purpose in what you do, and that purpose has to be understood and embraced by everyone in the organization.

I wasn't in a mood to fail when I came to Green Bay. And you should never accept failure either, not in any form. I won't let people or the culture or the atmosphere or history or lack of expectations bring me down. This is the essential attitude you must establish first before you can improve anything, whether it involves your company, your financial life, or your job status.

It also wouldn't matter if I was overseeing the Packers or managing a corner store. If you want to develop the edge you need to ultimately produce excellence, you have to introduce specific operating principles.

You need to strive for a smooth operating situation in which decision making seems natural and seamless instead of halting and inconsistent. If your philosophies of management are communicated correctly, no one should ever be surprised by your actions or the way the company evolves.

You need to develop a feeling of harmony in which everyone believes they've helped produce success.

You need to develop a business without deadwood—whether that means eliminating unnecessary employees, unnecessary layers of management, or unnecessary divisions and products. One of the worst mistakes a company can make is to undertake too much, and do none of it well, rather than focusing on a few areas and make those the best they possibly can be.

You need to put the company first over anything else. If priorities are different in your situation, you'll never be as good as you want. This means instilling an obsession within your business that dominates the landscape. In the process, you must eliminate the "I have a job and I'm happy" mentality that eats away at productivity.

By the final game of the 1991 season, I was convinced I had a good handle on the team itself. I had spent hundreds of hours sitting before a big screen in a room next to my office, watching tape of each player. The franchise had a great videotape collection, one of the best I'd ever seen, and I was able to review virtually every play and every practice over a six-month period, starting with training camp. It was an enormous undertaking, but I felt I owed it to the players and the franchise.

I broke down the team just as you would any company—section by section, department by department. I was pleasantly surprised by some of what I discovered, but I also soon realized the huge task that lay ahead. We were more competitive than our record indicated, but we were far from being very good. We had a core of talented players who could carry us and make us presentable while we went about improving the overall quality.

Instead of wreaking wholesale havoc on the roster, I concluded we could make selective changes. My intention was clear. Keep the players I respected the most, give them as much help as possible during the ensuing off-season and, at the same time, begin adding younger players who eventually could step in as their replacements and dramatically raise the quality of the product. It was a two-tiered approach—a Stepping Stone approach—that would allow us to be competitive soon while also setting the stage to get much, much stronger in the future.

I still had to decide how we should handle free agency. A modified free-agency system called Plan B was still in effect, but it was evident we soon would be dealing with a new world of free agency in the NFL, where a decent number of quality players would become available on the market—players good enough to improve our situation immediately. I wasn't sure if the Packers would become high rollers once free agency was instituted, but it seemed likely. It certainly would give us an opportunity to upgrade our ability level more quickly than if we had to rely strictly on trades and the draft.

Of course, businesses outside of professional sports always have functioned in a free-agency environment, and it probably seems funny to many executives that free agency eventually would create an enormous fuss and furor within our world. If nothing else, the introduction of unfettered free agency gave me a clearer understanding of what businesses encounter daily in their efforts to improve their personnel.

Now that my month-long study was completed, I could begin putting together an action plan that I would follow to improve specific positions on the roster. I had to prioritize the needs of our team, so I could avoid a helter-skelter approach where you blindly attack a bunch of weaknesses without ever deciding which is the most important. This shotgun method might help stem the lack of progress over the short term. But without a well-conceived, prioritized plan, you aren't ensuring the long-term stability and growth of the enterprise.

Our most glaring problem concerned quarterback, where we were woefully inadequate. Don Majkowski, the established starter, had never fully recovered from a shoulder injury, which took away the zing in his arm. Nor could he take the pounding anymore. I thought we had backup quarterbacks, not big-time starters who could win a title.

Tight end was in better shape with Ed West and Jackie Harris. A definite plus. Other than Ruettgers, the offensive line didn't have any big names. But guards Rich Moran and Ron Hallstrom and center James Campen were decent veterans who could buy us time as we rebuilt. Tony Mandarich, the right tackle, was the second player picked in the 1989 draft. Because of how high he was selected, I hoped he could become a good player.

We needed a big-time running back. This was a major area of concern. Receiver Sterling Sharpe was a Pro Bowl-caliber player, but he was all we had at that position. Chris Jacke was a quality kicker, a real strength.

The Packers had been running an offense that revolved more around the pass than the rush, and I didn't think we could be successful either in our climate or in our division employing that approach. We had to get tougher and more physical, and we had to run the ball better. In three of Infante's four years with Green Bay, the Packers averaged less than 100 yards a game rushing. Only two other times in the franchise's history had the team been below 100 yards. In the last 33 games under Infante, no individual back had rushed for 100 yards. I thought guard Billy Ard got it exactly right when he said after one game, "There is zero atmosphere of domination there."

I also kept returning to the attitude problem that overshadowed the whole team. Players thought they were doing well. Yet many didn't exhibit the work habits they needed to make them successful, or for that matter, they really didn't make the sacrifices necessary to improve their skills.

There's a huge difference between playing well enough to stay in the league and playing well enough to win. Just showing up is not enough, not at this level. I didn't see the dedication or the commitment I wanted. For both traits to emerge, we had to develop more effective team leadership, both on the coach and player level.

In your situation, eliminate those employees who are trying to survive instead of trying to improve. You don't want an office full of people doing only what it takes to preserve a paycheck. They work against everything you hope to accomplish. You must educate your staff so members understand the proper work ethic and ambition you expect.

Much like our offense, the defensive unit presented a mixed picture. The linebacking corps was impressive. Johnny Holland, Tony Bennett, Brian Noble, and Bryce Paup were quality players who gave us a foundation on which we could build. But, except for cornerback LeRoy Butler, the secondary was a disaster. I was impressed with the toughness of the two safeties, Chuck Cecil and Mark Murphy. They were both heroes in Green Bay, but they didn't have the speed to play at a high level.

That was a team-wide problem. The Packers lacked speed almost everywhere and without it, we had no chance of challenging for a title. I knew I eventually had to deal with the situation at safety. If we had to replace Cecil and Murphy, it would create a lot of local controversy. But a good manager must make difficult decisions and absorb the resulting criticisms. So often, we don't want to offend anyone or risk unfavorable publicity. However, as long as you always put the company's welfare first, you'll be motivated to do what's right, regardless of the reaction.

The defensive line had a bunch of hardworking, highly competitive guys. But they were overachievers, not exceptional athletes. We had to obtain bigger, more dominant linemen. The roster also lacked depth, and we needed more reserves who had the potential to become starters and stars.

Every rebuilding situation is faced with a list of problems as lengthy as the one I was contemplating. You can react one of two ways. You can stare at all the needs and wonder how you'll ever get them fixed. Or, more intelligently, you can accept the fact everything won't be solved overnight. Then you can methodically prioritize your solutions, knowing all the while that patience becomes paramount in these circumstances.

I came away from my study convinced that, at best, we were a .500 team. I needed to upgrade our quarterback and our secondary; those were the two glaring concerns. I refused to set a goal for the Packers in 1992. It didn't serve a purpose to announce, "We'll be .500," either privately or publicly. I truly never gave our short-term future a thought. I just believed strongly that if we followed our Stepping Stone approach, we would keep improving everywhere until we moved to the level we sought. We would bring in Player B and see if he was better than A. If so, B would stay. Then we'd bring in C and see if he could shove aside B, and so forth. We also would mix in draft choices. Player acquisition was my strength, and I knew I had to uphold my end before the Packers could realize all of our dreams.

Still, before anything substantial could be accomplished, I first had to resolve the Infante situation. It's never pleasant to fire anyone—if it doesn't trouble you, you've lost touch with your emotions—but I knew that Lindy wasn't the man I wanted to help reshape this franchise. On the way home after we won our final game of the 1991 season, beating the Vikings in Minneapolis, 27–7, I decided to let him go.

The next day, I went to Lindy's office. It wasn't a lengthy discussion. There's no reason to prolong such occasions. I told him I appreciated his dedication and loyalty to the organization, but I wanted to move in another direction. I'm sure he didn't agree with my assessment, but he was gracious and, as always, a gentleman.

I later addressed the team. If looks could kill, I would have been a dead man. The players knew things would never be the same. The free ride was over, the country-club atmosphere was gone, and now, performance would determine their future. The standards of the organization had changed. If that bothered them, good. Things needed to be shaken up. Mediocrity no longer could be acceptable. They no longer could feel secure within the Malaise of Excuses. It had to be different in Green Bay, and this was the day the new approach would begin.

I gave a brief speech, ended by saying "Go Packers," and left.

The analysis period was over. It was time to move to the second Stepping Stone: Hire the Best—Before Anyone Else Does. We needed new team leadership, and we needed it badly. During the months following the 1991 season, that would become my quest.

But first, here are the prominent points you should remember from Stepping Stone No. 1—Identify What Needs To Be Fixed:

• Carve out an extensive block of time to analyze all aspects of your enterprise before taking any steps to improve the situation. Never rush so much that later, you regret decisions made in haste or without complete knowledge of your problems.

• Don't depend on consultants or study committees to make decisions for you. Instead, rely on your own analysis and the input of trusted friends who have expertise in the areas within your organization that need fixing.

• Avoid preconceived notions about the organization or its employees. Don't automatically assume that employees of a business that's struggled are incapable and should be terminated.

Establish a consistent standard that allows everyone—inherited employees and new hires—to be judged the same way.

• Avoid establishing comfort zones in which you depend too heavily on people you bring into the organization instead of making sure you force initiative and progress.

• Constantly ask questions and don't be afraid of the answers. The only way to obtain the information you need to allow you to make proper decisions is to keep an open mind and maintain a relentless curiosity. Never adopt the attitude that because you have reached a certain professional status, you now have all the answers.

• If something needs to be fixed and you aren't an expert in that particular area, call someone who is and tap their knowledge for advice before proceeding. It's not a sign of weakness to seek help in areas outside your expertise.

• Test performances by applying deliberate pressure. Use the "stir-the-pot" technique to determine whether people will give you honest opinions or replies deliberately crafted so they won't offend you.

• Expect resistance and resentment to any changes, and deal with both attitudes by making decisive decisions concerning organizational direction as soon as possible, then move on.

• Eliminate the Malaise of Excuses that undermines any underachieving situation, no matter the size. Make it clear you no longer will tolerate the use of excuses as a rationalization for lack of production and progress.

• Exhibit a style of management that is both consistent and effective, not one that changes on whim.

• Once you finish your analysis, institute general operating principles that will guide the organization and implement a specific action plan that will govern the initial steps you must take to make improvements.

CHAPTER TWO

Hire the Best—Before Anyone Else Does

I read extensively about leaders and history. The subject fascinates me. We talk about leadership all the time, but what exactly is it? Why is it that someone who graduates No. 1 in his class at West Point might never become a successful general, yet Ulysses S. Grant, who was something like forty-eight in a class of forty, can develop into a military genius? Grant was this little man, very undistinguished. Stonewall Jackson wasn't very striking either. He would sit on a horse sucking a lemon and wouldn't talk to anyone. Still, people went through hell for him.

Why do people follow Stonewall Jackson or Jeb Stuart or even George Custer, for God's sake? Here's a lieutenant they made a brigadier general by mistake, and yet people were incredibly loyal to him. Imagine watching Abe Lincoln riding a horse and seeing his legs dangling almost to the ground. He was tall and gaunt and incredibly awkward. Yet he was so far ahead of his time it was unbelievable.

It can't be charisma. Chuck Noll is not charismatic, but he won four Super Bowls. John Madden's outgoing personality is as different from Noll's as you can imagine, yet John was very successful too. It has nothing to do with size or weight or the sound of a voice or education. History's great leaders have no common backgrounds, no common traits that are obvious on the surface—except they have somehow made *something* happen and inspired others to follow them. Leaders create a bond that encourages people to believe in them so much they're willing to buy into their words.

During my time with the Raiders, I got to know John Madden very well. But I also developed a friendship with Chuck Noll and being around him was a very good experience for me. It was during the mid-1960s, when Chuck was an assistant with the San Diego Chargers and then the Baltimore Colts. He was scouting college prospects when we met. It was intriguing to me how he would deal with people who asked him about pro and college players.

"Hey, Coach, what do you think of so-and-so, pretty good, huh?" another coach would ask him. I would have expected some sort of diplomatic reply, but that wasn't Chuck. If he didn't like the player, he would say bluntly, "I don't think he's that good." Boom. That stopped all the dancing and white lies. I thought, "That's not a bad approach. Why do I have to sit here and tell a guy that someone looks good when I know he doesn't?" It was a trait I liked, and a trait I wanted in any coach I hired.

Here's something else I try never to forget. I was watching the History Channel on television one night and they did a piece on George Custer and Marcus Reno, his chief lieutenant. Research showed that even though Custer is portrayed as the one who created the big mess at the Little Big Horn, Reno contributed to his downfall. Reno didn't follow his orders properly and failed to support Custer as designed. If Reno had been in proper position, Custer might not have been routed. It was a classic example of not having solid, reliable leadership in every essential spot.

As a manager, it's crucial that even if I can't figure out why someone can truly lead, I still better be able to determine who can successfully help me direct my organization. If I don't have the proper instincts to recognize leadership, I'm never going to fulfill my goals for my company.

If you're involved in a business of any size, it's obviously impossible and foolish for you to try to do everything. So your future success becomes inexorably linked to the leaders you hire to function under you. Your strength and will can only achieve so much. Without great complementary leadership around you, you're leaving yourself vulnerable. Finding and hiring top leaders is an incredibly important process that will give life to everything you want to accomplish. Yet, I'm convinced many bosses haven't worked hard enough to develop a feel for great leadership, nor have they prepared themselves well enough ahead of time to identify leaders they might want to hire. In the rush to select the best leaders possible, these managers risk losing out to more prepared peers.

Stepping Stone No. 2 sums it up succinctly. Hire the Best—Before Anyone Else Does. This may sound simplistic, but it's not. Because sometimes the obvious is also what's ignored the most. There are only so many great leaders available, whether we're talking about the sports business, running a computer company, building widgets, heading an advertising firm, or directing a fast-food chain. If you're in too much of a hurry and don't spend the time needed to get the leadership part right, you'll hire managers who aren't your first choices—and that will make it more difficult to succeed.

If your top manager leaves today, do you have a list, either on paper or in your mind, of potential replacements? If you don't have a ready list, you need to put one together immediately. If you don't have the authority to hire yet, you still should be thinking about the people you'd want working for you in case you obtain that power. It's too late to wait until you have been placed in a position of influence before mulling over potential names. What if one of your key employees dies unexpectedly or is incapacitated by a car accident? You need to have replacement possibilities readily available to avoid seeing part of your operation paralyzed by your inability to quickly alleviate the resulting void.

With the Packers, I had to fill two key leadership spots, head coach and quarterback. With some rare exceptions, teams in our sport have never become champions without top-notch leaders in both positions. I know, because I have studied our game's history. Most of the great coaches and quarterbacks we remember are notable because they've been champions. If you're weak at either position, you'll be forced to overcome difficult odds to win titles. It can happen, but your margin for error is so minimal that you can't afford any other major faults.

I'm a firm believer in learning from the past, and that wouldn't change even if I ran the McDonald's down the street. I would study how other franchise operations had done in the same neighborhood and in the same town, I would research shifts in population trends, and I would cultivate friendships with towns-folk, trying to determine what's worked and what's failed. I would attempt to identify similarities among both the successes and flops, and then work to duplicate the former.

I was confident we could fill the Packer roster with wonderful players and we could have a terrific staff of assistant coaches. But I was convinced that unless we truly found stars to become our quarterback and our coach, the Packers would never threaten for a championship.

I'm linking coach and quarterback together for good reason. You can't overemphasize the quarterback's importance. He has to be able to lead a team, he has to perform consistently, and he has to make the big play in the most critical times. The better that player becomes, the better chance the team has to win. So it is a no-brainer. What's the one position that can change the fortunes of your team the quickest? Quarterback. If you find a good quarterback, you can compete. If you find a great one, you have a chance to be great. But have an average one, and it's difficult to be more than average. And if he's poor, you're in deep trouble. Time after time, season after season, none of these certainties change.

It amazes me how many teams in our league try to compete without strengthening the quarterback spot. Maybe success isn't important enough to them to take the steps necessary to solve this one problem. But it was for me. When I was seeking a quarterback for my team, the Packers had no added advantage over anyone else in the league. We didn't have a pile of surplus choices or some secret bargaining chip. But I knew who I wanted and I was willing to give up one of my two first-round selections to obtain my goal. Amazingly, sometimes the reluctance to surrender a No. 1 pick can prevent a franchise from upgrading the quarterback position. It makes no sense to me.

Obtaining a quality quarterback is like hiring a sales manager with terrific potential and watching him grow and mature in the position. As he improves, he'll just naturally upgrade those around him. He'll be good enough to carry along the weaker employees and bring out the best in your more gifted associates. Your quarterback just as easily could be the night manager at your restaurant or the guy who runs your factory. The good ones will keep you even with or slightly ahead of the curve, but the great ones one will find ways to jump-start you into a much stronger position. Instead of settling for the good leader, make it your goal to find the potentially great leader. It'll probably take more work to locate excellence, but it's worth the extra effort.

My management style also makes it essential that I find a strong, extremely capable, independent person to serve as my key associate; in this case, the head coach. I'm opposed to micromanaging, that insidious approach where bosses absolutely want to know every detail of what's happening in their organization, have to sign off on everything and undermine the authority of their top assistants by interfering with and overriding both their decisions and the decision-making process. I'll discuss my feelings on micromanaging in greater detail in Chapter Five. But with regard to the coach, the worst mistake I can make is to think I should be involved in the daily supervision of the players and development of game plans.

As a boss, you must determine your strengths and concentrate on those areas within the organization. Then hire others to shore up your weaknesses. Don't try to be so good in so many things that you aren't a standout in any. Consider how a general contractor handles the construction of a building. He might maintain a specialty, but otherwise, he subs out the rest of the project to people who can deal specifically with the minute details. He doesn't have the time, or the ability, to do everything. If he tried, the workmanship wouldn't be as good, and it's doubtful the project would meet its deadline.

The same logic applies to my job. If I attempted to be general manager and coach, I couldn't do either as well as I would want—even if I was qualified to coach in the first place, which I'm not. The world is too complicated and sophisticated for any manager to be spread too thin. You can never think you're so valuable and irreplaceable that your stamp has to be on every one of your organization's movements.

I'm a personnel guy. My strength is in scouting, grading, and obtaining talent. If I executed those duties correctly, I could make a significant impact on the Packers' ability to become winners. I needed a coach who could take those players and turn them into a team. It was my responsibility to make sure the coach understood both my role and the freedom he would enjoy within my organization. He would be hired to do the best he could, without interference from me. I wouldn't be diagramming plays or sitting in on game critiques or participating in half-time discussions. That would be intruding on his territory.

It helped that Bob Harlan had done a magnificent job of defining where I fit into the Packer operation. There was a clear picture of my authority and what positions and areas within the organization fell under my jurisdiction. He eliminated any possible confusion, and he didn't include any responsibilities that I had to share with someone else. It was a huge change from what I had encountered in Tampa Bay, where my line of authority was never carved out properly and where many of the essential roles I was hired to fulfill eventually drifted from my control. If you're assuming a position of responsibility, you must have your power spelled out and your place in the organization must be clear to everyone else. Otherwise, you haven't eliminated the potential for major problems.

Bob's concept of my role was the one key element that allowed me to succeed in Green Bay. When he finished describing my organizational duties at my introductory press conference, there was no doubt I was fully in charge of football operations, could make any changes I wanted and would not encounter interference from anyone. No one would be challenging me or my decisions. Bob said fans had been confused about who was running this segment of the Packers. No more.

Once these lines of responsibility and authority are set, I expect them to be respected. If I encounter intrusions that undermine my authority and threaten my effectiveness, I'll quit rather than attempt to function within a weaker and redefined role. I tolerated that situation once in Tampa, and I won't make that mistake again. I was determined that no one within the Green Bay Packers would ever be uncertain as to what responsibilities fell under my jurisdiction and what ones fell to the head coach.

My search for a head coach and quarterback made my first months with the franchise into the most important I would ever face in Green Bay. I absolutely had to obtain the best coach and quarterback I could find. But, because I had spent a long time grooming myself for these moves, I felt I was well prepared to execute these decisions.

Let me tell you a story. The Packers are owned by stockholders, who select a Board of Directors to oversee the corporation. In turn, the board has a seven-member Executive Committee. Bob Harlan and I meet with this committee monthly. In one of our first meetings, I started as always by discussing our football situation. Now, you have to remember that the members hardly knew me. To them, I was just Bob Harlan's guy. So they were curious about my intentions—and they really paid attention to what I said.

I went over the team, position by position. When I got to quarterback, I told them that we had an opportunity to acquire an exciting player to fill that position. A lot of people in Green Bay still liked Don Majkowski, so hearing me say I thought we had a huge problem at that spot and that Majkowski needed to be replaced didn't thrill everyone in the room. Moments like that help me understand what it's like in businesses outside the

NFL, where managers have to answer to stockholders and be aware of public reaction. It's not like the Packers have only one owner and he's the only person that must be satisfied. The Board of Directors and its Executive Committee are representative of the public ownership of the team and there's a lot of emotion invested into this responsibility. You start messing with a popular player and it can cause ripples throughout the region.

As I continued my quarterback discussion, I became really animated. I told them not only did we have a chance to obtain a gifted player but also that this guy would be so good—and I'll always remember this—that he'll make people forget about any player who has ever worn a Green Bay uniform. I told them his number will become synonymous with the numbers of all the great players who had been Packers. I even told them he would wear No. 4, and he would be like what Lou Gehrig meant to the Yankee franchise. I felt very, very strongly about that.

Of course, after that kind of ringing endorsement, they wanted to know who I was talking about. When I said it was Brett Favre, you should have felt the silence and seen the looks. I explained he was a third-string quarterback for the Falcons, but he would be as good as it gets, even if he had done absolutely nothing yet in the NFL.

I'm not sure what they really thought. I can imagine some of them must have wondered if I had gone cuckoo. Here I am, practically putting Brett Favre in the Hall of Fame and he can't even carve out playing time for the Falcons. But they were being nice to me so they started to show some excitement too. They asked questions about him, and I'm sure my answers didn't provide much assurance. I could tell them all I wanted about how good he would become. But the cold facts were that Brett had proven nothing yet and was so lightly regarded by the Falcons that they apparently were willing to unload him. How good could he possibly be?

If Brett came to Green Bay and flopped, I know I was setting myself up for a huge fall. Still, I thought it was important that they understood we weren't being passive about trying to improve. I told them if we got Favre, we had a real chance to eventually move into the upper echelon of the league. I asked them not to talk about Favre outside the room, because if anything leaked out, it could jeopardize the trade. I heard later that they were impressed because it was the first time anyone in personnel had sat down and told them exactly what he thought.

But my talk with the Executive Committee went beyond making a dramatic statement to a room full of important men. I was informing them that I intended to treat the quarterback position with incredible importance. They soon would come to the same understanding about the head coach. My future in Green Bay would be determined ultimately by two people, Brett Favre and Mike Holmgren—Favre more than anyone because he has to perform on the field—and I saw nothing wrong with clarifying that situation with everyone.

Managers aren't helping themselves or their organization by being less than honest. Sometimes it seems preferable to be non-committal. But people are looking for you to provide decisive, strong leadership, and you can't fulfill their hopes by dancing around the obvious. If you don't have the guts to stand on your beliefs, I don't think you give yourself or your company a chance to maximize its potential. Your role is to give direction, and if you can't clearly define what's important to you and to your company, and then convey your feelings to those around you, you risk establishing a confusing atmosphere that hinders production and success.

I wanted to convey to this committee and to all our fans some sense that positive change was coming. I wanted to give everyone some sense that the losing would end and that things would be different in 1992 and beyond—different than they had been for the last 24 years. I wasn't about to exaggerate and give them false expectations. But I also didn't want to be so low-key that they thought I had no idea how to unravel the mess the Packers had become.

If you think you're right, why not say it? That's how you provide strong leadership based on reality, not whim. I'll never promise anything I can't back up, but I'll also never back away from speaking out just because I fear I may wind up being wrong. I give my best assessment based on the facts at hand. That's how you create a positive attitude.

From the first time I had scouted Favre in college at Southern Mississippi, I was drawn to his special abilities. He was not the best quarterback I had scouted, but the more I studied him, the more I felt he was unique. By the time he was eligible for the NFL draft in 1991, I was sure he was a first-round choice who could become a difference-maker in the league. Back then, I couldn't have projected what he's accomplished now in the NFL—no one is that wise—but even as a senior at Southern Mississippi, he stood out. When he played, he raised his team above its normal playing ability. He could make his teammates competitive in situations where they should have been out-classed. He was the major reason Southern Mississippi pulled off huge upsets during his career.

More than anything else, this is the trait I want in a quarter-back—the ability to instill in his teammates, when the task ahead of them seems impossible, the feeling that as long as he's playing, they have a chance to win. That belief elevates squads and allows them to accomplish more than they're really capable of. Inspirational leaders can have the same effect on your business.

I've seen quarterbacks who have wonderful physical abilities, yet never cross the threshold from good to special. It comes down to performance through example. John Unitas was a lot different than Terry Bradshaw, but they both won titles because they made the great play when they had to execute. I see quarterbacks as elite salesmen pursuing a deal. Can they close it when it comes down to crunch time? Lots of people can handle the small stuff, but the true leaders withstand the pressure and pull off the really big performances.

That's a leader. He performs when it is time to perform. No more lip service, no more hollow promises, no more words without substance. That's what leadership is all about.

That's what I saw in Favre in college, and that's why, when I was the Jets' director of player personnel in 1991, I had hoped we could put ourselves in position to draft him. We tried and failed, and he would end up being taken by the Atlanta Falcons in the second round. Ken Herock, one of my best friends in football, was running the Falcons' personnel department at the time, and I told him I would gladly exchange the two guys he had picked in the first round—Mike Pritchard, a receiver from Colorado, and Bruce Pickens, a defensive back from Nebraska—for Favre. I was convinced they had taken the best player of that draft. He was regarded that highly by the Jets.

When I joined the Packers, I can't say I immediately thought about trading for Favre. But I had never lost track of him. During the preseason of his rookie year, I watched a Falcons scrimmage against the Seahawks, and I thought he was outstanding the little he played. Even when he became buried on the Atlanta bench, playing behind Chris Miller and Billy Joe Tolliver, I didn't reconsider my evaluation of him. Then what I guess you could call football fate intervened.

The first game the Packers played after I was hired was against the Falcons in Atlanta. Long before kickoff, I was talking with Ken Herock. In our conversation, he mentioned that if I wanted to see Favre—he remembered Brett was a favorite of mine—I better take a look at him before formal warm-ups began because he didn't throw after that. It might seem like an innocuous remark, but in football terms Ken was sending me a message. Favre was available. I hadn't even brought up Favre's name. It was just two guys talking, but Ken wanted me to know what was happening with his team.

I was thrilled. I certainly didn't need any more encouragement from him. At that very moment, I just knew I would do whatever it took to bring Favre to Green Bay. He was so much better than anyone who played that day, and now Atlanta was basically handing him to me on a silver platter. I already was working a deal in my mind. I wanted to get him for a second-round pick, the same round in which he was drafted. But if it took more, I was willing to consider it. If they came to me and said, "Give us a first," I would do it. I wasn't going to haggle unnecessarily with them. I would do nothing to mess this up.

It was really pretty funny. I'm in this new position, this is my first game, and wherever I move, television cameras are following me. That had never happened to me before, and I was uncomfortable with the notoriety. Now I have all these thoughts about Favre going through my mind. Yet I had to go about my business and stay under control. It wound up I didn't even get to see Brett throw. That didn't stop my adrenaline from flowing. There already was pressure; if I blew this, I would never forgive myself. It was like someone saying out of the blue, here is a check for $1 million. But you can't tell anyone about it for a month.

However, all of that would have to wait. I couldn't show too much interest too soon, and besides, the season had to play itself out. I told Bob Harlan we had the quarterback we needed, and I reviewed what had happened. I know it must have been a blur to him. In the four days since my hiring, we hadn't been able to spend any time together, and now I'm carrying on about how I have just solved our quarterback problem with a player he barely recognized, if at all.

I knew he certainly couldn't be overwhelmed by my news. I couldn't blame him; Brett hardly had an exciting NFL résumé. Yet, I will always be grateful that Bob never questioned my sanity or debated my decision. He supported my enthusiasm wholeheartedly.

I had to be intelligent in my pursuit of Brett. It was important that I act as if I wasn't sure I really wanted this guy. After all, he wasn't playing, and that alone should have dampened my enthusiasm. Deep down, I didn't care one whit about what the Falcons thought about Favre. Brett had been having a great time in Atlanta, partying and not training very hard, and that's not good. But even that wasn't enough to change my mind. I asked for tapes of him from practices and preseason. By now, we had a new coaching staff, and they looked at this material, which wasn't very impressive. The coaches were lukewarm about trading for him, but I wasn't swayed.

This is what I mean about a manager having the courage of his convictions. I could have taken the safe way, I guess, and either not pursued the deal or assumed a strong position with the Falcons and refused to give up an attractive draft choice. If I had adopted either stance, no one on my staff would have thought I had made a mistake. I was convinced, though, that Favre had the ability to become a star. I wasn't being stubborn; I was just reflecting the instincts I had developed during my years of experience in personnel. Sometimes you just have to pursue what you think is right, even if it's a minority opinion.

I also didn't spend a lot of time making phone calls trying to determine what others might have thought about Brett. It's okay to solicit recommendations, but you never want to make choices based more on the feelings of outside sources rather than your own instincts. You can't set up excuses and escape routes, such as "I really didn't want to hire so-and-so, but jeez, he came so highly recommended I couldn't pass him up." That's the first step toward failure.

Once you allow safe choices to become more important than relying on your instincts, I'm convinced you'll be a less effective manager. Aggressiveness and self-confidence have to remain the strongest traits of your decision-making process. This applies whether you're determining the best stock to buy or a new line of business to add to your company or a new assistant manager to hire. If you have prepared yourself properly for your current position, you already have developed a feel for what's right and wrong. Now that you have the responsibility you've been seeking, why back away from those feelings?

That's another reason why it's a mistake to turn to consultants, search committees, or, as happens so much these days, headhunters. Resorting to any of these alternatives demonstrates to me you haven't put in the time or the research necessary to be a successful leader. Using these outside sources says to me: I need to fill a pivotal spot in my company, yet I have so little knowledge of my business world that I have to rely on someone else to find competent candidates.

It's management by fear, not feel—fear that you aren't good enough or smart enough or sophisticated enough to do it right, so you get someone else to increase your odds of success. It's lazy management. You don't want to invest the time needed to identify the potential standout leaders in your profession.

In a later chapter, I will discuss my feelings about why you need to maintain an "edge" in your enterprise. But one way to dampen the atmosphere of progressiveness and enthusiasm that a successful business needs is to begin taking a conservative route with your decisions. If you don't keep pushing, it's foolish to think those under you will keep striving as aggressively either.

Now, don't get me wrong. I'm not saying you should isolate yourself from the input of others. Just the opposite. So-called "networking" is a must. Otherwise, it's impossible to know the developments in your professional world that could affect your future. It's not a matter of having a network. It's more a matter of when you tap that network.

The way I handle networking is simple. I have developed a few confidants over the years who will tell me the truth, won't sugarcoat their information, and understand why I'm seeking the material I need. I reiterate what I said earlier: if you want answers, you have to ask questions, even if the information you receive might be unpleasant.

I'm on the phone frequently, checking in, seeking, probing, trying to reduce or eliminate surprises. I never want to be in a situation where I don't know a player is available or a trade is about to be made, just as you should never be surprised about a change in your line of work. I use the network to anticipate the future, not scramble to catch up to what's already taken place. If I hadn't established a relationship with Ken Herock, which in turn led to constant player-related conversations, I never would have known as quickly about Favre's availability.

Keeping on top of what's about to happen takes time-consuming persistence. You can't waste any of those valuable minutes gossiping. I see no benefit to you or your enterprise to pass along rumors, just for the thrill of being in the know. It's all a matter of priorities. I don't think gossiping serves you or your company well, and that's sufficient enough to make it off-limits. What I want is input that will help me perform my job better, and that's the only reason I network.

Recommendations garnered from your networking should aid in helping you formulate a list of potential candidates for positions, but they shouldn't become the sole determining factor of who you hire. If someone I especially respect says I should hire so-and-so for my coach, I would consider that endorsement very seriously. That's because I know he wouldn't give me an endorsement just to get a friend a job or hand off someone to me that he no longer wanted working for him. I would trust him to have my best interests at heart, not his.

But I still would rely much more on the thoroughness of my research. If I make a mistake in the hiring process, it could cost me my job. So I can't bail out and depend on what amounts to allowing others to do my work for me. Instead, I have to execute a complete interviewing procedure. Perhaps a confidant recommended a candidate who isn't compatible with my personality or my business priorities. Or, as I see so often, someone is hired on the basis of his reputation and résumé, not his performance. You might find out, if you dig hard enough, that it's an undeserved reputation, that his performance has never been acceptable. Just because the person might have worked for a Fortune 500 company doesn't mean he's an automatic hire.

You can't be dazzled by a candidate's pedigree. It should never cloud an examination of his production. The way baseball managers bounce around is a great example of rewarding failure. They can't win with one team, yet they are hired again and again by others. It makes no sense. These are classic examples of executives being too lazy to obtain the answers they needed before making decisions. It's easier to say, oh yeah, that person worked for a great company or that person has a master's from that school or that person managed before, so he must be qualified.

And so what if he was completely wrong for his previous position? Do your research, do your interviewing, then rely on your instincts.

I played the negotiating game with the Falcons for a few months in early 1992. Then it came time to finish the deal. We had started off willing to give up a third-round choice. By now, it had dropped to a second-round pick. One day, they said the trade could be made if I would surrender a first-round selection. I quickly said, "Yes." I knew that offer was coming, because if I had been in their position, I would have done exactly the same thing. I have to think they were shocked with my answer; they probably never expected me to agree, certainly not that soon.

I didn't care if people thought I overpaid for Brett; remember, here I was surrendering a first for a guy who had been drafted in the second round and then had disappeared on the bench. But if Favre was as good as I thought, a first-round pick would be a minor ransom to pay. I braced myself for an incredulous reaction from the local media, all the while convinced we had taken the one major on-field move necessary to make our rebuilding project work.

By the time I obtained Favre in early 1992, the coach I thought we needed to improve both our team leadership situation and our football skills already was on the payroll. To many, Mike Holmgren presented almost as big a gamble as Brett Favre. Since he'd never been a head coach in the pros or college, his ability would be questioned until he won. Coaching at this level is a complex and demanding job, and it always looks easier than it really is, even to assistant coaches who have spent years studying how the No. 1 guy fulfills his requirements.

A head coach in today's NFL is much more than a coach, just as a boss of a company today is much more than a businessman. The demands generated by stockholders, the public, the media, and societal pressures don't allow any of us to concentrate solely on what we love best, our immediate work responsibilities.

Like managers in the private sector, coaches have to deal with problems in the labor force caused by drugs, alcohol, financial strains, family differences, and other personal matters. They're conscious of customer/fan unhappiness, and, in many situations, they're aware of the need to pump their product so people will purchase the commodity—in our case, tickets. Any coach who says he's unconcerned about these factors isn't being honest. It's no longer possible to isolate yourself and hide behind x's and o's. In this era, coaches who do a poor job dealing with off-field aspects of their job have a difficult time succeeding.

What I wanted in our head coach was simple to describe but hard to find. I wanted an unquestioned leader who clearly was sophisticated enough and strong enough to take control of our situation and shove it in the proper direction.

I wanted an offensive-minded coach. By studying the game over the last decade, I was convinced that teams with head coaches who knew offense best had emerged as the most consistent winners.

I needed a coach who was anxious to work with young players and could develop them, because I knew so much of our success would depend on our ability to groom inexperienced athletes to become starters.

Most important, I needed a coach who would bring a certain aura of winning to Green Bay, so the players could look at him and be convinced he was right when he said, "This is what it takes to win."

No matter his qualifications, his credibility would depend so much on this kind of positive background. He could be an offensive genius, but if his former teams hadn't won, his players would always question the worthiness of his teachings. Eventually, he might prove himself, but I couldn't afford that kind of on-the-job training. I didn't have the time to allow someone to earn a reputation. His association with success had to be on his résumé now.

To find the right leaders to help run your business, you must take this focused approach. Seek winners. It gives you a broad umbrella that covers a spectrum of personalities and backgrounds, yet still eliminates the non-producers. Someone doesn't necessarily have to come from a major competitor or a significant company to be considered. If they've been associated with success even on a small scale, then they've seen what it takes to win. I look back at my years with the Raiders, even when I was a raw scout learning the trade from Al Davis, and realize how much it helped being around winners. You learn from their approach, from their decision-making rationale, from their demeanor under pressure. Plus, you develop a confidence in your own abilities that comes from touching success. And that's how a winning aura grows around an individual and an organization.

We didn't have that aura in Green Bay. We'd known so little success for so long that hardly anyone walked around feeling they knew how to make things better. My choice for a head coach would be a major step in turning around that attitude and starting a new feeling within our walls. To me, the hiring of the head coach would become a statement about our intentions for the future, so I absolutely had to get it right.

Just imagine the impact this kind of organizational change has on your employees. They'll scramble to find out every tidbit of information they can on the new person, and what they learn certainly will have an early effect on the new leader's efficiency. I'd prefer they obtain positive feedback from their network rather than hear negative reports regarding someone's reputation. I want them excited, not apprehensive.

I had a short list of coaching possibilities. They were people I had watched and followed, people that I had placed in the back of my mind, just to be prepared if I ever had an opportunity again to hire a coach. It would have been a colossal mistake on my part to begin churning out names *after* I was brought to Green Bay. You never want to scramble in a new situation. Instead, you want to anticipate and be prepared.

Two names quickly became associated with the job in the media. One was Bill Parcells, the other was Mike Holmgren. Those reports were accurate.

Parcells and I became acquainted through the years, and we

have become even better friends now. I like his honesty, his love of the history and integrity of the game, and his intelligence. He's one of the true coaching talents the league has ever known. But after winning two Super Bowls with the Giants, he retired because of bad health and became a television analyst. In late 1991, he was still out of coaching, but I thought he might be getting antsy in his new role. If I could hire him, his impact would have been immense and immediate; no one would question his ability to mold winners.

It all depended on Bill's desire to return. If he wasn't ready, we'd stop our conversations. If he wanted to come back, he would become a strong candidate for our job. Yet I never felt he would terminate his retirement. So it was imperative that I didn't confine my search to him. That would leave us too vulnerable in case he chose the broadcast booth. And that decision led me to Mike Holmgren.

I didn't know Mike very well—we would exchange greetings when we saw each other, nothing more—but I was very familiar with his coaching skills. The Raiders would play the 49ers in an annual preseason game, and, during his time as the San Francisco offensive coordinator, I became impressed with the way he coached his unit.

Frequently in these games, teams used their second- and third-line players. But it didn't matter with him. He could have a bunch of very average guys out there, and we still might be playing our first-string defense, but the 49ers always would move the ball consistently down the field. The caliber of player seemed inconsequential; they still gained yards. For example, he taught an average quarterback like Steve Bono well enough to be effective in their offensive system.

I had always been brought up in the business convinced that, when you hired a head coach, you concentrated on candidates with defensive backgrounds. Don Shula, Tom Landry, and John Madden were defensive guys. But that trend changed. Bill Walsh, Joe Gibbs, and Dan Reeves all became dominant coaches with an offensive background. And they all had been pro-level assistants under successful head coaches. Holmgren fit these "new breed" characteristics perfectly.

This change in my thinking was good for me. It taught me flexibility is important. We become so set in our ways that sometimes we get stubborn. That limits our managerial skills. Maybe what worked yesterday seemed just right, but today or tomorrow, the same solutions no longer apply. It doesn't do any good to convince yourself you know all the answers, and then stop watching and learning from what's happening around you.

Because I express my beliefs pretty strongly, I'm sure people get the impression that I'm stubborn. Yet if I was too stubborn, I couldn't survive in today's football environment—even though I'm not so sure what was wrong when we had only 33 players and 4 coaches and not all this specialization. Nor am I particularly enamored with our current free-agency system or the size of player contracts or the way we're all spending money. But I want to succeed in my chosen profession, so I have put all of those personal opinions aside and learn how to deal with the landscape as it's presented to me today. If I didn't, I would fail, and that's not an option.

Poor management stems from a lack of flexibility and an unwillingness to try to understand the changing trends in business. The worst thing any of us can say is, "Well, that's not how we did it in my day," even if you're absolutely, completely convinced that way was still better than what you see now. I never want to put on blinders, refusing to even examine what I despise. If you don't try to accommodate *everything* affecting your job, how can you possibly make an informed decision?

My first interview with Mike Holmgren convinced me I didn't need to extend my coaching search. Mike is a big man, about 6–4 and well over 200 pounds, and he fills a room with a presence that you can't manufacture. He has that Bill Walsh type of confidence where you feel he just knows what he does is right; that he never doubts himself for a second. That, in turn, produces a winning attitude. He's thinking, "I don't care if you're putting 22 all-pros against me, I'll find a way to play you hard and to beat you—because I'm smarter than you." His personality was far different from Bill Walsh's—he's much more outgoing and loquacious—but he had the same cockiness. It was refreshing.

Mike was also that off-season's coach du jour. It wasn't a matter of him being hired; it was just a question of what team would gain his services. During his time with the franchise, the 49ers were very successful, and his offense, expanding on a foundation established by Walsh, had become very sophisticated and very difficult to stop. It had gained the respect of every defensive coordinator in the league.

Besides, his pedigree was special. Over the last three decades, two men have had a huge impact on the passing game in football—LaVell Edwards of BYU and Bill Walsh—and Mike studied under both of them. He was BYU's offensive coordinator before he joined the 49ers. What I didn't know then, of course, is that he has the ability to take what he learned from them and make it even better, expanding upon it and giving defenses even more difficulty. That's what he would demonstrate with the Packers.

Fifteen minutes into our conversation, I was so impressed that I already wanted to hire him. His lack of head coaching experience didn't concern me. He was so confident he could succeed that I quickly forgot about that aspect of his career. We discussed in detail how he ran his offense and who he wanted as his coordinators. It was obvious he had prepared himself for this job possibility. This was an intelligent, thoughtful guy with strong beliefs and a background that gave him credibility. My instincts told me he had the traits to become an outstanding leader.

But I still felt it was essential to complete the interviewing process. Successful interviewing is designed to obtain certain answers that will either stimulate interest or serve as warning signs that this might not be the best person for the opening. I have put together a form containing mandatory questions. I keep the form in my desk, and I refer to it before the interview starts.

I want to make sure I ask every candidate the same essential questions.

The form evolved as I became more convinced it's crucial to do these interviews correctly and consistently every time. I must cover key elements or the whole process won't be as complete as it should be. When I start off an interview, I usually attempt to find topics that the person will feel comfortable discussing, like family. That's normally No. 1. I want to change what normally is a stiff, formal situation into a relaxed, productive atmosphere. I know how hard it must be to stay calm when your future might depend on this one interview, so I want to be as understanding as possible.

The rest of the interview branches off from those early minutes. What I'm trying to discover, more than anything else, is the candidate's ability to accept the parameters of the job, and his willingness to make the sacrifice it takes to do it right. Will the commitment I require be present?

You can interview yourself this same way when you are trying to solve personal financial problems. You'll find solutions only if you have the proper commitment and only if you accept intelligent parameters. Are you willing to invest the time it takes to start your own business? Are you willing to absorb the resulting restrictions on your life, including the lack of initial income and the limitations it will impose on your lifestyle?

Anyone, of course, can tell me they'll improve our situation and that they're willing to do whatever it takes to accomplish that goal. Then it becomes the same as picking a player in the draft. You cut through the bluster with your experience and instincts—the way they say it, the way they carry themselves, the way they react when you ask them something they might not have expected.

I don't ask inane questions, like what's your favorite flower or the last book you read. I want to know about their philosophies and approaches to various specific issues, and I want them to understand my feelings on those same issues. I ask job-specific stuff, not the idealistic probings of psychological tests. I already have done my research and background checks. I have talked to enough people who know this candidate to formulate a good feel for the person sitting in front of me. I have taken advantage of my network of close associates to get honest answers, not hollow endorsements meant to deflect or hide weaknesses. Before you sit down to talk, you should already be able to anticipate how the candidate will react in certain situations, how he will perceive himself, and how he will function in relation to other people.

With our coach, I wanted to know about his preparation. How quickly and successfully can he change during games to adapt to the unexpected? Does he maintain his composure or is he a madman, either in public or in the locker room? If he's baffled by the unexpected or if he explodes at every misstep, he isn't a good long-term investment. If pressure throws you, you can't be a winner. I want to know about his personal life, too. Even if I was running a company located somewhere else, it would be essential for me to learn about his private situation. But in Green Bay, I can't have a leader who has personal problems. If he does, they'll soon become community knowledge. I want to bring in quality people, period.

When the interview is done, I have to be comfortable with you as a person and confident that I can entrust you with the responsibilities of your job. Never forget that this person, along with everyone else you hire, will help determine whether you succeed, so you can't afford a mistake even with one new employee, particularly with leadership positions. If you spend too much time in interviews analyzing the candidate's business qualifications and neglecting his personality and ideals, you risk botching the hiring process.

With Mike, I felt it was essential to immediately establish what our relationship would be. I told him that as head of football operations, I wasn't out to do anything except make the Packers a success. I wasn't in it for the glory, and I didn't expect the head coach to function in my shadow. I would not be micromanaging his position. The last thing I cared about was notoriety or ego gratification. If we evolved into a championship-caliber franchise, all of us would benefit.

For this to work, the two of us had to function smoothly. This was our show, the coach's and mine, and we would either succeed or fail together. That appealed to him. Not having to deal with a lot of layers, not having a boss who was flamboyant—what else could a coach want, short of better players?

Mike also needed to feel comfortable with the city of Green Bay, which isn't a place for everyone. But he had a strong family foundation and strong family beliefs, and that's a great fit for the Green Bay area. If he yearned for the fast lane, we would never have had a chance. Fortunately, he liked what he saw of our region, and he was smitten with the history that surrounds the franchise. He has a love for the foundation of the game, just like I do, and we knew that if we could pull this off, we would be restoring the Packers to their proper place within the football ranks.

After our interview, he left Green Bay to visit a number of other teams. It was important that I deal properly with the ensuing days. I had to walk a line between putting too much pressure on him and not showing enough interest. I knew I had to let the other interviews run their course. It was good that Mike spoke with other clubs. It helped him understand what an ideal setup he would have in Green Bay.

I checked in with him pretty regularly. I didn't want him to think I was desperate, although I guess I was, because I didn't want to lose him. So I would tell him, "Hey, just wondering how things are going? I want you to know I understand what you have to go through before you make a decision." We would chat just enough for me to determine he still was interested.

Time had become a factor. If he talked to every club on his list, it might be up to two months before he came to a conclusion, and that was too long for me. I thought we needed a coach in place by late winter, before we started the final phases of our scouting process for the draft. I also didn't want to miss out on all the good assistant coaches who were now available. I conveyed these concerns to Mike, and I got word to his agent about the importance of a quick decision.

I never threatened them or told them that if he didn't decide soon, we would move on. I would never do that. I don't believe in deadlines. Maybe you can apply some subtle pressure—although I'm not very subtle—but never deadlines. What if you set a deadline and there's no decision and you really don't want to give up on the person? Why put pressure on yourself when you don't have to? You're the one who has the position he wants, so don't give him an out. Make him say yes or no. You should always control your situation and not surrender the power to someone else.

The waiting was difficult. Mike had the traits I desired in our coach. He was forthright, honest, and personable, and he came across with a sincerity and conviction that was really encouraging. He was goal-oriented and had a single-purpose approach that reflected my philosophies. He also left me with the impression he could lead men and turn them into winners. Don't ask me what exactly gave me that feeling, but it was there—and it was what this franchise needed.

If you have similar feelings about someone you have just interviewed, you'd better do whatever you can to make sure little things don't get in the way of the hiring process. You need to stretch your resources and your flexibility to find room for this person. The worst mistake you could make is to have something like travel rules or stupid job requirements thwart what would have been a positive move for your business. Don't risk losing a promising employee by quibbling over an extra $200—or $2,000 for that matter. It's essential for you and those under you who also have hiring responsibilities to always see the bigger picture and put the welfare of the company ahead of minor hang-ups.

It also can get tricky dealing with multiple candidates for a position. I was honest with Mike. I told him we also had talked to Bill Parcells, but in my opinion, he would not return to coaching. However, because of our friendship, I owed it to Bill to explore his candidacy. In our situation, Parcells's name was in the media, so Mike would have found out about him anyway. But I'm not afraid to be upfront with the people I interview. I'm not worried about scaring them off. They either believe they can do the job or they don't, so whether they're the first choice shouldn't matter. Instead, if they're hired, they should be determined to show we were wrong not having them No. 1 on the list.

This is when egos get in the way. If you're irritated by a pecking order, then I don't want to hire you. To me, that means you're not mature enough to handle the job requirements anyway, so I'm better off without you.

The key here is that everyone you're considering is a quality choice. Otherwise, you shouldn't be interviewing them. You never want to adopt a "just-fill-the-job" mentality. Once you've gone through the solid candidates, and still haven't hired anyone, then back off, regroup, and start over. You're selling short both your company and your own future by shoving someone into a position even though you're not sold on their qualifications.

I was feeling pressure with this coaching hire. I had to be right; I didn't have time to make a mistake and then correct it down the road. I believed Parcells was an alternate choice, but he was uncertain about what he wanted to do. Finally, he told me he wasn't coming back. When he gave me his answer, I had only one other guy in mind, Mike Holmgren. Marty Schottenheimer and I had talked at length about Bill Cowher, who was on his staff in Kansas City. Marty told me if I brought Bill in for an interview, I would hire him. He was that impressive. It never got to that. I wanted Holmgren, and the tension to sign him was building on me, even if I tried not to show it to anyone. I could feel it. Trust me.

I had even talked to Bob Harlan about the possibility of Mike turning us down. I told Bob that maybe we should consider hiring an interim coach, someone who could do the job for a year or two, which would give us time to identify a long-term candidate. I'm not sure if that's what we would have done. But it certainly was an alternative to staking the future of the franchise on someone I doubted could succeed.

After Mike had interviewed with the Colts in late January of 1992, I called him. "I want you to be our coach," I told him. "We need to work this out and make it happen." We talked, he came in, and we agreed to a contract. That's when I told him, "We're the only two people in America who can mess this up, just you and me. How many other people in football have this opportunity? Nobody."

With Holmgren, and then Favre, the Packers had the foundation in place to improve quickly. I might have been the only one in the early months of 1992 convinced that was true, but that didn't matter to me. I had brought fresh, intelligent, gifted leadership to the organization, and I had hired men who just as easily could have wound up somewhere else in the league. It was the kind of aggressiveness that I knew I had to display to be successful, and my hope was that the entire organization would be excited by our willingness to ignite the rebuilding process.

Now I was sure the Packers were ready to tackle the third Stepping Stone in our climb to the top. We needed to establish an obsession within the organization that would drive us to win immediately. But before we move on, here are the prominent points you should remember from Stepping Stone No. 2—Hire the Best—Before Anyone Else Does:

- Leaders in your organization should be hired on the basis of your own research and interviewing, not on their reputation or résumé. Develop a select list of candidates that reflects the very best who might be available for employment.
- Use the hiring of leaders to make a statement to your employees. Hire winners—those people with success in their background. Their tempo, work ethic, and enthusiasm will be essential in reinforcing the direction that you want the organization to pursue.
- Prepare a ready list of potential leaders you would want to

hire long before you assume a position of responsibility. It's too late in the process to wait until after you've been hired to attempt to identify the best available candidates.

• Prepare thoroughly for interviews. Compile and keep a list of mandatory questions that you ask of every candidate. Strive to determine whether you can be compatible in a work environment with the prospective employee.

• Hire leaders that complement your strengths, not those who duplicate them. You need to thoroughly identify your own role in the organization and clearly outline the proper delegation of authority and responsibility. Resist the temptation to micromanage.

• When hiring leaders, don't settle for the good ones. Spend the extra time and energy to find the great ones.

• Don't allow your hiring instincts to be muted by the opinion of others or by taking the "safe" route in decision making. Use networking to become aware of promising candidates and trends in your business, not to gossip.

• When making an offer, don't set deadlines and don't oversell the position. Don't let minor requirements and unimportant demands stand in the way of completing a hiring.

• Never adopt a "just-fill-the-job" mentality. Once you've gone through the solid candidates, and still haven't hired anyone, then back off, regroup, and start over. If you shove someone into a position even though you're not sold on their qualifications, you're doing yourself and your company a disservice.

CHAPTER THREE

STEPPING STONE NO. 3

Develop an Obsession with Winning Today

Winning must be your obsession.

Winning must be the obsession that drives your business.

Winning must be the obsession that determines every decision you make, that guides your thought process, that pushes you to be aggressive when everyone else is hanging back.

Winning is the attitude that gives you and your enterprise an "edge," that air of superiority and confidence that separates you from your competition and keeps pushing you to stay on top. It doesn't matter if you're involved in a multinational company or a corner franchise, you must develop this edge.

In football, measuring winning is easy. We have tests every weekend for 16 weeks. Anyone who cares can see the results and knows if we have succeeded or failed.

But winning is more than beating an opponent on the football field. It's an attitude that determines success or failure in every business and in every personal financial decision you face in life. If you don't think you can be the best, if you don't think you have the intelligence, training, and confidence to do it right, you'll never give yourself the opportunity to triumph.

From my years with the Raiders, when they were carving out one of the great success stories in sports, I knew how it felt to win. From my years with Tampa Bay, I knew how awful it was to lose. After going 0–26 and realizing the Bucs will always be remembered as the worst team in expansion history, I learned firsthand how losing eats into your gut and never really dissipates. Once I was exposed to the excesses associated with both situations—winning and losing—you become driven to do everything possible to avoid the despair of failure.

During my first months in Green Bay, I had been so involved in analyzing the football operations, hiring a coach, and trading for a quarterback that I didn't have time to attack the depressing attitude that hung over the organization. I knew eventually I had to address all the elements that contributed to this negative atmosphere: the belief that losing wasn't really awful; the belief that all the problems associated with having a team located in Green Bay perhaps made it impossible to be champions again; the belief that the country-club attitude that dominated the daily business routine was okay.

I adjusted my priorities after a conversation with Red Cochran, a former Lombardi assistant who was one of our scouts. We were watching tape of some draft prospects and he mentioned that Lombardi would have liked one of the athletes we were analyzing. Red's a great guy, but he's no diplomat. He tells you how he feels in blunt terms, which I really appreciate. I was curious about how it was under Lombardi. I was fascinated by his ability to win. That alone would have piqued my interest. But the fact he did it in Green Bay made my first question even more important.

"When he got here, how did he go about trying to build the Green Bay Packers?" I asked Red.

I will always remember what he said.

"He had only one thought, and it carried him through every day," Red replied. "He wanted to win, and he wanted to do it now. To Vince, anything else but winning today was unacceptable. He felt he was too old to worry about a program. He felt that was counterproductive. You start talking about winning three or four years from now, and all of a sudden, your thinking changes. You aren't pushing to win as hard and as soon as you should be. He wanted to win right away."

What he said made so much sense to me. We all talk about winning until it becomes almost a cliché. There isn't a coach or a business that doesn't proclaim that its goal is to win; it's the American Way.

But this was different; what Red was saying was better. If you don't demand immediate results, you're creating an atmosphere where less than the best is acceptable, where winning is some abstract goal that serves more as a public relations ploy than an actual quest. If you talk about four- and five-year plans, you've established an unproductive mentality. It gives everyone an excuse—well, we didn't meet our quota this month, but it's our first time under the new system, and you know, these things don't change overnight. Or I didn't get that contract signed, but we haven't been making calls on that company for long, so give it time and things will change. Or, we fumbled too much in the game, but it's just the first month under our new coach and everything is so new. And by the way, in four years it will be different.

But maybe it won't be—unless you're demanding immediate and uncompromising success.

LeRoy Butler, our great strong safety, understood what I meant. After I had addressed the team early in my tenure, he told the media he was impressed. "Ron was just like, 'Look, basically we're going to change this. We're going to start winning here. Regardless.' When I heard what he was saying and saw the things he was doing, I said, 'Now, there's a winner.' "

By emphasizing not only winning but winning today, you move everyone's thought process away from a general concept and direct it toward something substantial. It makes progress easy to measure. It makes everyone's performance easier to measure. It establishes a tempo for the organization, and it blows away any excuse about not understanding what our goal is and what I expect should be done to achieve it.

It also eliminates any thought that going backward first before you show progress is okay. Under no circumstances would I ever want to turn a bad situation into an even worse predicament by thinking that anything less than improvement is acceptable. That's why I would never dismantle a business under the guise of "starting from scratch." That's why I spent so much time analyzing the Packers. I wanted to identify our strengths as well as our weaknesses, so I could maintain those strengths and use them as a foundation to improve immediately. I would have been extremely disappointed if our 1992 record had been worse than 1991.

You should be in a hurry to be the best, and you should make sure this kind of tempo permeates every aspect of your business—and your personal financial life. This is the "edge" I mentioned earlier. What I want to see from my organization and from my own life is an attitude that won't settle for mediocrity, that feels any problem can be solved with enough hard work and enough intelligent thought, that takes well-grounded risks that could result in huge gains, and that never rejects a notion out of fear of failure. Call it an attitude with swagger.

Yet you see just the opposite every day, everywhere you look. You see people, businesses, and organizations content with their place in life, wanting to be better but afraid that the future might not be as pleasant as the present. So they do nothing except work to keep the status quo. They accept being less than the best. They put up with inadequate performance, using the excuse that "well, he may not be the greatest, but if we replace him, goodness knows what we might get instead." At least the poor performer is a known commodity, and that generates a sort of skewed comfort that eventually can produce only mediocrity. No one is thinking, if we make a change, we have a chance to get better.

I say, make the change because we *will* get better.

I see the cautious approach all the time in the NFL. Teams unwilling or fearful of making trades, of cutting players, of doing anything outside the conservative but accepted norms of well-established personnel guidelines that have grown up over the years. Clubs hide behind the lame lament that "we build through the draft" so they won't be revealed for what they are: afraid to be good. There's something inside me that couldn't tolerate being .500, yet there are franchises that have done nothing other than the ordinary for years, even when faced with still another .500 or worse season.

I walked away from my talk with Red Cochran carrying my own personal marching orders. The third Stepping Stone was in place. We would become obsessed with winning today.

In everything I did from that point on, I would emphasize winning today. And that meant everyone in the Packer organization had to have the same priority: the Packers had to come first, before anything else in their business relationships and decision making. Otherwise, we wouldn't have the focus we needed to produce a quick turnaround in our fortunes. It became my duty to convey this feeling to every employee—and make sure this "win today" attitude was universally adopted.

This is where your strength of character and firm convictions as a manager come into focus. I have certain personal guidelines that govern everything I do in my business relationships and decisions. Those guidelines became Packer guidelines. We needed to change an entire organization's mind-set, and these guidelines would be the foundation of the alteration:

To Thine Own Self Be True

Whenever I have questions about how to proceed, I fall back on this one constant. If I can't live with what I have done or with the ramifications of what I'm about to do, then I've failed. Because, ultimately, I have to answer to myself, not to the organization or my boss or the stockholders or the fans. This guideline cuts through the muddle, clears up the uncertainty, and points me in the right direction. In turn, it expedites and clarifies decision making throughout the entire organization because it eliminates hesitation on my part. I can be decisive and quick, and that sets a tone for everyone else.

It allows me to admit when I'm wrong. After all, it serves no purpose to try to fool yourself by thinking you're doing a great job when you know you aren't. It allows me to take chances because I know I'm trying my best to do the right thing. It allows me to avoid becoming misled by praise because I know the truth; I know what succeeded because of luck and timing, and what worked because of the organization's talent.

Being true to myself also allows me to focus on what I know best and let others handle the rest. One of the most foolish things I could do to myself and my organization is to pretend I'm an expert in everything. It's wiser to find someone better qualified to deal with those matters that fall outside of my expertise. I'm not embarrassed to recognize and admit my weaknesses. I also think I'm better at my job because I concentrate my time on my strengths.

With Resolve, You Can Be Whatever You Want to Be

To me, this simply means if I stick to it long enough and work at it hard enough, I can be successful. I simply won't fail from lack of effort, lack of commitment, or lack of determination. Nor will my organization. I don't care if I'm running a business from my home or if I'm involved with the largest corporation in America, my will to succeed won't change.

This gives me the ability to be incredibly narrow-minded, but in a good way. I'm not going to fail, therefore I'll push aside any distractions and make sure that I take care of the assignments that have the highest priority. You don't overload yourself with excess work; you don't take on projects outside of the company that will interfere with your job; you don't try to be everything to everyone.

You must convey this single-mindedness of purpose to the entire organization. You have a duty, and you need to perform it as well as you can and as expeditiously as you can. Anything short of your best is not enough, nor will it be tolerated. I'm a no-nonsense person. I can joke and laugh like anyone else, but we aren't at work to have a day-long social hour. We're here to do a job, and that's the attitude I expect everyone to have. My message is, do your darnedest and then enjoy the success of your commitment.

Fear of Failure

Someone asked me recently why I still keep essentially the same work routine I have followed for most of my football life. It involves extensive traveling to scout college prospects and long hours spent evaluating talent prior to the draft. In Green Bay, I'll inevitably come into work early and stay late. I'll even visit the office on weekends during the off-season, if nothing else just to check our newspaper clip service to see if anything has happened of importance within the NFL.

I guess I could back off, but I know I wouldn't be comfortable with myself if I did. If things unraveled after I changed, I would never forgive myself for altering my routine. This fear drives me. I refuse to allow myself or those around me to be content with our accomplishments. I want to be haunted by the specter of looming failure. That truly guides me. You should never fall in love with yourself or the trappings of achievement. I have seen others in my profession achieve a certain level of success, and then they become a desk jockey, letting others do the work they once relished. I couldn't let that happen to me.

Once you start looking in the mirror and liking what you see, you've got a problem. Out-of-control egos are a trap waiting to consume anyone who has ambition. And so is the belief that you need to demonstrate to everyone that you've made it by surrounding yourself with luxuries and expensive toys, and thinking you need limos and grand hotel suites. That's the quickest way to destroy everything you've worked so hard to gain.

As my economic fortunes have improved, maybe the fact that I picked potatoes for five cents a bag when I was a kid growing up in eastern Pennsylvania has instilled in me a sense of caution. It took two bushel baskets to fill a bag, so if I made $1 a day, I was a heck of a potato picker. I'd buy a moon pie and a Nehi grape soda for 50 cents and put away the other 50 cents. I know I have an appreciation for what's happened to my life that comes only through understanding how difficult it can be to earn a buck. It's an appreciation I expect from anyone who works for me. Just because you're hired by the Packers or just because you put on a Packer uniform doesn't mean you have it made. There's an obligation that comes with the position, including an understanding that unless you do your best, you won't have a job.

I don't manage by fear. I think that's a lousy way to do business. I do believe in setting standards and expecting those working with me to meet those standards, something I'll discuss in more detail in Chapter Five. It's essential to do away with the "I-have-a-job" mentality. To accomplish that, I'm incredibly demanding. But I'm not intentionally goading people by looming over them and warning them they'd better shape up or get out. That's management by fear. Instead, I want an internal force to guide my employees—a fear they'll be letting themselves and the organization down by not performing as well as they possibly can. I want to cultivate a glowing pride in their accomplishments and in the accomplishments of their company.

Everyone in my firm should have a chance to improve himself. The message has to be, if you stick with us and stay with the program, we'll show you how you can help us win. The reward is a promotion to the next level; for someone dealing with personnel in our league, that could mean running your own scouting department, or becoming a general manager or supervising the salary cap. You need to help the employee buy into the notion that he's contributing to the welfare of the company. He has to believe we can't be on top unless he does his part well.

It's not a simple process to change the mind-set of an organization. You don't walk in one day and say, "We're all going to act like winners now," and expect it to happen immediately. Instead, you have to bring about the desired results by presenting a consistent message, which has to be repeated relentlessly and can never vary or be riddled with exceptions: undertake only those tasks that will help us win. Get rid of the distractions and the busy work, and concentrate on your key responsibilities.

I consider myself a fair person to work for, but if you aren't capable of upholding your responsibilities, then I'll find someone else who can. I can function without any of you; I can find replacements, so don't try to pressure me or bully me. I think

fairness is determined by the clarity in which I explain procedures and the consistency in which I enforce them. Employees
should never have a doubt as to where the company or I fall on
any issue or how I might decide a problem. You can't declare a
new rule for people to adhere to one day and then three months
later change the rule. You haven't put enough thought into your
pronouncements. As a result, you are creating doubt and confusion among your employees.

I would think everyone wants to be the best; that's what we're
all about. Wouldn't you want to be able to do something better
than anyone else? If you don't, I'm not going to allow you to tag
along with those who do.

Early in my tenure with Green Bay, when a lot of changes
were being made, Mike Reinfeldt, then the chief financial officer
and now also the vice president of administration, talked to me
about the morale within the office. Employees were having trouble dealing with the new environment. I was sympathetic to an
extent. But I finally said to him, "Their morale? What about my
morale? What's more important? I was hired to do a job and we
need people who understand our goals. If they don't, we have
to fix that."

To win today, you have to change a person's perception of the
proper work ethic. That's how you prod underachievers into
becoming performers, that's how you eliminate a country-club
atmosphere. It means making difficult decisions and being very
firm in what you do. Sometimes, your methods will be popular;
oftentimes, they won't. It would be a mistake, though, to hesitate to make an unpopular decision out of fear people might
react unfavorably toward you.

Now, this doesn't mean you cut off any feelings about your
employees or lose touch with how you're affecting those around
you. I want to have a warm and fuzzy atmosphere in my business, where people wake up in the morning and can't wait to get
to work. But if I have to choose between warm and fuzzy and
accomplishing my goals, there's no real option. The goals come
first.

I'm no different than anyone else. I want people to like me. It's part of the way we think today. We all want to be known as good guys, and if we aren't perceived that way, it bothers us. But if people don't like me, it doesn't distress me.

When making the tough decisions, I always try to set aside any emotion and look at what I'm doing from a company standpoint. What's best for the business? I want to take that approach every time; occasionally I'm successful, occasionally I'm not. The toughest thing I do is to tell a player who has helped improve our team that he's no longer wanted. It's difficult because he's made the supreme football sacrifice—he's been a team player. Yet if we'll be better by letting him go and replacing him with a more talented player, I must make that move. When I know I'm helping the company, I can deal with the emotional part of the decision. It all goes back to looking at myself every day and remembering, "To thine own self be true."

I guess it's the Harry Truman theory of the buck stops here. Someone has to make the unpopular but necessary choices, so why shouldn't it be me? The further you rise in the corporate structure, the less frequently you can be a good guy. If you have a proven record and you're comfortable with what you're achieving and your ultimate goal is to be a winner, you had better do things your way instead of trying to accommodate people by showing you're a nice individual. I was handed an opportunity by Bob Harlan that I never thought I would receive, and only one person, Ron Wolf, would determine whether we would succeed or fail. I couldn't be running a popularity contest.

Even before you realize some success, you still can start creating a winning atmosphere. It's simple—fill your organization with winners. For us, the hiring of Mike Holmgren was a major advance. He represented winning. After all, he came from the 49ers, one of the two or three elite organizations in the league. And he wanted to be a Packer; that alone was an endorsement that helped change the tone of our organization.

He also brought in winners to be his assistants. His coordinators, Ray Rhodes on defense and Sherm Lewis on offense, were former 49er coaches, so they too carried that positive aura with them. All three men now were willing to stake their professional future on the Packer organization. They became examples for our employees. Winners walk with confidence, winners have habits that are molded from success, winners understand and teach what works—or they would be losers. They bring with them a mind-set that says, "You might not have been successful here, but I know what it takes to be the best and this is how we're going to achieve that goal together."

Even if you're involved in a small organization, why not bring in a retired expert in your field and ask that person to lecture and meet with your employees, just to talk about success? Socializing with excellence rubs off. Winners become your message carriers. They sprinkle throughout your firm the knowledge it takes to shake off the doldrums, to make a bad situation better, to turn a good company into a great one.

Mike also walks with a boldness and confidence that is instantly impressive. Once he arrived in Green Bay, I don't think anyone ever heard a hint of doubt from him about what would happen to the Packers. His message was consistent: they would become winners. It wasn't just hollow conversation; he talked with conviction and a tone that left no room for uncertainty.

By adding winners to your business, you immediately are exposed to habits of success. Even if our players still weren't good enough to be champions, Mike and his staff went about coaching them like they were. The players were exposed to the drills, tactics, and training used to produce 49er triumphs, with Mike's own views and variations mixed in. There was a consistency every day that was not affected by poor results. This staff and this head coach knew that what they were doing was right. They had proven it to themselves because these methods had won in a previous environment. It was up to our personnel department to upgrade the playing talent until it became good enough to capitalize on these methods. But at least the way to win was being established.

How can you expect someone to be a terrific salesperson if

they aren't taught the habits of success? And I don't mean by some textbook. The best teacher is always reality, not theory. To excel, you must be given the proper tools and shown the proper procedures and not be asked to work through the maze yourself. That's a waste of time and talent and a deterrent to your goal of advancing the organization. I just can't imagine how anyone would think that a coach who has never had a winning season in his career is capable of conveying winning ways to his players. Nor would I hire an executive from a company that has not been successful.

Winners function in a first-class manner. We strove to do anything and everything we could to provide the most productive atmosphere possible. If we didn't have the equipment or information we needed to win, we made the necessary changes. Bob Harlan did a marvelous job of providing a tremendous working facility, both for staff and for the players. It isn't lavish, because excess is not necessary. But you walk in the front door of our administrative offices, and you get an immediate and positive impression. And you see the symbols of our success, those NFL championship trophies.

We knew we couldn't develop an obsession with winning today if we had an organization filled with whiners and bad characters, both in our offices and in the locker room. You can't move forward if employees are pulling you back. As a manager, it is imperative you identify those who want to work with you and those who will always be unhappy. And you must unload anyone who would rather be negative than productive.

I'm not talking here about dousing opinions that differ from mine. As you will see later, my whole player-evaluation philosophy revolves around obtaining as much independent and strong opinion as possible before reaching decisions about a prospect. For an organization to function smoothly and consistently, this is the way it has to work: you need to encourage input, you need to discourage "yes" men, and you need to sincerely welcome debate. I want people around me who can tell me I'm wrong and who aren't intimidated by my personality. I know I make mistakes. Yet if my associates constantly tell me I'm wonderful, my ability to keep our decision-making process on track will be blunted.

The flip side of this process, however, is that once a decision is made, everyone must buy into it. The choice becomes a Packer choice, and we all embrace it. This is the overriding principle guiding our procedures and everyone needs to accept it. It's a team-first philosophy and it has to influence everything we do.

I will never tell you I'm so smart that I can't learn. However, my point to you is that to persuade me to change, I need to hear solid arguments for your position. If you aren't convincing enough, we'll continue to do it my way and you have to accept that conclusion. If the complaint is legitimate, it will be resolved because our goal is to make this the best possible place to work for everyone, players and staffers alike. Yet if you continue to grumble after receiving a fair hearing, you're ripping down the very organization that's providing you a paycheck. And it won't be tolerated.

This isn't a false open-door policy either. It's easy to say you have an open door, and then just as easy to show through actions and words that the door is anything but open. At Tampa and then with the Packers, I was determined my open-door approach would be honest. If people didn't take advantage of this policy, it wouldn't be due to my attitude in general or the way I treated them once they entered my office.

The Packers can't afford to shut off communication with players, just like you can't afford to remove yourself from interaction with your employees. We're constantly trying to sell our organization, and we'll do everything to make the workplace as positive as possible. If the word gets out we're unwilling to listen and change what's wrong, it will hurt our ability to upgrade our roster. To improve, you need to listen to your associates and react responsibly.

After his first practice as a Packer, Reggie White made an interesting statement. Someone asked him, "What's the main difference between Philadelphia and Green Bay?" and on his first day on the job, he said, "In Green Bay people talk to you, and in Philadelphia, they don't." I couldn't have said it better myself.

If an organization is willing to listen—and if it isn't, it won't win today or over the long-term—the whining has to stop. It has to be a two-way street. I'm not naive. Whether you have 2 or 2,000 people working for you, you'll have some unhappy employees who will complain. We all have things in our daily lives that rub us wrong and can create moods. The chronic complainers are a different issue. They can never be satisfied. You also will have those people who always believe management is backstabbing them, so they in turn back-stab management. It's the kind of loser's mentality that must be eliminated.

Sometimes you wonder what you have to do to satisfy people. We had a soft-drink machine, and employees began complaining because they had to pay for a soda. Why would they expect to get it free? But they did. You do your best to roll with this petty stuff, and just hope these people start seeing the big picture.

When the whining grows more insidious, your approach must change. You no longer can sit back and wish it would go away. The chronic whiners and the back-stabbers need to be identified and dealt with, because if they aren't, they'll impede your ability to obtain your goals. In a locker room, the biggest offenders usually are the older guys who can't hold up their end anymore and resort to concocting excuses. Their griping becomes detrimental to the psyche of your team.

This is how bad guys can mess up a locker room. Players are together seven months every year, six days a week. That's an awfully long time, and little things can become magnified. One player might start grousing about the trainer. Doesn't like him. Every day, the player sounds off about the trainer. His teammates hear him. Maybe a couple more join in. Even though the original complaint had no foundation, now you have a huge problem. What began as an unhappy whiner with a personal grudge against the trainer has exploded. You had better know this is happening, and then you had better stop it quickly before it becomes a major distraction. You give the player a chance to explain his grievances, but if they can't be resolved—and they probably can't—you get rid of him. And the locker room becomes a better place for everyone.

An office is really just like a locker room. There is constant interaction—and constant analysis of every ebb and flow of organizational developments big and small. Office whiners grab a gripe and refuse to let it go, magnifying it until it becomes an issue attracting attention far beyond its importance. The whining can be about anything—work hours, food prices in the cafeteria, dress codes, parking space allocations, how the boss does or doesn't say hello, perceived slights. So much of this complaining is absurd, but excess whining can become an office cancer.

Yappers have no idea what it takes to win. They don't have the work habits, the desire, or most important, the commitment. Winners are committed to be the best, losers complain. Winners strive to make things better, whiners tear down the entire operation. You want to postpone improvement? Allow yappers to remain employed.

Sometimes your message to these people just doesn't get through. Sometimes you think you've eliminated the whiners and yappers, only to have others carry on with the complaints. In these situations, I'm convinced you can make a statement with an unexpected action. Fire a whiner that everyone thought was safe. That'll catch the attention of the entire organization. And make sure it's understood why that person is no longer employed.

In my first off-season with the Packers, we had trouble re-signing receivers Charles Wilson and Perry Kemp. Kemp especially had been fairly productive in past seasons. He thought he was better than he was, though, and so did his agent, and he had this attitude that he was better than the Packers. I evaluated him differently. I thought he was an asset, but certainly not an elite player. He held out, as did Wilson. They both demanded increases that would have made them grossly overpaid. We finally signed them in August, and then let them go before the start of the season. No one picked up Kemp, so it confirmed our analysis of his abilities. Since receiver hardly was one of our strongest positions, it shocked people that we would rid ourselves of both men. But to keep them would have sent a bad message. We wanted people to know that while they may be talented, if they didn't want to be a team player, we'd fire them. After Kemp and Wilson, our players knew we weren't bluffing.

I also believe that if employees get another job opportunity and then seek a counteroffer from you, you shouldn't give them one. Instead, let them go to their new company. I'm not saying these people are necessarily whiners, nor do I begrudge them for considering a chance to increase their responsibility and income. I just don't want them to use that as leverage in my organization. I have them employed in a position I obviously think they can handle; if I thought they were ready to move up, I would have already promoted them. It would be a mistake to prematurely upgrade someone just to keep them, or give them a raise they don't deserve, just to change their minds. That would be detrimental to the organization's well-being.

Besides, I think anyone who considers an offer and then turns it down is never going to be happy again with his current employer. He'll always wonder if he made a mistake by not moving on and that doubt will fester and cut into his performance. It's far better for your organization and for the employee to allow him to leave. I never consider such departures a loss of a valuable asset. Once an employee feels compelled to look elsewhere, his value to me and the company diminishes. Unfortunately, many organizations don't recognize the true value of many of their employees until *after* they've received other job offers. Only then are they given proper compensation by their current company. As a manager, you have to be much more aggressive recognizing who deserves raises—instead of conceding that identification process to a competitor.

You absolutely have to be convinced that no one is too valuable to replace. I might try harder to keep some people happier than others, just to make sure they stay around. But if it comes to a point where I must choose between the organization and the individual, the organization wins. I'll always make up for the loss, if not immediately, then eventually.

What you don't want is a situation where you're being held up for ransom. If you take a stand on a personnel or salary issue and then surrender to demands, you open yourself up to discontent and confusion among your employees. That's why what you do and say has to be seriously studied and considered before it becomes policy. Shooting from the hip usually results from anger. You see or hear something you don't like, and you fire off a strong memo or call a meeting and unload. Most of the time, you wind up taking action you would have avoided in calmer situations. Then you either have to retract it, which you should do, or live with bad policy, which is unacceptable.

If you take positions that are tough enough and consistent enough, you'll reduce conflicts within the organization, and that will allow everyone to focus their energy where it should be—on becoming more productive.

If you want to develop an obsession with winning today, you need to deal with two other major issues. The first concerns the structure of your business, the second with how the details of your business are handled.

Your initial organizational analysis should have yielded a profile of both the structure of your enterprise and its decision-making speed. If you have too many layers, which indicates too much bureaucracy, you need to make changes. I look back at my early days with the Raiders in the old American Football League. We had four assistant coaches, a head coach who was also the general manager, and 33 players. And we got the job done at a very high level. Yet even though I think we probably could be just as effective today with this streamlined organization, we keep adding more and more employees and levels of staff.

If nothing else, you need to examine every new position, every new division, and every new element that would increase the size but slow down the efficiency of your operation. Growth for growth's sake, until it becomes more for show than substance, is a step backward. It will bog you down. Every potential growth step should pass a litmus test: is it really necessary to help us win? Use this test whether you want to add another employee to a five-employee company, move to a larger facility, or take on another job from your home. Is it progress or is it show—and will it eventually create so many new problems and eat into revenues and profits that it becomes a negative?

The way you handle details can also affect your organization's efficiency. I include planning under the detail umbrella. I want to lay my hands on things I need immediately. I must be able to grab it, read it, and get what I need out of it. As a result, it's important to me to have data properly filed and records maintained and readily available.

If a meeting is planned in June away from Green Bay, airline tickets should be purchased far enough ahead of time to get discount fares. If we need to order supplies before a certain date to save money, the order should not miss the deadline. If we know we'll need information for the draft, the material should be gathered methodically over months, not at the last moment. There's no excuse for constant fire drills in your planning process.

Attention to detail means there's a focus behind what you're doing. And to what your organization is doing. By working purposely and with a sense of organization, you leave room for those unanticipated developments that always cut into your available time.

Never think that anyone outside your enterprise wants you to succeed, either. If you do, you'll develop a false sense of security. I learned that lesson vividly in my first months with the Packers. When I was negotiating with Mike Holmgren, the league office called both Bob Harlan and me. An official informed us that if Mike signed with another team, he had a clause in his contract that required the 49ers to receive compensation. We had no reason to doubt this claim, so we negotiated a deal with San Francisco.

He was worth an awful lot to the future of the Packers, and I was willing to pay a decent price. We began by offering a sixth-round choice and wound up giving a second-round selection to the 49ers. We had begun the off-season with two No. 1s and two No. 2s and eventually surrendered a No. 1 for Favre and a No. 2 for Holmgren. I walked away pleased with what had transpired.

Later, Mike and I were sitting with Mike's agent, and he showed me Mike's 49er contract. Mike had never signed it, the commissioner had never signed it—it was invalid. We had been duped by the league office. I was livid. I filed a grievance, but it's never been settled. I learned that it does matter who you are. The league is supposed to be serving all 30 teams, but it plays favorites. When Mike was hired, the Packers weren't that important. We don't have a rich owner who can demand special treatment. It's the way the game is played. My chair was hardly warm, and they were sticking it to me.

It taught me a lesson. Look out for yourself because no one will be looking out for you. All I could think of was a cliché: damn the torpedoes, full speed ahead. Just see if they could stop us. I became even more focused and determined to win. Maybe it wasn't important to them that the Packers succeeded, but that didn't matter. We had been accommodating for so long. Not now.

That feeling spread to the team and the coaching staff. I went into the 1992 season without any feel of how good we might be, but there was a prevailing attitude within the organization that our tenacity would reap some immediate rewards. Considering we hadn't changed many of the frontline players off a bad team, prognosticators thought we would be woeful.

What transpired over the next months was one of the best coaching jobs in the history of the NFL. Mike Holmgren and his staff took basically the same key players from a 4–12 club and molded them into 9–7 winners who weren't eliminated from the playoffs until the final regular-season game. We weren't a playoff team that year, but the fact we almost made it gave credibility to everything Mike and I were doing with the organization. It was, after all, the franchise's second-best record in twenty years.

My conversation with Red Cochran had allowed me to clarify my thinking about how this franchise would be rebuilt not only on the staff level, but also on the player level. This is how the Stepping Stone approach crystallized into a methodical system involving roster improvement. The Stepping Stone philosophy gave me the proper mind-set for dealing with personnel issues. It was the basis of our decision not to unload a lot more players going into the 1992 season.

I visualized the Stepping Stone approach to building a winning roster this way: we needed to establish a solid foundation of veteran players by keeping the best athletes from the 1991 team who were willing to accept Mike Holmgren's coaching ways. These guys didn't necessarily have to be stars because that team didn't have many standouts. But they had to be good enough to give us a chance to compete. We would use trades and the free-agent options available to fill in the most glaring holes with other veterans. At the same time—and this was the most essential element—we wanted to use the draft to pick potential stars who could be groomed in Mike's system and who eventually would become much better than the starters we currently had on the roster. That was the key to making this work—by the time the youngsters were ready to blend with the best of the veterans, they had to raise our talent level far higher than it currently stood. If they did, we could compete for a title.

I considered Brett Favre to be the first of those potential stars, our first major Stepping Stone. He probably would be forced to play faster than we might have wanted, but our quarterback situation was so desperate we couldn't wait for him to learn as a backup. He would have to undergo on-the-field training, which at times became inconsistent and error-prone. Yet I remained convinced once he matured, he would develop into an elite quarterback, which in turn would give our offense a chance to dominate. If Brett lived up to my expectations, I could just envision what Mike could accomplish on offense.

I knew if we lost our patience too quickly with everyone from the bad 1991 team, we would botch the Stepping Stone philosophy. We had to buy time by improving our veteran players to a point where they could win enough games for us to show progress. Whether you are rebuilding or revitalizing or just trying to make a good situation better, it's important never to lose sight of maintaining continuity. A large degree of upheaval may be necessary to achieve your aims, but you also must cultivate elements of stability. If I had wiped out the bulk of the roster, it would be impossible to secure the quantity and quality of replacements needed to make us contenders. It made no sense to take that route, although I'm sure people outside the organization thought it would be a wise move.

My roster analysis during the final weeks of the 1991 season convinced me the squad did not play up to its capabilities. If I could upgrade our talent even a little, I thought our coaching staff was so good that we had every reason to expect improvement. I just didn't know how much.

We wound up winning three 1992 games in the last quarter and running off a six-game victory streak near season's end, the longest such positive stretch for the Packers since 1965. Our 9–7 record marked the second time the Packers had been over .500 since 1982. Sterling Sharpe became only the sixth player in NFL history to catch 100 passes in a season. After an injury to Don Majkowski, Brett Favre took over as a starter four games into the schedule and finished with 18 touchdown passes and 3,227 yards despite being sacked 34 times. His passing yards were the fifth-highest in team history, his 11 straight 200-yard plus games was a team record, and his completion percentage of 64 was the best ever. He played well enough to make the Pro Bowl.

He also made one of the handful of plays that I consider cornerstones in our march to the Super Bowl. One game before he took over as starter, he replaced an ailing Majkowski. We were trailing the Bengals, 20–10, before he launched a comeback. At 23–17 and under a minute left, he connected with receiver Kitrick Taylor for a 35-yard touchdown pass to win the contest. It was the first glimpse of Brett's wonderful ability to function in pressure situations.

It's amazing how these things work. A week before the Bengals game, I don't know if I've ever felt so low. Even though we had lost our opener to the Vikings, we played okay. Then the Bucs just throttled us, 31–3, and Mike and I began reassessing where we stood as a team. We both concluded the turnaround could take longer than we had expected. Then Brett moved into the picture, and everything changed dramatically. He already was demonstrating the impact of great leadership.

Other than Favre, the most significant immediate addition had been veteran tackle Tootie Robbins, who came over from the Arizona Cardinals in a trade. He was a veteran who had performed for years at a high level. Even though he played on so-so teams, he was a winner. He was just the kind of guy I wanted to bring to the Packers, so our young players could watch him train and perform, and see what it took to excel. I gave up a sixth-round choice for him, and couldn't have been happier.

We also had added Frank Winters, a Plan B offensive lineman from Kansas City. Plan B was the forerunner of the current free-agency system, and we tapped into it heavily during early 1992, figuring if we brought in enough new faces, we could find some help. We thought Winters would be a serviceable backup center and guard and a full-time snapper. He wound up starting much of the season at center and guard, giving us a glimpse of how good he would become.

Because of our solid offensive line, we managed to grind out running yards despite lacking a star back. A young rusher, Edgar Bennett, whom we picked in the fourth round of our first draft in 1992, showed intriguing promise. Tight end Jackie Harris had a good year, but no wide receiver other than Sharpe caught more than 17 passes, which was unacceptable. The offense didn't constantly hurt itself with mistakes, and the combination of Favre and Sharpe emerged as one of the most dangerous and productive in the league. If we could bolster our rushing game and upgrade our receiving corps, we could get even better.

Defensively, coordinator Ray Rhodes made a great move by switching cornerback LeRoy Butler to strong safety, replacing retired veteran Mark Murphy. Butler, who had been a decent cornerback, emerged quickly as a standout safety. It was an outstanding example of good management. The best leaders are the ones who determine the strengths of their employees and then place them into the right niche. That's what Ray did.

Working from a 3–4 scheme, linebacker Tony Bennett recorded $13^1/2$ sacks and made the Pro Bowl. Fellow linebacker Johnny Holland led the teams in tackles, and we saw a lot of promise in linebacker Mark D'Onofrio, a second-round choice in 1992 who was hurt in the second game of his rookie season. Other than D'Onofrio, veteran Lewis Billups, whom we brought in to start at cornerback, and No. 1 1992 pick Terrell Buckley, who took over from Billups during the season, the rest of the defensive mainstays had been on the 1991 roster. The defense had been competitive, but needed help. We didn't have enough domination along the front line, we had to upgrade the secondary, and we had to get faster as a unit.

Still, I can't imagine any franchise in NFL history being happier about a 9–7 record. No one in the league was having nightmares about the improvement of the Packers, but the impact this season had on our organization was immeasurable. The players had been struggling for so long, yearning for something to give them hope. Now we had reason to be optimistic. We fanned their enthusiasm and stroked their egos. We wanted to put the past behind us as quickly as we could.

Once you see even a slight change in what had been such a negative picture, it's amazing how attitudes change for the better. That makes everything you want to do in the future so much easier to sell. You've got people buying in faster—and the ones that don't become more and more isolated and are subjected to more and more peer pressure.

Once you prove your way is successful, you have people saying,

"This guy knows what he is talking about. Let's tag along." Don't you think members of our Executive Committee looked at me a little differently in 1992, once Brett Favre performed well, than when I first told them I wanted to trade for him? Obviously, saying you'll be successful doesn't guarantee it. Still, if you take the right steps to construct the proper foundation, you have given yourself the best chance possible to improve your situation. That is what this third Stepping Stone—Develop an Obsession With Winning Today—is all about.

With the start of success, you're ready for the fourth Stepping Stone: Play to Your Strengths. Before we move on, here are the prominent points you should remember from Stepping Stone No. 3—Develop an Obsession With Winning Today:

• Establish a mind-set that puts the organization ahead of any personal goals—and make all decisions based on this priority. Convey this attitude through your convictions and determination.

• Strive for an "edge" that sets the tempo for your company's work pace and constantly pushes everyone to do the best possible work.

• Never accept the concept of becoming worse first before you start improving.

• Forget instituting plans that establish success only after a set number of years. Approaches such as five-year plans create a mentality where an early lack of productivity is acceptable and excuses for failure aren't challenged.

• Make sure the standard to judge performance is clear to everyone: if you produce, you stay, and if you don't, you'll be replaced.

• Don't rule through fear; instead, create an environment where everyone fears letting down the organization through poor performance. Strive to make people believe their contribution is needed for the enterprise to succeed.

• Don't shy away from the tough decisions because they might cast you as a "bad" person. Remove emotion from decision making as much as possible.

• Don't waver once you have established rules and procedures. Otherwise, you create an atmosphere of confusion and mistrust.

• Bring in winners to your enterprise, and use them as role models who can teach employees through their conduct and their knowledge of the methods of success. You don't have to win before starting to create a winning environment. Establish winning habits and make them the guidelines for your organization.

• Rid yourself of whiners and yappers who impede improvement through negative behavior. Those who receive a fair hearing on their complaints and don't buy into the company policy need to be removed. If necessary, make a statement to the organization through an unexpected decision, including the dismissal of a supposedly "safe" employee who isn't producing.

• Establish a credible open-door policy by demonstrating to employees you'll listen and act on valid complaints and suggestions.

• Streamline your business, cut out unnecessary layers, and pay attention to details, making sure there's constant long-range planning.

• If one of your employees considers an offer from another company, let him take it. He never again will be happy with you if he turns it down. Never counteroffer and never give in to outrageous demands. It sets a bad precedent for future negotiations and policy debates.

CHAPTER FOUR

Play to Your Strengths

Reggie White a Packer? You've got to be kidding.

I know that was the reaction around the league when we revealed our intention to sign defensive end Reggie White, who had become a free agent after the 1992 season. White was, and still is, one of the most talented free agents to become available in this new era of player movement in the NFL. His presence could strengthen any team, particularly one like ours, which was sorely lacking a big-play pass rusher. If we could land White, it would mean we would secure the league's all-time sack leader and one of its most solid citizens.

It would also give instant credibility for our rebuilding program. After all, this wasn't just another player. This was Reggie White, with an impeccable résumé and incredible talent. Plus, he had star power, a charisma that few athletes possess. Spend time around him, and you could sense his charm. For us to pursue Reggie would be the same as if you were revamping a lightly regarded computer company and wanted to recruit one of the nation's elite programmers. Maybe it seemed to make no sense—after all, why would someone so talented want to hook up with an employer who wasn't at the top of his profession— but to me, it made all the sense in the world.

You'll never become No. 1 unless you think you can get there. And White was a player who could help us make that leap. It didn't matter what anyone outside our company thought. We had to believe we were worthy of a great talent, and then we had to convince him to join us. We'd never be able to continue the climb to the top without the best possible players we could obtain, and White surely fit into that category. We couldn't allow any negatives to douse our optimism.

That's the problem when you aren't any good—too many negatives and not enough positives. Negativism can rip apart an organization and impede its growth. It can trample morale, make recruiting all but impossible, and virtually doom a company to failure. The Packers weren't immune to this virus. And I had to figure out ways to make things a lot more positive— before we could even think about winning.

Reggie White certainly would be a huge positive. I knew we needed an impact player, and no one in the NFL fit that label better than Reggie. He had enormous strength to go with impressive agility. He also had a will to win that can serve as an example for a team. If your best player wants to be the greatest and shows it, your lesser athletes should get the message.

Our 1992 defense recorded only 34 sacks, which ranked twenty-first among the 28 league teams. Linebacker Tony Bennett recorded $13^{1}/_{2}$ sacks but no defensive lineman managed more than four. To build a solid defense, you have to start with the line. You have to be able to stop the run, but you must also put pressure on the quarterback. Otherwise, you have to resort to gimmick defenses, and that ultimately leaves you vulnerable to big plays. You also want players on both sides of the ball that grab your opponent's attention. No offense can enter a game against Reggie White and not devote a good chunk of the game plan to controlling him. The more they double-team him, the more it opens up opportunities for other defensive teammates to make plays. So adding White would allow us to upgrade immediately in some crucial areas. He certainly also would give us a chance to improve our overall defensive ratings. We ranked a poor twenty-third in 1992.

Most of all, he would accelerate everything we wanted to do with the Packers, which alone made him worth the hefty investment we knew it would take to sign him. I believe strongly that there are times a business, no matter the size, must commit to a major expenditure in order to make a pivotal impact on its future. The money might be spent to hire a highly regarded manager or buy an innovative piece of equipment that will immediately improve productivity. The key here is to envision the long-term benefits of your decision, instead of being hampered by short-term distractions.

Certainly, the choice might put a strain on your current finances, but your thinking must be swayed by the potential pluses that could result from your move. This "impact decision" can be something as simple as an extra phone line in your house dedicated only to fax calls or Internet usage. That extra line would allow information to flow into your home unimpeded by busy signals that served as a barrier in the past. The efficiency produced by the new line will more than offset the added monthly costs. It's worth the expenditure because it creates a strength where a weakness previously might have existed.

If you make the proper impact decisions, you'll later look back and laugh about the initial concern you might have had about these choices. Let me explain. After our rebuilding program concluded with a victory in Super Bowl XXXI, do you think anyone within our organization thought we had overpaid for Reggie White's services? If anything, his value to the team became so unique and important that our initial investment seems more than reasonable now. You need to have the strength, fortitude, and conviction to believe that, by stretching your resources today, your situation will improve appreciably in the future, so much so that this expenditure will seem like a bargain in retrospect.

If we signed White, his presence would do away with all this nonsense about how the football world had passed by Green Bay. Certainly, the perception was that no first-rate free agent would voluntarily decide to come to Wisconsin, not when he could pick among clubs with stronger rosters and better climates. But if we could land Reggie, none of that would be true anymore.

If White had been available following the 1991 season, I'm not sure we would have had a realistic chance of signing him.

When I joined the organization, the negatives surrounding the Packers were so strong and so entrenched that it was depressing. That's the trouble with negatives. Let them fester unchecked, and they stifle growth and morale. Yet, too many managers ignore them, or worse, accept them as part of their circumstances. That's even true when it comes to managing your personal affairs at home. You allow the negatives—I haven't enough time to organize my spending, I don't have enough money to make investments, I'm just a little guy, so what chance do I have against the big spenders—to serve as excuses for standing still instead of trying to improve your financial well-being. But it doesn't need to be that way.

First, you must acknowledge the negatives. Then you must either eliminate them, or if that isn't possible, identify positives and begin emphasizing them so strongly that they overwhelm the negatives. That's how you play to your strengths, the essence of the fourth Stepping Stone.

Let's say you are sole proprietor of a small furniture store. You're competing against two larger stores in the same area. They have more showroom space. This negative can be eliminated only through a substantial investment in a bigger location. That should be your ultimate goal. However, until you can afford that investment, talk up your advantages. You may be smaller, but your size allows you to provide more personal service to customers. Emphasize that strength. Tell customers your location is more convenient. Tell them you fill orders faster than anyone. Tell them they aren't just another number, another sale. Now your size is working for you.

With the Packers, we were being undermined on two levels:

• The players' underground network did not view Green Bay favorably. The perception was that black players would be foolish to join the team if they had other choices. There was no social life for them in the community, nothing to keep them busy once they left our practice facility.

• The cold weather was discussed so much that it seemed as

if we were located somewhere in the Arctic. I wasn't about to put an unrealistic spin on this problem, but I thought we could at least use it to our advantage. It may be cold, but so what? Playing in this kind of weather just makes the Packers that much tougher and stronger. Let other clubs worry about coming into Lambeau Field and dealing with the conditions. Turn the weather into a positive, and construct a team that could handle the situation and not be unnerved by subfreezing temperatures.

I looked at this last point and concluded we had to be intelligent about the way we put together our team. We would be foolish to ignore the fact we are dealing with unique weather patterns. Yet, instead of allowing those elements to rip into our thinking, we needed to do everything we could to capitalize on them. It would be like the Red Sox ignoring the Green Monster, that very short left-field wall in Fenway Park. You'd be wrong if you didn't fill your roster with right-handed power hitters who could feast on the wall.

In our situation, we didn't want a whippet team here. It made no sense to have a team streamlined to play fast football. We wanted hearty guys who wear short sleeves in the worst weather. This game didn't start in palm trees and sand, it started in Canton and Providence and International Falls and Green Bay— not Los Angeles or Miami or Dallas. You don't see any artificial turf at Lambeau; real football players work in the cold and on grass. Considering the potential for bad weather during our late-season home games, we would constantly be encountering conditions that would neutralize quickness and emphasize strength. So why not go with the flow?

It's as if we were a company with a bunch of divisions. Instead of concentrating on building up one division until it becomes the best in its area, we try to make all of them good. The result is mediocrity across the board. I would sell off the weak divisions and concentrate on becoming dominant in just one arena. The Packers would never be No. 1 if we had a team that played decently in bad weather and decently on artificial surfaces but never performed wonderfully in either venue. For us to be champs, we had to unload the whippets and focus our energies on becoming a great cold-weather team.

Mike Holmgren and I thought Lambeau Field was an exceptional facility. But teams didn't fear coming to Green Bay. We thought we could alter that, in great part by using reverse psychology. Let's turn around this whole weather issue, and let it serve us instead of hindering us. Let's sell our team on embracing the conditions—the worse it gets the better—and almost daring an opponent to beat us in November and December in Lambeau. Our goal was to make Lambeau the best home-field advantage in the NFL, with help from Mother Nature.

Okay, the weather was one thing. I couldn't alter it, yet we had an idea about how to use it in our favor. Figuring out a way to receive a more favorable rating from the players' underground network was another. Nothing was going to alter the fact that we have a small black population in Green Bay. Yet plenty of black players have enjoyed successful careers with the Packers. Stars like Willie Davis, Herb Adderly, James Lofton, Willie Wood, Elijah Pitts, Dave Robinson, and Willie Buchanon. They were all extremely talented athletes, and they wore Packer uniforms. That had to be a plus.

This was also the 1990s, not the Stone Age. If you want a more active social life, Milwaukee is a two-hour drive from Green Bay. Chicago takes four hours driving the speed limit. You would have thought we were so isolated that civilization had somehow missed us. Just isn't true. Besides, so many players are family men, and I can't think of a better place to raise children than in Green Bay. This may be the smallest market in the league, but it is one of the safest. You can leave toys outside, and nothing gets stolen. You can leave your car and your house unlocked, and feel safe. You can walk the streets and not be harassed. There are no traffic jams, rush hour is a joke, and you're never more than ten minutes from Lambeau.

We also could improve by making our black players more comfortable. We began bringing in a barber from Milwaukee once a week, since no one in Green Bay specialized in cutting the hair of black players. Twice a week, we started to serve soul food at our practice facility, ample portions of fried chicken, macaroni and cheese, spinach, lima beans, and other tasty items that our players enjoyed. They responded favorably and immediately to our moves. Not only did they enjoy the meals, but they appreciated the fact we were making efforts to show we cared.

What I needed to eliminate was the type of story Mike Holmgren told the day we signed Reggie. He said when he was with the 49ers, he would get his players' attention by threatening to ship them to Green Bay. From a coach's standpoint, that was a pretty good warning. No one really wanted to play here.

I was determined to create a comfortable, informal environment that would encourage all our players to linger at our facility instead of rushing out the door as soon as they could. It would be a clean, neat place, something they could be proud of and that would keep them happy. Maybe these weren't major developments, but I'm convinced they helped us win. Bob Harlan made a significant contribution by adding a family counselor to our payroll. She's in charge of taking care of the players' families when they come to Green Bay. She drives them around the community, helps them find housing, fills them in about the school system, and does whatever is needed to turn their introduction to Green Bay into a pleasant experience. She has become an essential resource for the team and family members.

With the construction of an incredible indoor practice facility, the organization already had initiated a major, much-needed improvement. That facility, which was named after Packer Hall of Fame receiver Don Hutson, eliminated any concerns that prospective players might have about how our winter weather would affect daily workouts.

In essence, we wanted to make the Packer facility user-friendly, so complaints would be cut to the minimum. Happy players don't grouse to their friends around the league. Let's face it, I don't care who you are, there isn't much to do during the winter in Green Bay. You are stuck indoors. But if the players found our place to be gentle, maybe they'd want to stay longer at the end of the day. And they have. They sit around and play dominoes, and they seem to watch a lot of extra tape before heading home. With the catered food, there's even more reason to hang around.

Bob Harlan has not limited the improvements to the players' area. The lobby entrance to our administrative offices is open and bright. It isn't ostentatious, yet it's incredibly pleasing. It makes you feel welcome; it creates a positive atmosphere and attitude. The rest of the building is just as tidy and well-lit, and very clean. It's very obvious that this organization has pride in itself and its appearance.

Look around your workplace. It should be clean and neat. It should be pleasant and friendly. The facilities should be as modern as possible, not drab and unappealing. Find out what your employees don't like about where they work. Maybe you need to install more vending machines. Maybe you need to lay new carpet or paint the walls. Maybe the lighting isn't sufficient. These things are remedied quickly and relatively inexpensively, yet they have immense impact. Even if you work from home, you shouldn't settle for dreary surroundings. You can make your workplace a strength. If you do, your morale and the morale of your employees will improve automatically. Coming to work should be a pleasure, not a drudgery.

We received a lot of favorable publicity from the environmental changes we made with the Packers, which also helped change the perception surrounding the franchise. Plus, it showed we were trying to jump-start the franchise out of its lethargy. But I had to do more.

The answer was encased in one word: history.

I kept asking myself, what was the Packers' greatest strength? I always arrived at the same answer. It was their past success, and not just in the Lombardi era. In fact, I thought the Lombardi era sometimes hurt the organization. All you ever heard was how great those times were, as if those years were a Camelot we could no longer visit. And all you ever saw were kids wearing Packer numbers from the past, especially Bart Starr's No. 15 and Ray Nitschke's No. 66.

At the annual Packers fantasy summer camp, where fans could learn and play football with Packer greats, the last session always ended with a re-creation of the winning touchdown in the Ice Bowl. That happened in 1967, but it still was the most vivid memory people had of the Packers.

It was as if the 24 years since Lombardi left had never existed. It was as if we once were the leading manufacturer of a specialty car that now had fallen behind its competition in sales. Yet you keep a model of a car from your heyday sitting in the lobby, serving as a constant reminder of past glory—and an indirect reminder of your current failure. We needed to update, clean up, and add some excitement to the franchise.

For the Packers to become the organization I envisioned, I had to use our past as a positive, not a negative. We had a strength that had been sorely neglected, and that had to change. I had to wipe out the feeling hovering over us that we could never come close to returning the franchise to what it had been under Lombardi. It was a belief that grew with each failing year. We were perceived as a relic, not a contender.

I would bet that your company, no matter its current position in the marketplace, could benefit from a large dose of historical pride. Research past successes and publicize them to employees and to the public. Build a portrait of a great organization striving to live up to its legacy. Use prior triumphs as incentives for the current company not only to duplicate but to surpass. Structure everything as a strength, a positive.

I am a lover of football history, and my curiosity about the Packer past soon gave me the ammunition I needed to start turning around our public image.

See, the Packers weren't successful just under Lombardi. Curly Lambeau, the team's founder and first coach, guided them to a series of triumphs long before Lombardi took charge. Lambeau, for goodness' sake, was there with Halas in the early days of the NFL, and he was there when the Packers won six world championships as one of the most feared teams in football. He remains one of five men to record more than 200 wins as a head coach.

Today, I can take you to City Stadium, where it all began for the Packers. I can take you across the street from Lambeau Field and show you the Packer Hall of Fame, which contains an incredible collection of memorabilia from a football tradition that began in 1919. When you think football, you have to think of the Green Bay Packers, the very fabric of what the NFL has grown to become. There's something about the name that's so, so special.

Today, I can walk you through the tunnel and onto the field at Lambeau. It's an awesome feeling, knowing what has happened over the years to make this place such a huge part of the NFL timeline. You look up and see the names of our great players written permanently on the stadium walls, high above the field, ringing the facility. You recite the names—Hutson, Nitschke, Hornung, Starr, Canadeo. . . . It sends chills throughout your body.

This is what I decided to emphasize. Not Lombardi Avenue, which runs in front of our stadium, not those five world titles in the 1960s. But all the great players and great coaches that have worn a Packers uniform in this small but incredibly loyal community. I went back to our roots, put the spotlight on everything good that ever happened to the organization, and made sure everyone was fully aware of what the Packers have been and should be all about. Only then could players and fans in the 1990s understand that what had been accomplished once could be accomplished again, regardless of the naysayers who predicted nothing but mediocrity for our team.

When I first came to the Packers' facility in 1991, a replica of one of Lombardi's championship trophies sat in the lobby along with a few banners hailing some of the past glories. But nothing in the lobby praised any player or team after the 1960s. Indeed, if you stood in that lobby, you didn't see much that would tell you the franchise existed before or after Lombardi. That had to change.

I found pictures of great Packer players from the past and had them framed. I wanted them hung on our walls as a constant reminder of our goal to return the franchise to a championship level.

If you visit my office, which once was occupied by Lombardi himself, you'll see what I mean about history. On one wall, I have pictures of our roots: Lambeau; Dick Wildung, all-pro from Minnesota; Billy Grimes, our first Pro Bowl player in the modern era; and Bobby Dillon, an outstanding player on some bad teams. Behind my desk, I have Don Hutson, who has been called the greatest to ever play for the Packers; Tony Canadeo, a Hall of Fame running back; a scene from City Stadium; and a scene from the first game played in Lambeau, with Ray Nitschke pursuing a runner. On another wall, I have Paul Hornung, who according to the guys who coached here was Lombardi's best player; Nitschke, who symbolized what Packer football is all about—toughness, meanness, determination; Hall of Famers Willie Davis and Henry Jordan; a trio of great players, Herb Adderley, Willie Wood, and Elijah Pitts; Donny Anderson running behind Gale Gillingham and Jerry Kramer; and Dave Robinson, Fred Carr, and Willie Buchanon chasing Fran Tarkenton. There are also pictures of our best two players in 1997, LeRoy Butler and Brett Favre. And a photo of Bob Harlan, Mike Holmgren, and myself with the Super Bowl XXXI trophy after we won it in New Orleans.

I look at those pictures every day. They prod me. If I was running a company with a storied past, I would hang pictures of past presidents. I would find newspaper reports of special moments in company history, and have them framed and hung. I would create a hall of fame, so employees would never forget how the past can be rekindled in the future.

When Bob Harlan remodeled our lobby, he carved out space to display our three Super Bowl trophies. The greatness of the Packers smacks you right in the face as soon as you enter our facility. But we needed to do more. I was concerned the players might not understand the past as well as they should.

So I introduced the concept of honorary captains. For every home game, we would bring back a great player from our history. He would be introduced to the crowd, and he would be able to mingle with our present players. Even if they already were aware of him, this still was an opportunity for them to touch greatness.

It became a remarkable deal. Our players and fans took to it, and so did the guys we were honoring. I began receiving calls from retired players, asking if they could be a captain. A private business could duplicate this feeling by bringing back successful retired executives to give speeches and seminars or attend a yearly homecoming-like activity. Everyone could draw something not only from their presence, but from their expertise. A winner never loses the instincts of success. An hour's conversation with current employees could yield an impressive array of tips and wisdom. Yet so many firms want to bury the past and treat their former employees with a lack of respect.

I understood none of the moves we had implemented would directly win games. Instead, these changes would help feed the kind of positive, aggressive, upbeat attitude and atmosphere we needed to pave the way for success. But we also still required on-field help. We needed a player to put us over the hump, not necessarily making us immediate winners, but a star who would give us credibility in the 1990s and draw attention to our Packers. At the same time, I wanted someone who would generate excitement within our organization and give us a rallying point.

Reggie White was that guy.

For all his greatness, he'd never played on a consistent winner and he'd never performed well in play-off games. He'd never been to a conference championship, much less a Super Bowl. We were confident that we could fill all those voids for him. He just had to sign up and become part of the ride.

It wasn't like he was seeking us out. The Browns, 49ers, and Redskins wanted him badly, and they had a lot more going for them, in terms of recent success, than we did. Art Modell's wife even went so far as to give Reggie's wife a $900 leather coat. This was serious stuff, and we started from way behind.

In fact, I'm convinced Reggie didn't need much of a reason to back out of the visit we had planned for him to Green Bay. On the day he was scheduled to arrive, he was in Detroit, and the weather at both ends was terrible. Flights were being canceled, and we were afraid he would change his mind and return to his home in Tennessee. Mike Reinfeldt, our chief financial officer, salvaged things. His father-in-law owns a plane, which fortunately was in Pontiac, Michigan that day. Mike made a few calls, and Reggie soon was flying to Green Bay courtesy of Mike's father-in-law. That's how close we came to losing him before even having a chance to talk to him.

I don't believe in pretenses and gaudy displays, so our courting of Reggie was efficient, serious, and sincere—but hardly fancy. We went to lunch at Red Lobster—you were expecting Sardi's in Green Bay?—and Reggie wanted his fried catfish filleted. The restaurant didn't serve it that way, but he was told if he signed with us, he would always be able to get what he wanted at Red Lobster. Go into the Green Bay Red Lobster anytime now, and order catfish filleted. They'll be happy to serve it to you that way.

We wanted to show him what we were all about as an organization. We didn't have any gaudy coats, just a great coaching staff, including two men who really impressed him, Mike Holmgren and defensive coordinator Ray Rhodes.

They did an outstanding job of recruiting him. Their sincerity came through loud and clear to Reggie. He liked them, and he could see how it would be a pleasure to play for them. They even took a special trip to Tennessee, so they could visit with Reggie in his home. I found out the favorite flower of Reggie's wife, Sara. Every other day for two weeks, we sent her roses. Every little positive bit helps.

I know it's standard operating procedure to bring in a potential new employee and send him through the interview routine, bouncing him from one manager to another so everyone can eventually have an opinion about his worthiness. But this process emphasizes the wrong approach. Talking to current employees shouldn't be treated just as a formality; you need to seriously involve key personnel in your recruiting and hiring practices. Let them serve as salespeople; let them explain the company's vision through their eyes instead of depending mostly on your view. This works only when you have employees who sincerely believe in the goals of the organization. These people have bought into your approach. They've become positive examples of your viewpoint, and elegant spokespeople for it.

Ray and Mike are the reasons Reggie White became interested in the Packers. They believed in this franchise, where we were headed, and how important Reggie was to what we wanted to do. That is the kind of loyalty and the kind of input you must foster and encourage within your business.

When recruiting new employees, keep your approach simple and direct. Emphasize the strengths of your business, be honest about your weaknesses, and always put a positive spin on your discussions. Be optimistic, but don't oversell. Don't overlook the small things; whatever can give you an edge over the competition becomes a strong selling point.

Consider our approach with White. While he was in Green Bay, Reggie wound up sitting in my office. I wasn't going to feed him a bunch of bull. "You're a great player," I said, "and if you play for the Green Bay Packers, you'll become a legend. The people here will take to you and they will love you." We talked about the past glories of the Packers; Reggie is a big football fan too, and I think he was intrigued by the possibility of playing on the same team as Nitschke, Willie Davis, and the other Packer greats.

I'm sure he thought I was giving him a salesman's spiel, but I really meant it. I had come to understand the city of Green Bay. The citizens are wonderful and sincere, and they truly love their Packer football. They take great pride in supporting the only community-owned club in the NFL. They appreciate great players, and they'll do anything they can for them. And Reggie could fill a void. We didn't have any big-time Packer heroes anymore. I thought Brett Favre could become a star, but he hadn't made his name yet. Guys like Chuck Cecil and Don Majkowski were revered, but they weren't Don Hutson or Bart Starr. I was convinced Packer fans especially would take to someone like Reggie, a God-fearing, clean-living man who has his priorities in the right order. But they would never be able to get to know him unless we could sign him.

To do that, we had to come up with the right amount of money. He was so important to our future that we were willing to dig deep to compensate him. A business trying to become a winner has to show that kind of determination and demonstrate that kind of sincerity if it ever wants to establish credibility. I'm sure you've been in a situation where your company frequently discusses what steps it needs to make a breakthrough, for example, in a product line. Yet the talk never is translated into action, and the business remains lethargic. That was a mistake I wanted to avoid. Talk obviously is cheap; we could say all we wanted about wanting to compete in the 1990s. But now we had a chance to back up our words, and we didn't want to blow it.

Let's not kid ourselves. We could have done the best selling job possible with Reggie, but if our financial offer was not competitive, he never would have signed with us. It didn't necessarily have to be the largest bid, but it couldn't fall far short of what others were willing to spend. I have to credit Mike Reinfeldt with doing a splendid negotiating job. He was able to obtain a good feel for Reggie's contract desires, and then he was able to craft an offer that showed Reggie we were serious.

It took a four-year, $17.6 million deal, the largest ever given to a defensive player in NFL history and the third-highest for any football player ever, to convince Reggie to become a Packer rather than sign with the two other strongest bidders, the 49ers and the Redskins. The 49ers offered $19.5 million over five years, and the Redskins were willing to make him a $14 million, four-year deal. But our edge came with guaranteed money. Because our franchise had been managed so efficiently over the years, we had a substantial sum in the bank that we could use for bonuses. Reggie got a $4.5 million signing bonus and $4.5 million his first year. Throw in another $3.1 million the second year and that's more than $12 million for two seasons. The Redskins and the 49ers couldn't compete with that much early money.

It's an impact decision I've never regretted. We received our money's worth and more from this great player—and equally great man.

His signing also is an example of intelligent negotiating, which is an essential part of building or improving a business. The better you can negotiate, the more effectively you can serve your company and do your job. It's a skill that extends to your personal life as well. Think of all the occasions in which you face negotiations at home, whether it's dealing with unacceptable service, reaching a compromise on a disputed bill, or even figuring out who's responsible for what duties within the house.

Good negotiating begins with good listening. You have to be able to listen to people. And not worry about time. Time is of no importance in negotiations. You take as much of it as you must because the key is to reach a successful conclusion, not worry about your next appointment. For me, that means if we sit down at 2 P.M. and we need to keep going until 2 A.M., then let's do it.

You also have to maintain a respect for your fellow negotiator. You must understand they have a job to do, just like you do. I approach all negotiations in a calm, matter-of-fact manner, and I try to stay that way. I save my outbursts for when I'm accused of something that isn't true, which happens far too frequently in many negotiations.

What you can't do is allow everything to become personal and worry more about the perceived insults than resolving the deal. If the negotiation becomes personal, you need to back off and let someone else take over. That's what happened to me with player negotiations. I just couldn't deal anymore with the junk that goes along with the discussions. I'd have some agent who knows nothing about my business tell me his guy should be paid $400,000 when he wasn't worth half that. Once I started getting angry all the time about such distorted claims, my expertise as a negotiator vanished. My attitude had become, "I really don't care, the guy's not that good, I don't want to pay him, and I'll never pay him what he's demanding." You don't conclude many negotiations with that approach.

But early on, I could wait people out. I just sat there, and they got tired. We would sit for ten hours, but I could outlast them. They could tell me they were very upset by my offer, and then they could scream at me and maybe I would scream back, but I would keep sitting. Eventually, we would iron something out.

It helps that I'm always prepared. You had better know what you're talking about before you start bargaining, particularly if the other guy is also well versed. Otherwise, it's easy to make a fool of yourself. Years ago, before a players' union existed and before we all knew what everyone was making, I was involved in negotiations over a player. His representative had a partner who negotiated for a player from another team who played the same position as my guy. The first agent and I really got into it. He told me what this other player was making, and I told him he was lying—I thought I knew but I really didn't—and it turns out the agent was right because his partner shared the information with him. So I was as wrong as I could be. I apologized to him. If you spend the time it takes to background yourself properly, you reduce the likelihood that you will wind up with a bad deal.

I always try to negotiate in the other guy's territory. I have read that if they come to you, it gives you an edge. But I disagree. If you go into their place, you show them you're very confident about your approach and you aren't embarrassed by your offer. In other words, you've made the trip because you intend to negotiate seriously, and not play games.

It's like using their edge against them. I can sit in their environment and not be intimidated by it. It allows you to say, hey, no preliminaries, no fussing around, none of this you-submit-an-offer, I-submit-an-offer stuff. Let's get on with it and get it done. I'm also not interested in leaving the table always feeling I have "won." To me, success is resolving the debate. A really good negotiator makes the other person feel he has won—and still gets the problem settled.

You have to understand that most of my negotiations prior to Green Bay were undertaken with Al Davis as my boss. With Al, whatever you did wasn't good enough. If I sign you for $1, it should have been 50 cents. If I signed you for a nickel, it should have cost nothing. This is an okay approach, but I got to a point where the only element that mattered was getting the guy signed. That was the most important thing. Then you worry about the ramifications later.

I'm not saying you give the person an exorbitant amount of money. You still negotiate within a framework. Bottom line is, however, I would rather have the person than kill my chances by not being realistic in my negotiations. Looking at bargaining in this manner makes you more flexible and reasonable, and, I believe, allows you to best serve your organization.

Let's say you don't do the deal because of some stupid hang-up over a contract term or because of a few thousand dollars difference. You hold the line and lose the guy. The next year, he signs with your chief competitor, and instead, you hire some-one who is better than the person you are replacing but not as good as the person you couldn't sign earlier. And, because of market changes, you have to pay the new guy twice as much as you were offering the person who got away. You look back and kick yourself for not being more flexible. When you become unreasonable, this is the scenario that inevitably results. I know because I've done the research. Maybe this is cliché, but it rings true in negotiations—a bird in the hand is worth two in the bush.

I try not to get myself in a position where I have to resort to intimidation. That's because I know I turn to intimidation only after I've been stripped of leverage and I have no other choice. Problem is, the other guy knows you have no leverage either, and you feel naked. It becomes a dance, and I'm not always taking the lead like I want to be.

The key, though, is to never let them see you sweat. We went through a test in 1995 when we traded with Miami for tight end Keith Jackson. We gave up a second-round choice for Keith and receiver Mark Ingram, and then Jackson didn't show up for camp. At one point, I was fearful I had surrendered a second-round pick, which I could have used to select a quality prospect, for a guy who would never play for us. If that turned out to be right, I would really have harmed the organization. I wondered if I should trade away Keith for a draft choice and then move on.

But the more I thought about it, the more I decided unloading Keith was a bad idea. Once my players realized they could force a deal by holding out, I would have a line at my door. I told Mike Holmgren and Bob Harlan we needed to take a stand, and fortunately, they agreed. It helped that tight end Mark Chmura was having a heck of a 1995 season. I felt bad over how the holdout was harming the organization and how it appeared players still felt they could walk all over us.

At our annual stockholders meeting, this guy gets up and really goes off on me. He wants to know how I could have traded off a second-round selection for a guy who says, before the deal, that he will not play here. The guy wants to know who's responsible for such a bad situation. I told him I was—and I told him, "Don't question the decision." I told Keith and his agent that he either would play for the Packers or he would sit out, and that meant he wouldn't be paid for a year. I remained firm with them, but believe me, I was sweating on the inside. We needed Keith in uniform; otherwise, our team wasn't as strong as it could be.

The trade deadline passed, and he reported. Money was a key element. It's hard to pass up this kind of income just because you don't want to play in a city that you've never taken time to know. Keith wound up being a major contributor on our Super Bowl winner, and he enjoyed his two years with us, so everything turned out great. And no one was more pleased about the results than I was.

It was a much more pleasant experience seeing Reggie White standing at a podium in Green Bay, explaining why he had signed with the Packers. I was pleased about the message he provided to the public that day. He said he was impressed with the coaching staff, the organization, and the direction in which the Packers were headed. He said when he began his free-agent trips, signing with the Packers was the furthest thing from his mind. But once he visited, everything changed. He said the Packers were a team on the rise, and that was important to him because he had to play with a contender. He said he had become intrigued with the franchise's history, and he wanted to help restore its championship feeling. He said he was taken by how we went about selling the franchise to him, concentrating not on glitter but on football issues.

He couldn't have said it better even if I had written the script for him. He was verifying all the messages I wanted to broadcast about the franchise. Everything was so positive, so upbeat and so different from how it had been in November of 1991.

His signing proved the Packers could take on premier franchises like the 49ers and Redskins and come away winners. It proved our unique style of ownership was modern enough to be competitive in the 1990s. It proved that an elite player could look at Green Bay and see promise, not the Arctic. It proved we could make the positives stand out and weaken the negatives.

It gave us instant credibility along the players' underground. If White could embrace Green Bay, why couldn't other athletes? It wasn't as if his signing started an avalanche of free agents rolling into our city—we couldn't afford that many more—but we no longer were viewed by future free agents as some sort of novelty act. We now were a star in the free-agent market, and our drive to rebuild the roster had received a major boost.

Reggie, of course, has given back so much more to us. Besides his exemplary performances on the field, where he continued to dominate from his defensive end spot, he immediately became a major leader in the locker room. His strong, loud, clear voice provided a rallying point for the rest of the defense, and the rest of the team. He was positive and tough; he played hurt, and he played well, and he made it difficult for others to slack off or take a day away from practice because of minor ailments. No one ever knew how much Reggie might be hurting. He just ignored the pain and never missed a step.

His status within the community can't be measured. He's a genuine hero. Mere mention of his name during games ignites an incredible response. His evangelism and caring ways have touched the hearts of Wisconsin residents. His decision to move permanently from Tennessee to the state solidified his status; imagine, if you can, what it means to Packer fans for a player to love them so much he's willing to spend the rest of his life within their midst.

With Reggie under contract, I thought we were on our way to erasing a lot of the major negatives that had been hanging over the organization. Now we could concentrate on trumpeting our strengths. The opposition had to take notice of us. For too long they had looked at the schedule, and if they saw us on it, they automatically wrote down a W, even if the game was in Lambeau. But that was going to change, thanks in large part to Reggie White. He gave us the jump-start we needed to spring to the fifth Stepping Stone: Use the Four C's to Measure Performance.

But before we move on, here are the prominent points you should remember from Stepping Stone No. 4—Play to Your Strengths:

• Recognize that all businesses will have negatives. Instead of ignoring them in hopes they might somehow disappear, you should confront detrimental situations. Otherwise, negatives can stifle growth and trample morale, making recruiting of new employees all but impossible. Even in a home business, you can't allow negatives to serve as excuses for standing still.

• Determine all the positives that exist within the organization and figure ways to use these as a foundation to begin the turnaround.

• Understand that your business, regardless of size, needs to commit to large expenditures when necessary in order to make a pivotal impact on its future and create strength within the organization. The money, for example, might be spent to hire a highly regarded manager or buy an innovative piece of equipment that will immediately improve productivity. The key here is to consider the long-term potential for the investment instead of worrying about the short-term financial strain created by the expenditure.

• Examine the history of your company and see if it's possible to draw successes from the past that can be used to bolster current morale. Bring back retired standout executives from your company's past and let them conduct seminars or speak to your employees. Set aside an area at your headquarters to hold symbols of your organization's past triumphs. Encourage your employees to take pride in their company's history and use those glories as measuring sticks for future achievements.

• Add special programs and services within the company that could ease complaints and build positive goodwill. Your goal should be to make your business warm and fuzzy, not cold and threatening.

• Examine facilities objectively, and improve and upgrade them when necessary in order to provide the most positive working environment possible. Find out what your employees don't like about where they work and make changes to reduce the grousing. If you work in your home, don't be content with dreary surroundings. You want to make your workplace a strength.

• Negotiate from a positive position, with the idea of getting the deal done. Don't allow petty issues and egos to interfere with or block a resolution. Carry into the negotiations an attitude that your goal is to hire the person you want or to obtain whatever you need and that you must be flexible enough to fulfill your mission. You never want to look back and be upset that you botched something good for your company because of your stubbornness.

CHAPTER FIVE

Use the Four C's to Measure Performance

A car dealer friend of mine once told me he learned to run his organization more efficiently by watching how the Packers conducted their daily business routine. Of course, I was grateful for the compliment. But I was also curious. What exactly did he mean?

"You have based performance on measurable standards," he told me. "It cuts through the uncertainties and helps both management and the employees. Management has a system to make judgments and employees know exactly what it takes to do their job right."

He said he adapted what he learned from the Packers to his business. He began evaluating his personnel by putting up a chart and establishing performance levels. Those who matched or exceeded the minimum expected results were rewarded. Those who didn't were either terminated or given a warning. Although he made some allowances for potential and inexperience, he relied almost exclusively on the chart to form opinions about how his business was functioning.

The Packers don't have a chart posted in our front office. We aren't in the automotive business, so setting quotas to measure our performances doesn't make sense. But we have reduced the gray area in job evaluations as much as we can. We've done that by being as precise and as firm and as consistent as possible about what it takes to be a top-notch employee for the Green Bay Packers—and what won't be tolerated from our associates.

It doesn't matter where your business is situated on the developmental curve. You must have in place the specific standards and expectations by which performance can be judged. But this is particularly essential when you're either introducing change into the organization or trying to revitalize and reorder an enterprise.

Change always creates turmoil and anxiety in varying degrees, depending on the amount of alterations being instituted. The more confusing a situation becomes for employees, the more important it is that they find stability in some part of the business function. If they clearly understand how they should go about their duties and how their performance is being evaluated, they will adjust to the new atmosphere more easily.

I knew that if I wanted to accomplish the goals I had established for the Packers, I had to introduce instability and managed chaos into a structure that had been mired in stability for too long. So, in these early years, it was essential for me to remain steadfast in my expectations and judgments in dealing with my employees.

When I took over, the Packers had stability. But it was the wrong kind. It was lax in its demands and comforting in its judgments. In this form of stability, employees function in a safe zone that shields them from job stress and rarely requires extra effort. This environment is characterized by its tendency to produce lots of employees with long tenures. The organization is top-heavy with people who've been around for years and believe the business owes them a living. Dismissing them is virtually impossible, if considered at all. The result is the equivalent of a mellow song. It sounds good and feels good, but it generates no excitement, no message. That was the Packers for too many years after Lombardi. A nice song that didn't offend or inspire anyone.

These determinations became the cornerstone of the fifth Stepping Stone: Use the Four C's to Measure Performance. This was the last step I needed to take within the organization before our full attention could be focused on the development of the football team—and to the system that would be employed to upgrade the talent level.

The cornerstones of the fifth Stepping Stone are four principles. Expect Certain Devotion. Expect Certain Dedication. Expect Certain Work Ethic. Expect Certain Results. I was determined to develop each so completely that it would eliminate any questions or doubts about how the Packers would function and how each employee was expected to perform. In the process, I would use the four C's to ignite an enthusiasm that would push the business toward excellence and shake off the lethargy that had plagued it for so long.

It was essential that these standards apply to every layer of the Packers, including top management. What was good for my scouts was also good for me and everyone who worked directly under me. There wouldn't be a double standard in my organization. I find double standards abhorrent. They produce ill will and mistrust within the staff, and they generate resentment toward management and fellow employees. If you have standout employees, reward them with raises and promotions, not with special treatment, relaxed rules, and soft demands. Double standards inevitably lead to lousy morale within the enterprise, and poor morale can cut into production and waste energy.

Yet, too many bosses utilize this damaging management method. They adopt favorites among their staff and single out these people for obviously preferential treatment. The favored few leave early when everyone has to stay late. They can miss deadlines when everyone else must adhere to the standards. They can overspend their budget or violate company rules and never be reprimanded.

Taken to an extreme, double standards can severely hamper the smooth operation of an organization. Those receiving special treatment suddenly aren't as productive as they need to be. They grow increasingly difficult to deal with and incredibly demanding. The burden of carrying the business falls on others who must make up for the lack of output from the select few. The end result is that an enterprise's ability to utilize talent to its full potential is limited.

If you have some employees who aren't carrying a fair load, no business can function at peak capacity. It's like having a star player who decides he only wants to play in the second and fourth quarters or on first and second downs. He still may contribute, but he'll never be as good as if he played a whole game. You can't have employees who won't travel on weekends when everyone else does, who refuse to work overtime when everyone else does, or must always have a lunch break at a certain time, unlike everyone else. If they're given privileges that are denied to the majority of their peers, it's a sign of management weakness. And employees won't waste any time taking advantage of this wrongly placed generosity.

Instead, you need to EXPECT CERTAIN DEVOTION from everyone, without allowing exceptions to develop. What I mean by "certain devotion" is simple, yet sometimes so difficult to obtain. I want my employees to truly embrace the Green Bay Packers and develop an incredible loyalty for the organization. That's one of my paramount goals as a manager. I will make a commitment to you by hiring you or maintaining your employment. In return, you need to give your utmost to the company to help us succeed. Both sides must uphold their obligations.

Just because you work for me, I have no mandate to carry you. Nor should you ever think you are owed a job by this organization, that you can slack off and still expect to be paid. I once operated under the premise that no one really wants to fail, that we all have a drive to excel. But I've changed my mind. There are members of our workforce who believe that businesses are set up to serve their needs, and not vice versa. This "owe me" mentality, with the resulting hands-out requests, is contrary to everything I believe makes an organization successful. To erase that type of selfish thinking, it's essential that the relationship between employee and employer stems from a mutual bond, not a one-sided deal. It's a mutual devotion to the same goal. As you work to best serve your firm, my promise to you is that I will do nothing to take away your respect. You will always be treated with a dignity you deserve.

This is not a pipe dream. I've seen this kind of devotion develop with the Raiders, and now, with the Packers. A vast majority of the people who work for us take incredible pride not only in what they do, but also in the accomplishments of the organization. Maybe they didn't play a down in Super Bowl XXXI or XXXII, but they rightfully still felt they had made a major contribution to the team's on-field success.

I'm not talking about lip service here either, where employees go along with our expectations but really don't embrace our goals. Your aim should be to make your enterprise so appealing and so invigorating that it becomes a pleasure to be an employee. This doesn't mean lax rules, soft demands, or easy goals. It does mean creating a fair and rewarding environment that generates pride and discipline.

You want to create a self-policing situation in which those employees who don't embrace the prevailing attitude are nudged along by their peers, not their supervisors. Once this happens, the people who leave before the work is finished, who are first out the door at quitting time, or who extend their breaks unreasonably, feel peer pressure. They're reminded that they aren't putting the welfare of the company—and the welfare of those who have to pick up the slack—ahead of their own selfishness. This self-policing is the certain devotion you want to generate.

I previously have referred to the philosophy of "buying-in" as one of my fundamental management principles. Devotion is all about buying in. It starts with a strong statement from management about what's expected from each employee. To me, it's elementary. You produce, you stay. You don't produce, you leave. Whether, in our case, you're a player, a secretary, a scout, a trainer, a video guy, or a receptionist. Any business that doesn't have a clear, precise operating tenet like this has not established the foundation that allows its enterprise to grow.

Our message to the players has been repeated constantly: we

expect you to perform at a certain level, which will be made clear to you through training and repetition. If you don't perform at that level, we move on. You make big dollars, you had better play like big dollars. If you make big dollars and talk a good game instead of playing it, you're gone. In other words, when it's your time to produce, you had better be up to it.

I expect my employees to buy into this operating tenet. When they're hired by the Packers, they absolutely know what's expected of them. It's great if they have a wonderful sense of humor and a terrific family and an admirable work background, but if they don't live up to our expectations, they'll soon be looking for other employment.

It's up to me to do everything possible to allow our people to produce. I must examine our business operations with the aim of removing obstacles that stand in the way of maximum production. It's unreasonable to expect a certain level of performance while at the same time impeding everyone's ability to reach that goal because of barriers instituted by the company.

Nothing frustrates me more than idiotic rules. Want to order paper clips? Got to sign a form. Want a vacation week? Fill out all this in triplicate. Got a question? Oops, can't ask that person unless he's your direct supervisor. Want to stay in a certain hotel near your primary account? Nope, a room costs $10 more than the company limit. None of these barriers makes any sense. They become nuisances or, worse, impediments to job performance. The aim shouldn't be control; it should be to make people feel they're professional and trustworthy and that the company isn't paranoid about their behavior.

I don't ask any employee to drive my car, wash my car, shovel my driveway, or do any other "off-the-job" duty. I understand a lot of teams take their college scouts off the road occasionally and have them evaluate current NFL players. We don't do that. It would interfere with the duties my college scouts were hired to perform. I want them to be the best scouts they can be, not the most versatile personnel men in the business. I don't want to do anything that slows this quest. I wouldn't ask them to, say, scout an NFL game just because they're visiting a college in the same area.

These college scouts are asked to do one thing: evaluate players to the best of their abilities. They're given plenty of time to do their job and the freedom it takes to do it right. They don't fill out foolish forms; their energy is funneled into meeting their obligations. Their task is not easy. They're on the road for extended periods, then they spend more months helping to put together our draft board. Once that's finished, they have $3^1/_2$ months of downtime to recharge their batteries. During that period, no one from the Packers is badgering them for information or interfering with their relaxation.

This is what contributes to being a good manager. I understand people have needs. I give them an opportunity to do their job without additional strings attached. I treat them in a professional fashion by keeping loose control over their schedules. I create an atmosphere in which it's obvious I believe in them and their abilities. If they fail, it won't be due to unnecessary obstacles constructed by the Packers.

You must be mindful of the spirit of the people who work for you. If I expect devotion, they should expect my acknowledgment that they're not faceless individuals merely around to pick up a paycheck. That's why little things can mean so much. We had a rule governing our charter flights to the Super Bowl. Space was available to our families. If seats remained, people outside the operation could buy them. But interns weren't allowed to participate. I thought that was wrong. Other than gaining job experience, interns do lots of unexciting but necessary work for little reward. By letting them go along, we had a chance to thank them in a big way. Yet they weren't included. Bob Harlan listened to my arguments and agreed with me.

We can't divide employees into informal, separate sections, then treat each section differently, and still expect everyone to have the same level of devotion. The lowest-paid employee should be governed by the same rules and expectations as the highest-level personnel. Once an organization loses sight of how far it's come and of the people who helped generate the improvements, it's setting itself up for a fall. You stomp on employees long enough, and the word gets out. Your company becomes an undesirable place to work, and that impedes your ability to bring in the best workers you can find.

Unfortunately, businesses frequently trample employees who are in the embryonic stages of their professional development. Why penalize the guy who's working for next to nothing, who just wants to learn, who so often has served the organization well?

I've noticed that businesses, once they start having success, also have a tendency to add restrictive rules. It's a reaction, I guess, to a fear that if they don't institute strict controls, things might move backward. I've cautioned my people that we can't fall into this restrictive rut. The better you become, the harder you must work to remain just as aggressive. You can't ever stop striving to be better.

I do have workplace standards. We ask people to be neat. We ask them to be presentable. When they are representing the Green Bay Packers, we expect their conduct will never reflect badly on the organization. I want people to look at us and say, "They've got some class." In turn, everything we do as an organization will be as first class as possible. Our scouts are given Packer shirts and jackets. I want them to wear this attire with pride, because I want them to be glad they work for us. We'll set the standard high for ourselves, across the board, no exceptions. This is as good as it gets in my line of work—and pettiness and stupidity won't be allowed to tear it down.

Within my operation, we don't have rules regarding hair length or earrings, that sort of thing. You come in looking like a slob and you'll be told to clean up your act. People understand that. We dress casually because the most important thing to me is not whether you wear a shirt and tie, but your accomplishments. I've seen colleges where the trainer comes to work in a jacket and tie. That's okay, but his job isn't enhanced because he looks like he walked out of the pages of *GQ*. I'd be much more concerned with how he performs his responsibilities. I'm convinced that companies that have relaxed dress codes won't see a drop-off in production. Instead, they have done themselves a huge favor by taking the focus off needless requirements and putting it on the right priority, the performance of duties.

If I hired you today, I wouldn't tell you to dress a certain way. I wouldn't tell you to shave your mustache or trim your hair. I wouldn't tell you to take out your earring. None of that. I would tell you that I expect you to be productive and to uphold your responsibilities. Immediately I have put the emphasis on the right area. I haven't allowed peripheral issues and rules to become dominant. I have focused on what's important to me and the organization and I have begun your initiation into the Packer Way.

The CERTAIN DEDICATION I expect evolves as you fulfill your job requirements. You're dedicating yourself to winning. You're dedicating yourself so completely that you eventually understand you aren't in this alone. Instead, you're part of a team, so that if the team succeeds, you also do, and if the team blows it, you share in the blame even if you upheld your duties. That's when "we" becomes more important than "I." That's when losses upset you no matter your contribution. That's when bad news bothers you even when your contributions were positive.

Here's how I can measure dedication. Take one of my scouts. Let's say we're scheduled to discuss one of his prospects. He might think the prospect is an outstanding player. So before we get together, he's taken it upon himself to study all-star games or look at tape of other players with comparable ability. He now has the background to make a much stronger case for his guy rather than just telling me, "I think he can play." He's busting his butt to increase his knowledge and do a better job. The guys who have the wherewithal and determination to take that extra step become the best scouts. They would be elite workers in any organization because they're stretching themselves and seeing beyond the minimal requirements. That's dedication.

Ultimately, it comes down to this. You have to be willing to make the sacrifices that enable you to reach the top of your profession. If you aren't willing to accept that and put in the time it takes, then you can't work for us because that's what we constantly demand. If you shirk your duties, I'll know it, and more important, you'll know it, and you'll be replaced.

As a manager, you have to realize not everyone automatically understands what it means to be dedicated. I always sit down with our new people and explain life as a Packer to them. In my business, you can never know enough. It is a constant quest for knowledge. For scouts, it means learning enough about their business to be able to identify who can play and who can't. You don't learn that by working the fewest hours possible. And they have to understand how I feel about these issues. I don't want our people guessing at what it takes to meet our standards. I tell them straight out.

When I first started with the Raiders in 1963, I knew nothing about scouting. Al Davis wanted to hire and train someone who was good with names of NFL players. A mutual acquaintance from my brief tenure as an office worker with *Pro Football Illustrated* (now *Pro Football Weekly*) recommended me to Al. At that time, I had finished a stint in the army and gone to the University of Oklahoma, where I was concluding studies in my major, history. I then planned to join the Central Intelligence Agency. Al called me the day of my last final and gave me a test. He would ask me about a player, and I would tell him where he went to school, his number, and other information. Then he offered me a job. I had always wanted to work in the league. But I lost hope when the letters I wrote to teams as I was leaving the service failed to generate any response. I couldn't believe how my luck had changed.

I spent my first months with the Raiders listening and learning. I would sit in a room with Al and the coaches—there were only four coaches back then—and look at film and watch as they broke down players and performances. I slowly began developing a feel for what characteristics separated the good player from the bad and the great from the good. I couldn't have picked up the knowledge I needed without a certain amount of dedication to my job.

I was trained to the finest detail. I wasn't just tossed out on the road and left to wander around, unsure of my duties. I knew I'd better fulfill my responsibilities to the fullest because that was the demand placed on me by Al. When I went into Al's office, I realized I couldn't buffalo him about a player's talent so I had better be prepared. He was too sharp and too well-informed to mislead. Inevitably, he would ask a question I hadn't thought about and wasn't prepared for, and it would throw me off. But this wonderful knack made you work incredibly hard so you could handle anything he tossed out.

I'm amazed how organizations hire people and don't train them properly, yet expect complete dedication. Instead, they risk spewing out employees who are left to guess how they're supposed to function. No matter your dedication, this lack of preparation is a quick way to fail. When we hire a new scout, we assign him to somebody like Ted Thompson, our director of player personnel, for direction. Then we'll send someone out with him on the road, so he will learn firsthand it's not the glamorous life it's made out to be.

If I expect you to uphold your end of the obligation to the organization, I can't shut you out from learning your job as best you can. I have the experience to help you, and I'm willing to share as much of that knowledge as you want. That's why a truly "open door" is necessary. My employees need to be able to come into my office anytime they want, for whatever reason, and ask questions. I'd rather have them do that instead of refusing to seek help and messing up a project that they couldn't handle. If you admit you lack all the answers, I won't think less of you. Instead . . . welcome to the club. It's essential that if you can't handle a responsibility, you let me know. I will think more of you as a person for being honest. Once you accept a job without protest, it tells me you're capable of fulfilling it and I expect it to be done right.

There aren't any shortcuts to excellence. You can't deviate very much off the path that leads to success. If you manufacture concrete, no matter how your industry has changed, that concrete still must have the correct consistency and have the proper ability to harden or you've messed up. Modern technology, for example, has made it easier for our scouts to file reports. They can put all the information into their laptop computers. But the steps they take to compile that information haven't changed, and their investigation had better be just as painstaking as ever. You can't shortchange your dedication to your job, no matter how the workplace evolves.

I consider work hours a test of dedication. I detest clock-watching. I find it incomprehensible that you can turn it on at 9 A.M. and turn it off at 5 P.M., walk out the door, and not think about what you might have accomplished by coming in earlier or staying later. I'll never monitor your hours. I don't want to know when you started your lunch break. Nor do I care when you returned. What I care about is that you know there's a job to be done and you're willing to put in whatever time it takes to finish it, even if it means extending your day.

This nine-to-five mentality was far too prevalent with the Packers in 1991. When the work day ended, you'd better not be blocking the door or you'd risk getting trampled by the employees rushing to their cars. I was appalled. In their minds, they were striving to be successful, but only if it could be accomplished within their parameters. Heaven forbid that it might mean working more. That would never do. I had to change that loser's attitude.

I'm not talking about encouraging "show" hours either, where people sit around and wait for the boss to leave. They really aren't productive. Instead, they realize if they go home too early, they risk a reprimand. I'm always looking out for these types. I'm also repulsed by the employees who come up with the great ideas after the fact, who talk the good talk but can't perform. They really don't know anything about winning. Nor are they ever happy with what you give them. Hand them $4, and they want $8. Hand them $8, and they want $80. I'd rather hand them a termination letter.

I also had better not hear from a third party that you're unhappy. You need the fortitude to come to me and make your complaint. Whenever I read in the paper about a player who's complaining, I seek him out immediately and tell him, "Let me set the record straight. My door is always open and you need to come in and talk to me. There's no excuse for failing to air your problems." These people are a cancer to an organization. Get rid of them.

Treat braggarts the same way. I can't tolerate those employees who want to make sure you know how hard they work. I don't need to be constantly reminded how brilliant you are. Our goal is to make the organization brilliant, not its individuals. You were hired to do a certain job, and that hiring demonstrated we had a respect for your brains and your ability. If you perform up to standards, I don't have to be told. It will be demonstrated by results, and you'll be rewarded.

Nor do I think the level of your dedication should be influenced by the amount of money you make. Let's say I'm earning $20,000. Maybe if I dedicate myself to improving my skills and maybe if I become more valuable to the organization, I'll be promoted and my salary will increase. The key here is for the employee to know that improvement truly is rewarded and not acknowledged by a mere thank-you.

I know dedication pays off because I proved it. Al Davis paid me $60 a week when I first started, and I told him we couldn't live on that salary. So he raised me another $100. We rented an apartment for $110 a month and lived off the rest. But he also gave me an opportunity, and I tried to take advantage of that chance and make something of myself by giving everything I could to improve. I want an organization full of employees who are dedicated to pushing themselves up the corporate ladder. I don't want the demands to be so overbearing that employees are denied a life. But they need to develop enough pride in their work that it gets done to the best of their ability, regardless of the time it takes.

Mike Holmgren and I talk all the time about our expectations regarding those around us. We both realize we have to be careful. We expect so much of ourselves that we also expect others to care as deeply. Most times, that won't happen. We both get frustrated when a deadline is missed or when a request is not fulfilled quite as thoroughly as we wanted. I can't judge everyone by my standards and my drive; not everyone is governed by my internal fear of failure. Still, there's a certain level of dedication that is fair to expect, and that is what we try to obtain.

That's why I won't hire friends, unless I want to lose their friendship. Your relationship automatically establishes a test of dedication. If you aren't happy with their efforts, it becomes difficult to approach them and discuss it like you would with another employee. There's a built-in comfort zone between the two of you that permits lax performances and a decrease in demand. If I like someone, it's natural not to want to hear anything negative about the person. My antenna will shut down, and that's wrong. It's the incorrect way to fulfill my responsibilities. I have to apply the same standards to every employee, friend or not. I certainly wouldn't hire a friend to do a menial job; that would be demeaning to him. I'm not sure anything good can come from bringing in friends, so I don't do it.

The same applies to people who have previously worked with you. In Tampa, I hired some people I knew, and it turned out they weren't as good as I thought they were. It created a lot of tension and slowed production. It's better just to go another route.

I also refuse to beg people to work for me. If I try to hire them and they turn me down, I move on. The initial refusal casts doubt in my mind about their long-term commitment. They either refused at first because they didn't think they were capable of meeting our requirements or they really wanted to stay at their current job. To attempt to nudge them from either mind-set doesn't benefit our organization. If they don't jump at the opportunity to work for us, I'll find someone else. I certainly don't want to be involved in a bidding war for their services.

I'm more tolerant of someone's personal problems. Although

I would never condone the use of drugs or excessive drinking, I also don't necessarily believe either is a sure sign of lack of dedication to the organization. You can't arbitrarily dismiss someone who is entangled with a societal problem. You can't bury your head and say these problems don't exist or that your firm is exempt from their effects. Nor can you fail to help someone seek and receive rehabilitation. The organization has an obligation to try to aid a person with problems. But there's a limit to how far a business should go before it should reconsider the situation.

If our production level falls because of this person's failure to properly rehabilitate himself, you have reason to dismiss the employee. First, though, I want to give the person every opportunity to improve himself and salvage his life. It'll become obvious whether the rehabilitation has been successful or whether he's no longer an asset to the organization.

Because society is constantly changing, it's important that a manager, as he grows older, keeps young employees around him. I'm still listening to oldies stations. I don't have a clue about heavy metal and the rest. So I have younger guys talking to me about how college life is these days. These conversations enhance my understanding of today's athlete, which, in turn, helps me to fulfill my personnel duties more responsibly.

My younger associates talk to me constantly about the nineties players, how so many of them don't have a male influence in their lives, how they've been raised by a mother or aunt or grandmother. Their home life is different than the one I knew—and it changes them. We talk about their music and their dress, all the things that my generation has a difficult time accepting and understanding. They talk to me about the temptations of their generation that are different from the temptations that confronted mine. I still have my standards and beliefs, but these discussions at least broaden my view of the world around me. It makes me a more effective manager and, I hope, a smarter person.

My desire for a CERTAIN WORK ETHIC hinges on the ability of our employees to flourish under a freewheeling atmosphere that encourages constructive thinking and initiative. Ideally, I want an organization where people are allowed to work without constant monitoring. If I find a task is not being performed correctly, I always reserve the right to interfere. But it's preferable to surround myself with self-starters who understand our mission so well they can function as sort of independent contractors.

To establish the work ethic I'm seeking, it's crucial to properly delineate lines of authority and responsibility. I don't want to micromanage, which is evident in the way our office functions during the large chunks of time throughout the year that I'm traveling.

From late August through November, I'm constantly on the road scouting. I try to leave the office on Tuesday, and sometimes I don't return until after our game on Sunday. Obviously, I can't coach the football team from a hotel room, nor do I try. Mike Holmgren has the responsibility and authority to direct the Packers. We talk frequently, but I don't want him to run every little piddling thing by me. From training camp on, he sets everything up. I only ask that I know what's happening before I read about it in the newspapers.

When something unexpected happens, particularly pertaining to an injury, we communicate even more than normal. But if I meddled constantly, it would belie the confidence I showed when I hired him. He wanted the opportunity. So it was up to me to get out of the way and let him prove himself. And he certainly has.

I have enough trust in the rest of my people that I can be away frequently and still feel assured the internal operations of our organization will run properly. I don't expect, nor want, to be informed about every development. The major ones, yes, but as far as overseeing every aspect of what we do, that's not going to happen.

My faith, however, had better be rewarded. If you tell me you'll be in a certain place at a certain time to do a certain job and you don't show up, it'll eventually get back to me. I've been in this business long enough to have a network that keeps everyone in line. It's just like excuses. Give me too many of them, and you have begun your walk out the door.

I expect the leaders in my organization to use their authority wisely. Power can inflate people's egos far too quickly. I try very hard to anticipate how someone might handle power. I don't want to promote anyone who will turn into a pocket dictator, running roughshod over the people under him. This again becomes an abuse of my faith in that employee, and it won't be tolerated.

I foster leadership that works, not leadership that abuses. I will constantly push those with leadership potential. I will praise them, stroke them, do anything to help them realize their promise. Still, until someone is placed in a position of leadership, it's impossible to predict how well they'll do. How could anyone foresee the type of leader Mike Holmgren has become? He embraced the responsibilities he was given and expanded on them. You watch how people react to him and see how he can make players conform to his wishes, and you understand the incredible importance of strong leadership to a business.

You get constant feedback about your organizational leaders, so you had better make sure you're listening. In my business, everyone is willing to share their opinions about anyone who's a Packer. I hear opinions from fans, from the media, from players, from other people in the building. But you too have opportunities to receive input. Talk to your immediate supervisors. Encourage a suggestion box. Hold regular lunch meetings with various segments of your operation. Engage in impromptu conversations with employees. You only need to be willing to hear what they say. Just as I do, you can use this information to form an accurate picture about how your leaders handle pressure, how they deal with other people, how they inspire those around them to perform to their maximum talents.

Your ability to mold a proper work ethic depends substantially on the faith you show in your employees' capacity to think. If you give them freedom and then constantly second-guess their decisions, you'll shut down your efforts to produce independent wisdom. I go out of my way to establish an atmosphere in which everyone is aware how much I appreciate aggressive thinking and decision making.

When I hire people, I tell them, "Okay, you're the person for this job. Here's how we run what you're going to do. Now, run it." They run it, I don't. I'm not standing over them, watching them every day, every week, every month. The only time I'll come to them is if someone is having a problem with them in another part of the business, or maybe a piece of equipment they supervise doesn't work, or they ordered something incorrectly. Then I want to know the "why" behind the problem. I'm not going to jump them. We'll handle it professionally until they show me they're incapable of performing. I will meddle only after I have attempted to address the situation with advice and warnings. If I don't receive the improvement I want, I act.

I want to avoid bouncing in and out of a situation. When I'm around, I resist the temptation to undercut my managers by intruding into their daily operations and either offering unsolicited advice or, in essence, doing their job for them. You're weakening your enterprise with this kind of blatant interference. In the process, you're draining authority and respect from your top leaders.

Within a year of being with the Packers, I had a new trainer, a new equipment man, some new scouts, a new head coach, and a group of new assistant coaches. These new people exert themselves and execute their responsibilities with the independence I'm seeking.

I demand strong personalities. We had a new, young scout who told us we should bring in a free agent to test. I deliberately jumped all over him and asked him why. He gave his reasons, but I didn't think he was persuasive enough, so we didn't follow his suggestion. It turns out the player performed well for another team. During a later meeting, I told the scout in front of everyone, "You were right and we were wrong. We should have listened to you. It would have been a heck of a deal for us, and

I'm kicking myself for not doing it." I turned to the room and said, "Let that be a lesson to everyone. If you have something to say, don't be afraid to say it and stick with it. No matter what I do, don't be afraid to stand your ground. What I want is the right decision for the organization. It doesn't matter who gets credit as long as the organization benefits."

By admitting my mistake and praising him for his evaluation, I accomplished two important goals. I showed that I wasn't infallible, so they should be less concerned about making their own mistakes. And I showed how important opinions are to me, that I want people to speak out loudly and strongly. As much as possible, I use positive reinforcement to draw them out, open their minds, and build their ability to think clear of my control. I'd love nothing more than a roomful of people so confident that they virtually demand we either sign or draft a player. Or, if I was in another business, demand I buy a company or take on a new account.

Because of my position, I receive a lot of credit when we are successful. While I appreciate it, I also strive to make sure the people who really deserve the praise are acknowledged. I never look upon a successful draft choice, for example, as "my guy." Rather, the whole operation is responsible for the selection, and everyone who works for us should feel that way. That's the aim of everything we do—to forgo individual credit for the good of the Packers, because if the business benefits, the individual will benefit.

I'll also use praise to accomplish another goal. I want people to understand that if they do something that improves the Packers, I'll make sure everyone within the organization knows it. At the same time, if I hear someone is taking credit for an achievement I know darn well was due to another person's labors, I'll straighten out that misconception immediately. I'll make a public show of placing credit on the right shoulders, and if I have to accompany that with a private meeting to correct the offending party, I will. I want the people who do the work to benefit, not anyone else.

It's also important to understand the personalities of your employees. Some thrive on positive reinforcement. Others require a swift nudge. It would be a mistake to treat everyone exactly the same. You can't scream at everyone, nor can you be low-key with everyone. It's worth the extra effort needed to learn about each individual. Once you're armed with the proper knowledge, you can tailor your methods to each person.

Let me use players as an example. In 1997, we had a young kicker, Ryan Longwell, whom we claimed on waivers after he was cut by the 49ers. He wound up replacing Brett Conway, our 1997 third-round choice who got hurt in preseason. Some kickers you leave alone. They're in a different world. But Longwell is unique. He could give it back as quickly as I could jab him. I enjoy walking by him and exchanging a few opinions with him. He'll smile and not give an inch. He's mentally tough. He has grit, and a kicker needs that. What other position in sports asks you to be perfect every time you perform? Other guys would have wondered why I was riding them, or maybe they would have thought I disliked them. Not Longwell. But I would use another approach with a more sensitive player. Otherwise, I might needlessly offend someone for no valid reason.

If I'm not pleased with the staunchness of the opinions I'm hearing from my staff, I turn to some techniques I've developed that break through the reluctance and foster some strength of character. Sometimes, I'll jump all over an employee and really push him to be honest with me instead of telling me what he thinks I want to hear. I'll prod him by informing him that although I might be happy with his performance, he needs to step it up even more to become a producer worthy of his potential. I'll tell him he's too talented not to fully utilize his gifts. Sometimes I'll stir the pot, a method I discussed in Chapter Three. I'll question someone spontaneously about an issue, just to test his ability to give me an honest opinion without a lot of preparation. I'm always goading staffers into being their own people.

Everything we do depends on constant communication. And it all starts at the top. I won't allow anyone, including my chief aides, to hide behind e-mail and other such isolation-provoking technology. Nor can they depend on memos. We all work for the same firm; how can you tolerate someone in the office next to you sending you an e-mail or writing you a memo instead of walking over and having a discussion? Our managers have to be anxious to rely on face-to-face talks, the more informal the better. They have to establish a rapport with their colleagues that allows a free flow of information, eliminates yes-men–type approaches, and demands honesty. We want continuous feedback, not computer-speak. As a boss, you can't be intimidating or cop an attitude that indicates to everyone you really don't want an opinion but more a confirmation of your view.

If you're doing something I don't like, I don't go home and agonize over it or send you a message. I tell you straight out what's wrong and how I expect you to correct it. I attempt to be tactful, but we're not in this to worry much about egos and hurt feelings, either mine or my employees. The main priority is to do everything we can to succeed. No one in our organization should ever be able to say they didn't know whether I thought they were doing well or needed to improve. They know, because I talk to them.

My employees also know their achievements will be rewarded financially. If I EXPECT CERTAIN RESULTS from my associates, I also must show my appreciation for their efforts in concrete ways. Like any manager, I have a certain expectation that employees should fulfill their job requirements. That's why they're being paid. Beyond that, though, I'm constantly pushing to see performances that far exceed the minimum. If I do, I don't think a mere thank-you or a hearty pat on the back is sufficient.

As I mentioned earlier, the obligation between the organization and the employee works both ways. If I expect a certain standard of performance from our staff, they also should have expectations from me. My obligation to them starts with a pledge to make them better. You create an atmosphere where everyone believes they have a chance to improve themselves. It's simple: find the best, reward the best, and train the best to be even better. I'm convinced any company following this philosophy will find itself filled with ever-improving employees who are raising the bar to new heights.

If someone has worked a year for you and hasn't improved noticeably, you and your organization have let both that person and yourself down. You need to rethink your training approach and your motivational techniques. Your responsibility as a manager is to put every employee in a position that will allow him to flourish, and never ask anyone to perform a task that exceeds their capabilities. Otherwise, you're setting someone up for failure.

I understand what it's like to work very hard, make strides, and not be rewarded in a manner you feel acceptable. Working for Al Davis was a great experience in so many ways, but when it came to financial rewards, I learned how not to handle the situation. I really never felt I was appreciated monetarily by the Raiders, and it bothered me. A good manager should never forget what it was like when he wasn't in charge. He should take the best from those experiences and toss out the behavior from his bosses that he found distasteful, vowing never to repeat it. If one of your old managers constantly screamed or lost his patience quickly and this behavior destroyed morale, your goal should be to avoid these inefficient traits when you're put in a position of influence.

I still believe it's important for someone to prove his value before he reaps the rewards. I tend to hire people at relatively low salary levels and then give them plenty of room to grow. The results I expect from them are spelled out clearly and succinctly. They're expected to be a team player, to think for themselves, to have independent work habits, to constantly strive to make our organization better, and to take extra measures to exceed their job requirements. I tell them they will eventually make a significant contribution to the club, and they'll be rewarded accordingly. This approach has worked very well for us.

If employees live up to your expectations, they should benefit through salary increases and promotions. Because I think all raises should be performance-driven, I don't believe in automatic cost-of-living increases. If you don't deserve a jump in your income, you shouldn't get one. I'd rather give substantial raises to someone who has really bought into what we're selling. I always keep in mind that adage, "If you pay peanuts, you get monkeys."

We also create positions for those who've earned promotions. As the Packers improved, it became apparent that some employees needed to be elevated, so we carved out spots that gave them more responsibility and more money. At the same time, I have little tolerance for those who constantly have their hands out, wanting additional increases. These people generate an unhealthy buzz within the organization. I use a direct approach dealing with this problem. I talk to the individual, and either figure out a way to satisfy him or determine when he should leave the club.

I never use evaluation forms to make any personnel decisions. I don't need a form to help me evaluate a performance. Besides, what if the form is filled out on a day I'm irritated with you? Maybe that would be unfairly reflected in my evaluation. Evaluation forms also become substitutes for an on-going analysis of an employee's performance. Managers back off from giving constant feedback, which is the right way to conduct business, and wait for a formalized situation, such as annual reviews. By then, a problem that should have been handled months ago has been allowed to fester, and that's not efficient management. Even if your company policy requires formal evaluations, don't substitute that procedure for ongoing, informal conversations with your employees.

I don't give out individual bonuses, although if the Packers do well, we have a bonus system tied to the play-offs. Employees receive money depending on their length of service with the organization, and it can be a substantial sum. Used properly, bonuses have their place. I learned that from Bob Harlan, who awards an annual Christmas bonus to every employee. I'd never been in an organization with that philosophy, and I found Bob's approach eye-opening. I believe it's a superb gesture by a company to its employees. It shows we care, and because the bonus is handed out at that time of year, it has a particularly warm aspect to it. It reminded me that you can't lose sight of the value of the human element. What did someone once say — it takes 3 muscles to smile and 14 to frown? Companies frown too much.

Unfortunately, sometimes you have to fire an employee. It's perhaps the most difficult aspect of my job, and that never changes. You understand you're affecting not only the life of the employee, but usually his family and his economic future. But you also understand that, in these situations, the needs of the organization become paramount.

Firing is a process of evaluation. You come to realize that an employee isn't capable of handling his job. It's an admission, really, that you failed as a manager because he's been in a position where he couldn't succeed. You aren't happy, and there's no way the staffer in question can be happy trying to meet unobtainable expectations. If I can find another slot in the organization that better utilizes his skills, I'll move him. If that isn't a viable alternative, I have to remember that our business can only be as good as its weakest link.

If I can ease the situation by finding the employee a job somewhere outside the organization, I will. I won't dump an incompetent worker on anyone else, but if the individual has abilities that just weren't right for my operation, I'll do what I can to help him. For example, maybe we have a scout who's been promoted to a management slot. Let's say he can't handle the added tasks. It doesn't make sense for him to go back to his old job with us, yet he still remains a good scout. So I would attempt to locate a scouting position for him with another team.

For many years with the Raiders, I was the "turk," the guy who cut players in training camp. I had to develop a technique to try to soothe egos and make it as easy as possible for them and for me. It still always came down to this: the player couldn't uphold his end of the deal. It didn't matter how nice he was or anything else. You needed to look at it strictly from a performance standpoint.

They would argue with you. I had one guy tell me he was going to kill himself. I told him not to put that on me, that he was the guy who didn't meet the standards. I was offended that he would lay his failures and lack of ability on me. It woke me up. I had to make sure my priorities were correct. If I want my business to succeed, I must have achievers working for me. Otherwise, I'll fail.

At the same time, I would never tolerate being ordered to fire somebody. If I feel the firing would be unfair, I wouldn't do it. I would also probably quit because the lines of authority obviously have broken down. Interference like this destroys a manager's credibility and ends his effectiveness.

I will give you every opportunity to succeed. Al Davis once taught me a great lesson about tolerance. On the first round of the 1983 draft, the Raiders chose offensive lineman Don Mosebar, who played for Southern California. He was my guy, and I urged his selection. On draft day, Mosebar was in a hospital recovering from disk surgery 24 hours earlier. I didn't know about the operation, and I should have. Prior to the draft, we had sent someone over to USC. We were told he was okay. I should have been better informed. Al could have fired me and should have. Maybe because I had been doing a decent job, he gave me another chance. As it turned out, Mosebar enjoyed a fine career, making the Pro Bowl three times. Al's handling of the situation showed me patience and understanding can have positive benefits, particularly when dealing with an employee's future.

Dismissing someone gets even more difficult when it involves a longtime employee. Sentimentality and loyalty become factors, yet to be effective as a manager, those considerations can't be allowed to cloud your judgment. I have to operate in a consistent, single-minded fashion. Once an employee no longer performs up to expectations—even if he has been around for 20 years—I have to correct the situation. If I lose confidence in his ability, I must make a change. Otherwise, I'm messing with my chances to succeed. It comes down to whose morale is more important, mine or the person who's failing? What's your primary purpose? Is it to be a nice guy or to be successful in what you do? I can't allow sentimentality to become a hurdle. It may sound cold and calculating. But if you want to win, that's the only way you can approach it.

It's inevitable that you'll be faced with this loyalty vs. production question. You have a comfort zone with this longtime employee. He's a pretty good guy, he understands how we function as a company, and, by keeping him, you'd save the time it would take to find and train a replacement. Let's say he's selling Breckenridge doorknobs and he's been doing it for 20 years, and by God, he knows the ins-and-outs of Breckenridge doorknobs probably better than you. So what if his sales are off 50 percent and he's pulling everyone else down because of his lack of production? To me, there's only choice in this situation. Make a change.

I'll strive to carve out the most dignified exit possible for a person with seniority. Maybe he can take an early retirement, or maybe I can locate a job for him somewhere else. I'm surely not moving him into another spot in the company; that would only serve to switch the problem, not solve it. I don't want to strip anyone of his dignity. Still, when remaining loyal to an employee becomes more important than doing my job properly, my priorities aren't in the right order.

I'll always remember what a fan told me the night after I fired Lindy Infante. I was eating in a Green Bay restaurant, and the fan walked over. "Don't worry," he told me, "it's not your fault he didn't do the job. He had his chance, and he couldn't perform. That was his responsibility, not yours." This was a businessman assessing the situation properly. When I'm dealing with these difficult personnel decisions, I always remember what he said. People wind up firing themselves by not fulfilling their obligation to the company.

With the Four C's in place and functioning, I was ready to turn my full attention to implementing the personnel system that would enable us to capitalize on our surprising 1992 season. This would be the sixth Stepping Stone: Making It Work. But first, here are the prominent points you should remember from Stepping Stone No. 5—Use the Four C's to Measure Performance:

• All employees must conduct themselves in a professional manner that won't bring disrespect to the organization. While no dress or appearance code should be necessary, they should always be presentable and representative of the company's high standards.

• Require certain devotion, certain dedication, certain work ethic, and certain results. Standards and expectations should be clearly defined and explained, eliminating any gray areas among employees.

• Everyone should be expected to put in the extra time and take the extra step to make things better for the company. To accept the minimum effort is unacceptable. The goal is to create an atmosphere where "we" comes before "I."

• Everyone should be allowed to function without idiotic requirements that impede maximum job performance. Clearly define the duties of each position and give each person the ability to perform these tasks without interference. Allow people to flourish without strings.

• Allow no double standards when it comes to rules or treatment of employees. Eliminate the "owe me" attitude and clock-watching. Your aim should be to make the organization so appealing and invigorating that it's a pleasure to be an employee. The goal is to have everyone "buy into" the company philosophy.

• Everyone should understand that, no matter his seniority or loyalty, lack of performance will lead to dismissal. Firing someone is never pleasant, but if people believe they can coast without producing, the organization won't function correctly. Sentimentality can't be allowed to cloud decision making when dealing with evaluations.

• Make sure you constantly demonstrate appreciation of a job well-done through raises, promotions, and consistent praise. Find the best, train the best, reward the best.

• An employee has an obligation to the company to strive for the best possible performance. A company has an obligation to employees to give them every opportunity to improve so they have a chance to rise to the top of their profession.

• It's essential to have measurable standards by which to judge performances within the organization. You need to have some flexibility in job evaluations, but those who don't perform should be weeded out. All evaluations should be weighted heavily around one question: has the employee's performance enhanced the ability of the company to succeed?

• An organization should attempt to help rehabilitate employees plagued by personal problems, including drug and alcohol abuse. But if they don't improve and their performance suffers, they should be released.

• Create a freewheeling atmosphere where opinions and aggressive thinking are nurtured, lines of authority are clearly delineated, and where those who make too many excuses or take credit when it isn't due are not tolerated.

• Communicate constantly, but don't hide behind e-mail and memos. Management by isolation isn't effective.

CHAPTER SIX

STEPPING STONE NO. 6

Making It Work

To win, you need to believe in a system. Without a systematic approach, you'll never generate the consistency of effort and the unflagging determination you need to develop a successful organization. To a great extent, you should be utterly predictable in how you go about moving your enterprise through the Nine Stepping Stones to Building a Winning Organization. There's room for spontaneity, but if you're consistently unpredictable in your decision-making methods, it'll be impossible to achieve the stability you require to allow constant improvement.

The first five Stepping Stones establish a foundation upon which all progress can be constructed. Now you have to put in place the Stepping Stone that will provide the fuel to energize the rest of the process. Your system must be well-grounded, it must be proven, it must be easy to comprehend, and it must be embraced by all your employees.

Let's say you've hired people to sell widgets. How do you want them to proceed? I don't believe in telling them to wing it. Before making their first sales pitch, I want them to do enough research to be completely comfortable both with our product and with the client. I want them to be properly prepared, so they're reciting only factual information. I want them to understand how they're expected to represent our firm in regards to appearance, punctuality, and manners. I want them to know the limits of their authority when it comes to making agreements—what they can commit to without needing permission and what must be approved by their boss. I want them to be comfortable with production schedules, discounts, and incentives. I want them to be so well-informed and so impressive that the client never once doubts their sincerity, ability, and class. The system becomes the company way.

It doesn't matter if you're doing home publishing, running a grocery store, directing a car dealership, or managing a large corporation, your steadfastness in embracing a system that makes everything *work* can't waiver. I could hire the greatest leaders and the best support staff and have all the resources I wanted. But unless I have a structure that gives everyone the same direction and requires the same consistency, I would have very little chance of realizing the goals I have established for myself and my enterprise. I may bring about some improvement, but to become excellent takes commitment and a methodology that gives you structure.

I knew the Packers would never be champions unless we drastically upgraded the level of talent on our roster. Without top players, we couldn't compete on a consistent basis. These are easy generalizations to make, no matter your business. You take over a magazine that is floundering and to fix it, you need to increase circulation or advertising. To grow your landscaping firm, you need new clients. To broaden your florist business, you need more walk-in customers.

But how do you turn those needs into victories? I spent years studying and analyzing the best ways to identify quality players, and I spent the same amount of time learning how I could obtain enough of these athletes to improve my team faster than anyone else in the league. I prepared myself so if I was given an opportunity to run my own personnel department, I was ready to install a system that would govern our scouting and player procurement methods.

You can't wait until you're in a leadership position to formulate an operational system. As you work your way into more authoritative roles, you need to project your future. How would you increase sales? How would you make the product better? How would you attract more customers? You can't waste time dabbling in theories. You need to become very specific, relying on what you've seen succeed or fail and crunching all this information into guidelines that will bring about the desired results.

I'd never allow myself the luxury of feeling I had lots of time in a new position to determine how I want things done. Impatience is becoming the rule, not the exception, in business today. Stockholders demand immediate results, bosses demand immediate improvements, customers demand immediate changes, and no one is willing to wait for the good signs to show up. All you need to do is examine the sports world to see the effects of this impatience. Coaches are being fired at a faster rate than ever before because owners no longer have a mentality that allows a "program" to be implemented over drawn-out stages. That's why I believe so strongly in the third Stepping Stone— Develop an Obsession With Winning Today. You've got to prepare yourself well enough so when the opportunity comes, you're ready to establish your system and get things moving.

Just like in your business, I have certain tools available to me to make my system work. To upgrade our roster, I could use the draft, I could use trades, I could sign players not under contract to other teams—so-called street free agents—and I could use free agency, first the Plan B concept and then the free-agency method that now functions in the NFL.

I prioritized these tools, just like you should. I wanted to rely most heavily on the draft because I felt the long-term stability of the roster depended on the number of young, quality players we obtained, and the draft was the best method to acquire these youngsters. I wanted to trade as frequently as possible because this was a solid way of securing a special player or two, particularly if I had to fill a need. I wanted to bring in a limited number of street free agents, although I was confident that early in our rebuilding program, we could identify players from this category who would upgrade our roster. At the same time, I needed to see how formalized free agency would evolve: what caliber of players would be available and how we would absorb the limitations and rules of the salary cap, which put a ceiling on our player expenses.

Too often, businessmen don't fully utilize all the resources available to them. They don't take the time or make the effort to keep up with trends and to familiarize themselves with the best possible means of improving. I'm not the most technologically advanced person, so I surround myself with employees who are aware of technological advances. I want them to propose ways we can utilize the available technology to enhance our system. With the Packers, we have tried a lot of new things. Some have worked, some haven't, but I don't want to squash anyone's enthusiasm. That's a good way to limit your potential success. I want innovation to help improve our efficiency and time management, but I'll never allow it to distract us from being as methodical and thorough as necessary to make the system work correctly.

It's essential you don't withdraw so much from the daily business function that you develop a sense of isolation from the system. That's why I continue to be hands-on with the Packer personnel department. I never want to forget that the lifeblood of our organizational quality rests with the system we have installed to procure players. If we neglect that one area, we're setting the stage for failure. The same philosophy should be applied to your endeavor. If it means walking the factory floor or sitting with salesmen on calls, or reading major employee reports, or monitoring sales meetings, you need to do it. If you spend too much time involved in policy meetings and long-range planning and not enough time staying in touch with the ongoing daily aspects of your enterprise, you risk losing your ability to identify potential problems before it becomes too late.

No matter your business, the principles that move the system along are the same. The system should be designed to maximize production. Any parts that detract from achieving this goal should be eliminated. The system should be easily taught. The system should be flexible enough to absorb unanticipated developments but rigid enough to insure an across-the-board standard of excellence and compliance. The system should have well-defined goals so that everyone understands if things are executed properly, certain expectations, such as specific personal rewards and company glory, will result.

Let me give you a football example as illustration. Mike Holmgren installed his version of the so-called West Coast offense with the Packers. He alters the scheme every year to absorb offensive innovations and to respond to defensive adjustments. But the way he teaches his system and what he demands from the players within the system have not changed. The players are instructed in a manner so they understand the reasons plays are run in a certain fashion, and they're indoctrinated in Holmgren's beliefs about toughness, execution, and the destruction caused by mistakes. Whether we win or lose, the fundamental aspects of the system won't change because he's convinced that if his teachings are executed correctly, the Packer offense will outplay any defense.

This is what I mean by belief in the system. If you lose out on a bid for new business, it's no reason to scrap your methods or raise major questions about their effectiveness. You certainly should analyze why you failed, just as Mike Holmgren and his staff search for answers by breaking down game tape. You should use any results of your analysis to refine your approach. But until you determine that the system has fundamental flaws that are preventing you from winning, you need to show the dedication, patience, and belief in your methods to hold firm until it works.

Ever wonder how a successful entrepreneur can build a multimillion dollar business, then move on to another endeavor in a separate segment of the business world and repeat his triumph? Besides obvious intelligence, he also has developed a method that he can apply to any situation, and turn an opportunity into a slam dunk. His system is so universally sound that it can be used in every enterprise. A man like Wayne Huizenga is a perfect example. He built Waste Management from a small company to a huge firm, then he moved on to Blockbuster Video and did the same. He's trying now to revolutionize the used-car industry. Don't bet against him succeeding again. Those companies are vastly different. He is the one constant within all three, and it's his system that has allowed him to win.

Vince Lombardi was brilliant as coach of the Packers. But I have no doubt his offensive system, based on his famed "run-to-daylight" concept, would have been just as unstoppable if he had installed it for a high school or college team. It was so beautifully conceived, so simple and so superbly taught. Lombardi didn't preach anything very fancy, but his concepts were fundamentally sound and were repeated over and over again until they could be executed flawlessly. Defenses knew what to expect from his squads, yet the players' ability to stay within the system and their knowledge of that system overcame the preparation of opponents.

When I see head coaches in the NFL changing their offensive or defensive schemes in dramatic fashion, such as switching to the run-and-shoot and then back to a more normal offense, it indicates to me they aren't convinced which approach really will work. Without that belief, they have a fundamental flaw that puts them at a disadvantage against other coaches who are much more consistent in their teachings.

One of the traits that appealed to me about Mike Holmgren was the strong conviction he held about his offensive system. Although he intended to alter the West Coast approach in Green Bay to reflect his opinions about the scheme, he still was an enlightened disciple of the concept and would continue to teach its basic principles. That's exactly what he's done with the Packers. Much of what we run on offense today is different, formation-wise, from what Bill Walsh designed, but the philosophies behind how Mike attacks defenses and searches for flaws haven't changed. And that's why the offense continues to dominate.

In the months after I came to the Packers, I knew it was crucial for me to begin installing my player personnel system as rapidly as possible. But I didn't have sufficient time before the

April 1992 draft to completely put in place everything I wanted. I was working with scouts who weren't nearly as familiar as I was with the system, and I was still deciding whom I would retain among current Packer employees. Still, the April draft was incredibly important. Even after giving up a first-round pick for Brett Favre and a second-round choice for Mike Holmgren, we had 11 selections, including three very high picks. We needed a solid first draft to initiate our Stepping Stone approach to building the roster. I also knew we couldn't forget this was a long-term proposition. We weren't going to remake the Packers overnight, so it was important that we exhibited the patience to allow our system to function properly.

In the early stages of a situation in flux, you have to caution yourself to keep things in perspective. You must remember the big picture. If you do things methodically and correctly now, but with a sense of urgency, eventually you'll reap the benefits. If you aren't patient and if you don't persevere, you risk a worse "P"—panic. When you contemplate the scope of your task, you inevitably have to deal with panic. I look back at those first months, and I know I panicked at times. I would glance ahead and think about our potential player matchups against division opponents, and I'd convince myself we didn't have a snowball's chance of prevailing. You have to talk your way through these moments and make yourself stay patient.

As a manager, you must acknowledge that your employees are watching you closely, particularly during moments of stress. When you're trying to jump-start a program and have initiated a concerted effort to improve things, your ability to remain consistent every day and keep prodding and not have tantrums, no matter the size of any setbacks, contributes greatly to the ultimate result. If you show signs of panic, it'll soon overwhelm everyone.

For our first draft, we had to combine information that the Packer scouting department had already gathered with the material I had compiled while working for the Jets. By the following draft, everything would function exactly as I wanted. For now, we worked to put together the most intelligent effort we could, knowing that we couldn't allow a lack of time to hinder us from making correct choices. That's an important point to keep in mind when circumstances conspire to prevent you from dealing with an ideal situation: never allow excuses to compromise your decision-making process. Even if you have to temporarily modify your system, you must remain wedded to the principles you know will work.

During this period, I also spent a lot of time with Mike Holmgren, discussing football and his preferences in players. As a personnel guy, I can't force my coach to accept my concepts of what it takes to play certain positions. I have to adapt my thinking to secure the kinds of players he feels most comfortable using. It didn't matter if I believed we should be employing quick, small receivers. If Mike thought his offense functioned better with tall, power guys, that became the player type we'd seek.

His schemes also require cerebral players. They have to understand the intricacies of the tactics and execute them properly. I would come to realize that no matter a player's abilities, if he constantly made mental errors, Mike wanted to unload him. If we brought in players who couldn't think, we would be impeding, not expediting, the rebuilding process. Since the bulk of the scouting was finished before Mike was hired, we were pressed to alter our thinking to more accurately reflect his desires.

We also had to train our scouts so they understood what I wanted from players, which in turn was what Mike wanted. We would spend a lot of time in the off-season, before and after the first draft, training ourselves in the Packer Way regarding players who fit our system. The closer we could come to meeting Mike's ideals, the closer we would come to achieving our goals as an organization.

These discussions with Mike served another purpose. They gave us a chance to know each other better, which was essential to our ability to function as a team. Even though I was his boss, we both had a specific responsibility in our quest to produce a champion. If I did my part correctly by obtaining top-notch players and he did his part correctly by coaching them well, we had a reasonable chance to succeed. But none of this would happen if we didn't establish smooth, ongoing communications built on trust.

We had to feel comfortable with each other, and we had to be honest with each other. Personnel, to a large extent, is subjective. I may like a player, you may not, and we have to learn to agree to disagree. Just like in every other aspect of my organization, however, once Mike and I came to a conclusion about a player, we had to move on and not brood about the outcome. It now was a Packer decision, and we had to deal with it in that fashion.

This kind of free-flowing, open exchange of opinion doesn't happen automatically. You've got to work at it constantly, on every level of your organization. The more you understand the nuances of your relationships with employees, the more consistent your communication will become, and the more productive your enterprise will be. Nothing stimulates a business more than an environment where people talk to each other, exchange ideas, and seek to improve both themselves and their company. If I can't convince employees to tell me what they really think rather than what they think I want to hear, I've failed as a manager.

The genesis of what became a championship team started in those first months, in great part from my talks with Mike. We hit it off quickly and that helped. He likes personnel and understands both its intricacies and his own strengths and weaknesses when dealing with this part of the business. I soon started to envision the type of player that could turn things around. For example, we'd be seeking big cornerbacks—physical guys who could handle the strong receivers in our division. To be successful, those corners would also need sufficient quickness and speed to hold up consistently on our level. Our receivers likewise would be big, just like in the 49er system. We are talking 5-11½ and up; ideally, we would like them to be at least 6–1. Our tight ends needed to be large; same with our offensive linemen.

Knowing these requirements narrows your player search. You may see a Darrell Green-type cornerback in the draft, but because he's small, we'd shy away from him. I realize he's played in the NFL for years at a high standard. But he is an exception, not the rule, and I like to stay with what'll work the highest percentage of time.

A top-rate manager knows the exact traits he wants in the people who will make his system function. He knows what kind of personalities he needs in certain spots, he knows the educational background he desires, he knows the experience level he requires. And he makes sure everyone who hires personnel also understands all these requirements. By being so specific about requirements, you expedite the job search. If a candidate falls outside the priorities, don't interview him. It's critical that the company doesn't back off from these requirements when filling positions. If that happens, you risk reducing your organization's efficiency.

To determine the specific qualifications for different positions in my company, I would study the history of those slots, so I could understand exactly what traits have worked in the past for each. Let's say, for a certain assistant manager's position, we've had more success hiring MBAs from eastern schools than any other single trend. That would guide me to recruit heavily from these schools, concentrating on people with advanced degrees. That doesn't mean I wouldn't consider other candidates, but I certainly would give weight to the favored category. Unless you profit from the past, you always risk mistakes in your hiring process. It won't guarantee you'll be error-free—as you will see in Stepping Stone Eight, I have made plenty of mistakes—but it's still far preferable to blasting away wearing a blindfold.

The personnel system I brought to Green Bay is very precise in its structure. We divide the country into six geographical regions and assign a scout to each. They're responsible for the schools within those regions. We begin the process in May when we assemble names of potential draftable players from a pool of

3,000 rising college seniors. We rely on our own information and input from the National Scouting Combine, which also represents ten other NFL teams. Our preliminary pool could consist of as many as 1,500 players, and we could wind up actually looking at most of them, plus anyone else who emerges during the ensuing season.

The scouts stay on the road virtually nonstop from late August through the end of November, visiting their assigned schools, which usually number about 60 each. They normally will be gone for ten days, refresh themselves for two or three, then leave again. In December, they revisit prospects that we like or that we need to research more.

I also have a scouting schedule. During the NFL season, I try to leave on Tuesdays and either come back on the team charter after Sunday's game, or if we're playing at home, I return to Green Bay sometime late Friday or Saturday. I have a number of major schools I visit every year, and I add programs with promising prospects. My study of the draft has shown me that as many as 80 percent of the guys who play in our league come from 85 schools. So we'll visit, let's say, Notre Dame every year even if the Irish didn't have anyone on our preliminary list. We'll make sure the major colleges are covered, then we'll delve into the smaller institutions. Otherwise, we aren't using our time efficiently. I also determine potential weaknesses of our team, and I want to scout players who might solve those problems. I'm trying to concentrate on first- and second-round prospects. If I can visit 30 colleges, I feel fortunate.

You follow virtually the same routine at every stop. You arrive early, move into an assigned film room, and watch as much game tape as you can on the prospects you're scouting. Ideally, we want our scouts to analyze five games of each player as a junior and five as a senior. You also try to talk to coaches and other school officials about the players to help us compile in-depth background information. If you're allowed, you watch practice. Every night our scouts file a report on each athlete they've just analyzed. I want to read about the player's potential. I want my scout to project how good this guy could be and whether he's worth draft consideration.

In January and December, we follow up this work by attending all-star and bowl games to have more looks at the players in a different environment. In February, we attend the league scouting combine, where most of the best players work out.

In late January, we begin the preliminary process of assembling our draft board. When I was with the Raiders, we went about player evaluation a little differently than we do now. Back then, it was a matter of personnel men gaining an understanding of how each position should be played, and then deciding how prospects measured up to the standard. Was A better than B and if so, how good was A compared to a previous No. 1 choice? When I went to the Jets, I was exposed for the first time to a much more formal system, and it changed the way I went about putting together my board.

The Jets utilized Dick Steinberg's system as taught to him by Bucko Kilroy, the much-respected former personnel expert for the Patriots. It was a mathematical approach based on a model developed by IBM to help businesses hire quality executives. This method aims to move away from relying too much on instincts and emotion. Instead, it depends more on cold, hard evaluations. With the Raiders, we put guys on the board according to the round we would draft them, and if there weren't enough players to fill up each round, so what? With Dick, if there were 12 rounds, you would put up 12 rounds of players, each with a numerical rank and a letter grade (A, B, C, or D). They were assigned the ranking by Dick after he assembled everyone's opinion and averaged out the various assessments. The incredibly thorough scouting form required for each prospect took 50 minutes to fill out.

The problem was, when it was their turn to pick, the Jets would rely too much on where the guy was on the board instead of whether he could really perform or not. Even if he wasn't first-round material, he might be listed in the first round because we had to fill up the board. With the Raiders, we would put only players in the first round we thought belonged there, and we never added anyone who didn't meet these standards. Unlike Dick's system, we relied on a seat-of-the-pants instinctive feeling that you can't remove from scouting or, for that matter, any other kind of evaluation involving humans.

Let's say you're looking at two candidates for a job. One has an impeccable résumé with all the qualifications you think would indicate a high degree of success in the position. The other also is well suited for the job, but doesn't have quite the experience or educational background. Yet there's something about the second candidate's enthusiasm and attitude that makes you feel more comfortable about him than about candidate No. 1. Dick would probably hire candidate No. 1 because the indicators of success pointed in that direction. He would override his instincts. If my instincts felt right, I would override the system and go with No. 2. I'm convinced your abilities to hire the right person depend largely on your knack of mixing instinct with fact. If you stick by the book, you'll make more mistakes than you should.

Dick was a volume guy. He wanted as much information as he could obtain about a player, so you could wind up with 20 reports on someone. I'd rather have specific details and opinion. If I trust you as an evaluator of talent, I only need one report. Still, a lot of what Dick did is reflected today with our draft board. Even with all the years I spent in the Raider system, my short time with the Jets had the most impact on my drafting philosophy. Dick's relentlessness and thoroughness drove everything and everyone around him, and I felt I needed to enhance my approach by putting more emphasis on those two traits.

My experience with Steinberg taught me a great lesson. Regardless of your business achievements, you have to remain open to change. If I thought I was so experienced and so good that I couldn't possibly improve, I would have been unreceptive to Dick's philosophies. Instead, I now know what a terrific move it was for me to switch from the Raiders to the Jets and expose myself to a new situation. It made me a stronger talent evaluator, and it prepared me better for my role with the Packers. I think it's a lesson all managers need to heed.

Dick's attention to detail was magnificent. In any business pursuit, it's essential to be as detailed as he was to give your system any chance of excelling. We never want to feel we have neglected to do as much homework as we can when we're studying a draft prospect or any other assignment, for that matter.

Still, we continue always to remind ourselves not to neglect the human element in our evaluations. I'm a stickler for knowing everyone's height, weight, and speed—what we call measurables—and I use those to limit the people we consider. In theory, the Raiders' Napoleon Kaufman, because he's shorter than we want our running backs, wouldn't be a high-round pick on our board even though most teams would place him in the upper rounds. You have to adhere to your standards. At the same time, we always have to ask, "Can the person play?" He may be a wonderful physical specimen, but that doesn't tell you one thing about his heart or his instincts or his aggressiveness. Kaufman was tough and productive. He was a player. So Kaufman would become an exception and would appear on our board.

Accordingly, when you see an exception to the standards you have set, you must examine him thoroughly. Running back Warrick Dunn of Tampa Bay, who wound up being the 1997 rookie of the year, was an exception in the 1997 draft. If possible, we would have selected him. That's because he could flat out play, and that was enough for us. You'd be hurting your organization if you weren't flexible enough to give special exceptions a fair hearing, even if you have doubts about them.

Yet we still don't wander much from the philosophy that former Cowboys coach Tom Landry once described to his scouts in Dallas. He told them he didn't want Joe Washington, a talented but smallish running back, on his board because he was too short and not fast enough. His reasoning was that you make one exception, and pretty soon, you have a team of exceptions.

I constantly remind our guys of that. I'd rather look bad and pass up an exception who makes it somewhere else than have a team of players who don't meet the standards that we're convinced lead to winning. We want a squad, for example, full of big, fast backs. Over the long haul, you are more effective with these runners. I'd also prefer to miss on a linebacker such as Sam Mills, who had a wonderful career but was too small for us, rather than wander from our commitment to large, quick, mobile linebackers. I'd rather let someone else be the genius by uncovering the sleepers. I'm not in this to take what I call "shots," those selections where you project a future for a player that probably is far beyond his actual capabilities. For every reach you might get right, you'll miss on far too many to make the gamble practical.

In your business, you also must avoid too many exceptions to the standards you have set, whether it involves personnel, policy, procedures, or any other aspect of your system. Once you start ignoring your base concepts, you risk undercutting the potential of your operation. You must have the discipline to stay with what's right, not with what's attractive.

Having a system that you sincerely believe in helps make your job easier. Our approach continues to help streamline our draft pool by eliminating a chunk of potential prospects who don't measure up to our minimum physical qualifications for various positions. And during our initial years in Green Bay, it also dictated some of our roster cuts. A few veteran players we inherited fit into Lindy Infante's offensive and defensive concepts but not into Mike's, so they had to go. Anytime you inherit a new situation, you'll find employees who don't mesh with your system. They may flourish somewhere else, but that's not important. If you have technical writers who produce good copy but can't meet deadlines—and your business has changed to a point where you now constantly are presented with deadlines—you're hurting your goals by keeping those writers. It's that simple.

Since coming to Green Bay, I've also learned that we need a special kind of player to thrive here. This is a different place to play in November and December, and not every athlete functions well in this environment. Guys who like warm weather won't relish playing in Lambeau during a snowstorm. We've adjusted to that now, and our draft board reflects these considerations. If you're recruiting for a business located in a small town, you need to be sure your new employees will be comfortable with a nonurban environment. I've lived in Los Angeles and in New York, and they're vastly different from Green Bay. Not everyone can be happy in either situation.

So much of a manager's success comes down to having the courage of your convictions—and the flexibility to know how and when to adjust. Maybe you have a standing rule that no order can be filled in less than four weeks. Whenever you've done it sooner, you've had poor quality. Yet a major account absolutely has to have its order filled within 21 days. Because of the size of the account at stake, it's up to you to figure out a way to satisfy the request and still maintain your quality standards. However, if you allow too many exceptions and fill too many orders in less than four weeks, you risk compromising your quality and losing valuable future business. The key is to have the proper instincts and the guts to know when to say yes, let's make an exception, and when to stand firm.

Putting together our draft board takes weeks. We begin in late January. The entire personnel department participates. We work seven days a week, from 7:30 A.M. to 7:30 P.M. with a 90-minute break for lunch. We consider players who have received a grade of 5.0 or higher; that's the minimum rating for a draftable prospect. Anyone below 5.0 is considered a free-agent-level player.

We take each position and go through each player at those spots one by one. Each of these prospects has a file. In it will be the report from our scout, the combine report, and a questionnaire that we've sent to the player, which, hopefully, he has filled out and returned. We also include a copy of his write-up from his college media guide. We read out loud each guy's height, weight, 40-yard and 20-yard time, his arm length, and hand size. I then ask the scout who has seen him and has graded him how he arrived at his decision. I ask him if he's changed his mind because we're constantly reviewing our information. I ask him if there's anything he wants to add to what we know. At this point, he'll tell us whether we need to look at tapes of the prospect.

If we do, we'll pull out five games against his best opponents. The NFL has a central clearing house that receives tapes from all the colleges, copies them, and sends them to the member teams. So we have a massive tape library to support our scouting effort. Everyone in the room watches the tapes—we have this gigantic screen, and I run the tape machine—and we start talking about what we're seeing. If the player isn't showing very well, maybe I'll ask the scout if he'd rather put up another game on the screen. By now, the scout is melting in his seat because his evaluation isn't holding up. It's amazing how your perception of a player can change, sitting in that room, watching him on this big screen in front of everyone. After two or three tapes, you get a feel for the prospect. You give him a final grade, which could differ from the scout's. The player winds up in one of two categories. If he's bad enough, he becomes a reject and doesn't go on the board. If he has what we call a makable grade—he has enough ability to perhaps play in the NFL—he goes on the live board.

Eventually, we have to determine not only if he can play in our league but also at what level. Reserve? Starter? Can he start now? The reserves will wind up below the fourth round, the quality guys will fill the higher rounds. That placement unfolds as we get further into this process. For us to consider exceptions, a persuasive case has to be made about the prospect's talents. As an example, if you have scouted a 6–1, 300-pound center, he darn well should resemble an all-pro center like Dermontti Dawson. Otherwise, he doesn't have the right proportions, in our estimation, for that position.

The point is, we can't sit there and say, well, we better look at all the midget running backs because we don't have any big backs to examine. I won't accept that. Work a little harder and find the guys we need. Maybe we have to lower our requirements just a bit. Let's say, instead of the back having to be at least 6–0, he can be 5–11. Just a slight adjustment, but it's not the same as opening the gates and letting in 5–7 players. I also don't want our scouts eliminating guys from our consideration just because they think they're exceptions. I want that to be a group decision. What I want from our scouts is an opinion: can the prospect play well enough to have a shot? If he can, present him to the group.

If we're lucky, we review 20 players a day in these draft meetings. They continue for five or six weeks, athlete by athlete, with each player allotted enough time to be evaluated properly. If you rush, you could make mistakes, which is what this process is trying to avoid. The pace changes according to position. If we like a receiver, we'll take a look at every pass that's been thrown to him during his career, whether it was a completion or a miss. Same with running back. Every run. On quarterbacks, we just watch them play as much as we can. This is a long and arduous process. How many times can you review people blocking each other? But you have to maintain an edge. You have to be correct.

You could consider this process a governor on organizational decision making. It prevents you from making quick, rash, angry choices that could hurt your enterprise. Instead, this method allows you to flush out every possibility before coming to a conclusion. If more businesses followed this methodical process of decision making, they would make fewer regrettable declarations of intent—and policies would be much sounder.

Let me give you an example of what we're trying to avoid. In 1968, I went to scout a prospect named Bill Bergey. He played for Arkansas State in Jonesboro, Ark., which wasn't exactly on the main roads. I had all types of travel problems and got lost, then when I arrived at the river to cross into town, the water was too high and the ferry wasn't running. I finally got to the school, and they took me into this room to watch film. The room had a potbelly stove. I mean, it was really cold. I was tired and cold and annoyed, and it wouldn't have mattered if Bill Bergey walked on water, I would have given him a poor scouting report. And I did. He wound up being a heck of a linebacker for the Cincinnati Bengals and Philadelphia Eagles. I want our draft-evaluation process to eliminate those kind of bad-judgment episodes from determining our final grades.

I don't want to miss a Bill Bergey because of one scout's personal troubles. Nor can your company suffer because you made a rash decision on a day you were angry with the world. You need a system that won't allow these individual quirks to have a long-term impact on your business. As much as possible, you should eliminate emotion of any kind from your decision-making system. I know at times I've said the heck with it, we're choosing a certain player and I don't care what others think. That'll happen, but it shouldn't. As a manager, you have to resist the temptation to be a Lone Ranger.

When we're finished, we have identified all the players we think are worth drafting, and we have placed them in the rounds where we think they fit. By early March, we're back on the road, attending formal workouts held by the top prospects and visiting players we think are worth more evaluation. In the meantime, when I'm in the office, I put prospects back on the screen and review them. I can go through two or three a day. We'll constantly shuffle the board, moving people from round to round until we think we have it right. In the days before the draft, we'll meet with the coaches to finalize the board. We get their input, and, in turn, they come to understand our reasons for who has been placed where. What I don't want is arguments on draft day. None of this chalk-throwing stuff.

I want a board that contains no puff. If a guy is in the first round, it's because he's a first-rounder, period. He's not there because we *think* he might have that kind of ability. The cosmetics are gone. I want to look at these names and know we've given it our best shot.

Our draft room is no place for the timid. You function within a tough, hard-nosed atmosphere that becomes incredibly demanding, intense, and, more than anything, intimidating. It takes a lot of conviction to stand your ground in there, especially when everything is exposed on a big screen. I have to eliminate any chances of having yes-men in those meetings because they'll help create mistakes. I don't need people agreeing with what they perceive is the majority opinion. I need someone to stand up and say, "I don't care what you say, I think this guy is a player and we're going to make a huge mistake if we don't draft him." That is often difficult to do because you might be wrong, and if you are, everyone in that room will eventually know it. It's up to me to make sure you understand mistakes are inevitable and that I would much prefer forcefulness than middle-of-the-road behavior. It's simple. You have a 50 percent chance of being right, so why not go for it? I also can't have employees so stubborn they won't listen to other opinions. I call them Pittsburgh guys, people so hardheaded there's no compromise. They rip apart your process, not enhance it.

The wonderful thing about scouting is that it eventually exposes the truth about your evaluation process. Maybe the first two years in the business, you think you're a genius because a number of your guys get picked. By the third year, you see they can't play a lick. It humbles you. So if I can start off a meeting talking about one of my botches, it lightens things up and makes the conversations easier.

If the boss can admit he's human, it helps everyone to relax. I'll never maintain I'm infallible or display such an inflated ego that I can't be questioned. For example, I tell them the story of Ray Guy. The Raiders took him on the first round of the 1973 draft, an unprecedented spot to select a punter. He was an organizational pick. By that, I mean everyone within the organization agreed on the selection before it was made. So now he's in his first game with us, and his first two punts sail over John Madden's head on the sidelines. They average something like 26 yards. Shanks. I'm standing there, and Madden turns to me and yells, "I thought you said this (*blank*) guy could kick?" I was looking for a place to hide. It turned out that Ray was an incredible punter, maybe the best ever. For a while, though, I thought John was correct—and it made me sweat.

Sometimes, we make draft mistakes the same way you could commit an error in your business. All of us give too much weight to rumors, media reports, and the way we think trends are moving. We allow this kind of information to sway us to make decisions that violate both our instincts and the evidence produced by our research. Sometimes it requires great strength to be in the minority on an issue, but showing courage in these situations can lead to dividends for both you and your company.

In the 1983 draft, Dan Marino was a talented quarterback from the University of Pittsburgh. He had gifts you admire in a quarterback: size, strength, a quick release, and toughness. He should have been a top-five pick. Then the rumors started. He had struggled at times his senior year, and there had to be an explanation. So the speculation began. His arm was dead. He was on drugs. The innuendos piled up, making a case against taking him very high. I was one of the people who accepted these reports without verifying them. Dan slipped almost out of the first round before the Dolphins took him. The rest of us messed up.

Yet we really didn't make a mistake. Why? Because we had what is so prevalent today, the "CYA"—Cover Your Ass—mentality. If anyone questions your decisions, you have all this research, test numbers, and measurements to back up your conclusions. Plus, how about those rumors—even if no one proved they were right. So we weren't wrong—at least, if you go by all our information. Blame the facts, not us. As long as you have piles of paper to back up your position, you always have your rear end covered.

In scouting, we keep adding tests to protect ourselves. We use vertical jumps, we use 20-yard shuttles, we have psychological quizzes. We pile on the information. But you're always dealing with the ultimate unknown mechanism, and that's what lies inside a person's heart. We can't cut someone open and see his insides, so you really never know what makes that person tick.

You can't see his toughness or his belief in himself. You never know why a free agent off the street can compete at a higher level than a first-round choice. But it happens time after time in our business.

We allow all this overwhelming detail to cloud our instincts. So much of proper management still is determined by a seat-of-your-pants feel, whether you're a scout or a president of a major company. Yet we've attempted to strip away the nuances and turn everything into a by-the-numbers, bottom-line decision. Those of us who still allow our instincts to influence our thinking have a better chance of being right more often.

To develop these instincts in my employees, I work to make them braver. I might point out how they've been right in the past on their players evaluations. I go out of my way to compliment them on just about anything I can. I'll tell them how important it is to stick to their gut feelings. I'll bring up examples from my experience, where I backed off a prospect and we didn't draft him and then he developed into a decent player. Or I bring up someone like Ray Guy. What if the Raiders had decided it was foolish to pick a punter in the first round, since no one else had ever done it? If we hadn't stayed with our convictions and dared to be different, he would have become an all-pro for another franchise.

You need to be a stroker. If I have a meeting where I'm doing the bulk of the talking and only a few brave souls are participating, I won't allow the situation to go unchanged. I'll confront the silent ones and push them to speak up. If I can get enough people in that room to talk, everyone else eventually will join in. Otherwise, you're wasting everyone's time. You don't have a constructive dialogue, so you might as well put your thoughts down on a memo and distribute it. But you've got to prove to them that this isn't an academic exercise in which you already have your stance determined and you're just being nice, listening to their voices. You really have to listen. If they're still unwilling to become involved, I'll find others who are more willing to cooperate.

Our system is fueled by only one goal: select the right player. It doesn't matter whose player it is. It just has to be the right player. By that, I mean it's not important if you're the guy who scouted the player we picked in the draft. It's more important that the athlete is a Packer choice, that everyone in the room buys into the decision, and when it's finalized, no one is grumbling or second-guessing or walking around with a "they-should-have-listened-to-me" attitude. You had every opportunity for months to speak out and make your case, and if you lost the debate, it was because you weren't forceful and factual enough to swing the room. Now it's time to become part of the majority.

We have to put aside all our petty jealousies and strive to make sure the board is rated correctly and the players are in proper order. It's the ultimate in teamwork, a principle that every successful organization must promote.

I'm not seeking watered-down consensus opinions, nor do I believe this method leads to that result. Because the debate is so sharp and focused, our thinking in these meetings carries a decisive edge. If you can generate this kind of atmosphere within your organization, I'm convinced the consistency and efficiency of your decision making will increase noticeably.

This systematic approach to making choices, as reflected in our scouting philosophy, is adaptable to a myriad of situations. Whether you're debating the purchase of new equipment, an expansion of a division, the need to move into new office space, the wisdom of adding more employees, or building a new store in the next town, a reasoned discussion featuring frank comments and credible opinion will produce a valid result.

You obviously aren't drafting players, but any time you have to hire someone, you're in the personnel business. Many firms, for example, are heavily involved in recruiting new employees from college campuses. The Packer Way can serve as a model of how to analyze potential new hires and figure out who's best suited for your company. With our system, you wind up seeing a broader picture of someone's qualifications and how those traits fit into your enterprise. This approach reduces the possibility of making major mistakes in your hiring process. I don't think any business can afford many, if any, poor choices in new employees. Too much time and too many resources are invested to botch it very frequently. Otherwise, it becomes a distracting drain on organizational function.

I also believe any business would profit by being as attentive to detail and as precise as is required in the Packer Way. I'm driven by the deeply held principle that you can't be too prepared or too conscientious about any aspect of your situation. We spend so much time on the draft because to take shortcuts would risk the future of our team. But this kind of overwhelming precision also sets an example for the entire organization. We establish a standard in the draft that other Packer employees understand should be met within their area. Everyone should pursue every aspect of his job with the idea of being thoroughly prepared and by giving the maximum effort it takes to succeed. These are company-wide expectations that don't have to be formalized. Our people see it and feel it every day they work.

The same principles we apply to the draft process govern how we handle two other tools in our personnel system: our ability to sign free agents and our ability to make trades. Since both trading and signing of free agents involve mostly players with pro talent, we have a separate section within our personnel department that helps us in these areas. These employees track player movement within the NFL. We follow every player in the league—all 1,700-plus athletes—whether they're active, hurt, on injured reserve, or on a practice squad. We have scouting reports on each of them, complete with a grade, so if someone gets cut or we want to make a trade, we can turn to a file and familiarize ourselves with how we rate that player's ability. It eliminates surprises or being caught unprepared.

We assign colors to differentiate the players' ability levels: blue, red, gold, purple, brown. Blue is a ten. No one is a ten—at least, not yet. Anyone who is brown is a reject. We focus our energies mostly on gold, because that means the athlete could play for any team in the NFL.

At least once a week, we meet to talk about the league. We want to make sure we haven't overlooked a player, and that we're fully aware of everyone we might consider later for our roster. We're always updating each club's roster. We also track players who have been released or cut. We have a board listing their names—five deep of the best guys currently not under contract at each position. If someone gets waived, we know whether he's more talented than one of our current players. If he is, we might try to claim him. If we try out a street free agent, we want to see if he has more talent than a current Packer: is B better than A? If so, he stays and A goes. Then later, maybe we'll see if C is better than B.

I'm not saying that you should track every potential employee in your line of work. But you can modify our approach to fit your situation. You should identify prospects from other companies who are recognized as being among the best around. You can follow their movements and be mindful of indications that they might want to change firms. This kind of preparation gives you the ability to move quickly if a potential future employee becomes available.

Our system helped us immensely when we wanted to execute a trade. I say "helped" because the art of trading in the NFL isn't practiced very much anymore, particularly when it involves exchanging players for players. The new free-agency system has all but killed your ability to deal off athletes, because now you have to worry about salary cap implications and the commitments you would pick up with the new player's contract.

You once could use trades to strengthen your team. This is how it would work. If I had two tight ends and only needed one and you have two halfbacks and only needed one, I would trade you our backup tight end for your backup halfback and we both would benefit. Trades also could help players. As you improve, you always have a group of athletes who no longer are good enough to make your roster. I like to deal them off rather than cut them, so they would have an opportunity to compete on another team. In exchange, we might get a player or draft choices.

To me, trades are a solid way of building your roster. You know what you're receiving because you've studied the player's performance in the league. With a draft choice, as thoroughly as you scout him, he's still an unknown quantity until he plays in the NFL. But some clubs are just happy to exist without the need for change. They have seven draft choices, and they'll use all seven, and never try anything different. I'm not saying that's bad, but it certainly eliminates a viable alternative way to improve. And getting better is what this is all about.

Now, trades mostly involve draft choices instead of players, especially right around the draft. For example, I might give up this year's second pick for multiple selections in the same draft. You make this kind of trade when you're convinced the draft has depth and there isn't a player at the higher choice you think is worth that pick. I'm still aggressively seeking this sort of trade because it's helped us in the past. During our building years, we've benefited by obtaining extra draft choices that allowed us to bring in more young players at a time when we needed that type of transfusion.

I've learned that as good as you think your system is, you need to remain flexible and receptive to suggestions and trends. Otherwise, I'd probably still be trying to make player trades instead of conceding to the changing times; or, I'd still be stumbling into the same mistakes I made in Tampa, where I discovered that some of my theories on roster building didn't hold up.

In Tampa, I made some idiotic trades. Because I was comfortable with players who had been with the Raiders during my tenure with that club, I would trade draft choices to bring some of them to the Bucs. I thought we could plug them in and they would make us better. At the same time, I would assign a draft choice to each of these veterans. My thinking was, that player really is the same as the third-round choice I just gave up. It turned out our talent improved over the short-term, but when I looked at the next year's draft, I realized we could have obtained much better players if we had kept those picks and used them for college prospects. I vowed to never again import older players in exchange for choices.

Only George Allen, the former Rams and Redskins coach, was successful using the picks-for-players approach. Yet, you see coaches who move to new teams attempt this method all the time. Pretty soon, the coach will start collecting some of his former players. Allen was smart; he obtained mostly core players. But most of us concentrate on bringing in reserves or second-line performers. These are guys you think were ready to be starters with your old team and just needed an opportunity to step up. So you give them the chance, and you soon realize what they are, really, is average. And average is average, no matter the uniform. Mike and I imported very few players to the Packers who had been with us in Oakland, San Francisco, or New York because we didn't want to risk making the same talent mistakes.

I decided to violate my beliefs with just one trade, and it only served to reinforce what I knew was right all along. In 1993, I traded with the Jets for quarterback Ken O'Brien. I thought Brett Favre was at a stage in his development where he needed to see how a veteran quarterback conducted himself—his work habits, his preparation, that type of thing. Yet I also knew that Ken's style of play wasn't suited for our offensive system. It asked him to do things he couldn't, and that's poor managing. Never instruct an employee to undertake tasks that he can't handle, either from an experience, training, or skill standpoint. I blocked out the part of my instincts that told me Ken would be a bad fit and made the deal anyway. Ken didn't last through training camp.

Your company would be better served if you don't bring former business associates into your new situation. They usually aren't as good as you thought, and they also immediately become, in the eyes of current employees, favored sons who will receive special treatment from management. The resulting potential damage to morale is not offset by the quality these former associates can add to your firm.

An effective manager also should always be willing to review the way he operates his system and make changes that are warranted by results. In essence, he's using on-the-job experience to constantly hone his own skills and, in the process, improve his firm's level of production.

As we finished implementing the system that would govern the Packer Way to building a winning football team, I felt we now could make the transition to the seventh Stepping Stone: Keeping It Going. But first, here are the prominent points you should remember about Stepping Stone No. 6—Making It Work:

• To succeed, you need to believe in a system that will make your decision making and your methods of management predictable, and will lend stability to your organization. Your system must be well-grounded, it must be proven, it must be easy to comprehend, and it must be embraced by all your employees.

• Unless you have a structure that provides everyone with the same direction and requires everyone to produce the same consistency, the chances of realizing the goals you have set for yourself and your enterprise are limited.

• Don't wait until you assume a position of responsibility to begin formalizing a system of operation. You need to determine the principles as you gain work experience and strive toward a management role. In this era of immediate fulfillment, you likely won't be given a prolonged period to demonstrate that your system works properly, so you'll need to strive for early, positive results.

• Work diligently to identify and incorporate all available technology that will improve your system. This means remaining open to change and being receptive to suggestions. Never believe you have reached a level in your business life where you no longer can learn.

• Remain hands-on no matter your position in the company,

so you'll always be able to identify whether the system is functioning properly.

• Establish key principles that will become the foundation of the system and never allow those principles to deteriorate.

• If you aren't patient and if you don't persevere as your system is being implemented, you will risk the possibility of panic, which could destroy even minimal progress. The way you react to hurdles and setbacks will be noticed by employees and will set the tone for the rest of the organization.

• Emphasize the importance of adhering to the principles of the system and avoiding exceptions to the rules. Approving exceptions should come only after careful consideration and should not become commonplace.

• Pay particular attention to thoroughness and detail. You can't be overprepared, nor can you have too much information on a subject. At the same time, this methodical approach to decision making shouldn't eliminate the human element. When determining policy or hiring employees, instincts still must be involved. A good manager must maintain the flexibility to adapt to the unexpected.

• Never portray yourself as infallible. You should admit mistakes when they happen and use these errors as teaching points when dealing with associates.

• It's usually a mistake to bring former associates into your new company. They frequently show they're not as good as you thought.

CHAPTER SEVEN

STEPPING STONE NO. 7

Keeping It Going

During our early years in Green Bay, I expected Mike Holmgren to rush into my office one day and start screaming. I knew exactly what he'd say. "Ron," he would yell, "I'm trying to coach a team here, and you keep bringing in all these new players. We teach them the system, and then they're gone and somebody else takes their place. How do you expect me to do my job if we don't have some stability?"

To Mike's credit, and with my everlasting gratitude, he resisted the temptation to explode. He had every reason to become frustrated. He was trying to win games in the midst of what was organized chaos. We both knew what we had to accomplish. We needed to upgrade our roster and, at the same time, remain competitive on the field. To fulfill those goals, however, meant constant upheaval. First, we kept remaking the bottom part of the roster. Later, we undertook difficult changes at the top.

To a great extent, how an organization deals with the trauma created by a systematic plan of improvement determines the firm's long-term ability to win. There's nothing more demoralizing and frustrating than change, both to individuals and to companies. Longtime habits are disrupted. Friendships are disturbed. Everyone has to absorb new rules and procedures. Uncertainty and anxiety become daily emotions. During the transition, it becomes difficult to envision a brighter time ahead. Certainly, I don't think many Packers back then were dreaming of Super Bowls. They were more interested in surviving. Everything else seemed far-fetched.

Yet the way in which our organization not only overcame

those unsteady days but used them as lessons to help us grow contributed greatly to our ability to play in back-to-back Super Bowls so soon after my hiring. We pushed everyone very hard and made a number of difficult decisions that weren't always popular. But our employees' belief that our system could eventually construct a winner kept us going until we were able to compete at an elite level.

Bob Harlan and I often talk about how the difficulties we encountered in those early days helped build the character and strength of our present organization. Bob says that as wonderful as it was to win Super Bowl XXXI, he actually became more emotional after we beat the Carolina Panthers to capture the 1996 NFC title. I understand why. Late in that game, with the victory assured, we were standing together in a tunnel at Lambeau Field. We both knew how bleak the situation had been in November of 1991, when Bob decided to shake up the franchise and change the leadership at the top of his football operation. Now, to be in Lambeau, where we were about to win our eighteenth straight home game—a streak that turned this stadium from being one of the weakest home-field advantages in the league to the strongest—and to glance around the upper deck of the facility and read all the famous names from past Packer glory painted on the facade—Lombardi, Nitschke, Starr, Hornung, Lambeau, Canadeo, Hutson—and know that the franchise had returned to its rightful place among pro football's best created a special moment that left us speechless. All we could do was hug.

As we examine the major points of the seventh Stepping Stone—Keeping It Going—that scene in Lambeau can serve as a constant reminder of how effort and a well-conceived, well-executed business plan are capable of producing beautiful results . . . Super Bowl appearances . . . Record profits . . . Home-run investments . . . A spot at the pinnacle of your profession . . . A merger that makes your company an industry leader . . . Enough income to open new stores . . . A prestigious promotion.

To reach these major goals, however, you must have the commitment to see the process through. You can't allow short-term obstacles and shortcut solutions to obscure your vision. You must develop an ability to measure progress even when those outside the organization see none. You must be able to transmit to your employees the happiness you feel from even the smallest of positive signs of improvement. You must resist the temptation to doubt yourself or your system, even when critics do. You must protect the attitude of the organization by downplaying your own dark moments and presenting a consistently optimistic face to your employees.

In the dark hours after a loss, I am a madman. If I had to make decisions in those moments, I would likely be tempted to clean out half the roster. If I allow that anger to linger and become the fuel that ignites how I execute my authority, I surely would harm the organization with my rash actions. It's extremely difficult to accept disappointments, yet a businessman's ability to deal constructively with these emotions helps to determine his effectiveness. How do you react to a bad stock purchase? How patient are you when a salesperson botches a call? How understanding are you when an employee has a problem with a customer? These are the times when your experience, intelligence, and persistence must take over, so you can keep your enterprise on the correct track.

By never protesting about the roster turmoil, Mike Holmgren knew exactly what it took to make the Packer Way work. He was intelligent enough to understand the complexities and roller-coaster nature of what we were trying to accomplish. He understood that this was a Stepping Stone process that required a methodical system to realize our goals. Even after our surprising 9–7 record in 1992, he didn't lose perspective, which could have happened easily considering the heady manner in which he was being treated in Green Bay. He was the emerging hero of the franchise, a sturdy, affable, energized symbol of the franchise's future. But he didn't let this ego gratification interfere with his work ethic.

Amid the growing adulation, his commitment never changed.

We knew that our achievements in 1992 had been a godsend to an organization that desperately needed a glimpse of hope. We also knew that we weren't ready to make the jump from 9–7 to champions. We needed to correct too many weaknesses on our roster before we could become contenders. We continued to believe this was a long-term process. That understanding would prevent us from speeding up our maneuvering to the detriment of the franchise's future.

A company's drive to stay on a successful course is similar to daily changes in the stock market. We're told that the "buy-and-hold" approach to stock buying is the most effective of any market philosophy. Yet, when prices drop suddenly, you're always tempted to sell to cut your losses. And when the market rises unexpectedly, you're always tempted to sell for a quick profit. You understand it's more intelligent to look at the long-term picture, but the emotions generated by the market's quick fluctuations make it difficult to adhere to your convictions. Still, if you're convinced you'll be better served by staying in the market until your investment is maximized, you can't cave in to these tantalizing alternatives.

In the months following the 1992 season, we probably could have rushed to cash in on our early success by signing a bunch of older, limited players in hopes we could challenge for the Central Division title. But that approach contradicts our organizational philosophy. As we worked constantly to improve through our Stepping Stone theories, we weren't about to add too many Band-Aids to our roster. Instead, those spots needed to be filled by younger players who could develop into Packer stars. We would pursue a division title—but only by staying within the context of the structure we had established for roster development.

Occasionally, you'll see an NFL team improve considerably from one season to the next, then drop off drastically the following year. If you examine how its executives built their roster, you'll probably find that the squad went backward because the managers attempted to win a championship by adding too many players who were no longer as good as their reputations. They believed these aging athletes would continue to perform at a high level and would do so beyond one season. Instead, the players' production dropped off quickly, and the franchise tumbled, wiping out all the short-term progress. The club compromised sound personnel philosophies, and now its future had been seriously damaged.

Along the same lines, you also have to resist the desire to stretch beyond your current capabilities and try to hit an organizational home run—that one splashy decision designed to put you over the top. You want to achieve your goals so desperately that you'll compromise your instincts regarding intelligent management and approve that one risky but spectacular chance. In essence, you become convinced that you can leapfrog some of the Stepping Stones and accomplish everything faster if only you can implement this one "home-run" move. So you shorten the deadline on a new product line by two months. Or you go way over budget on an advertising campaign designed to secure a record year. Or you hire a new manager by paying far above market norm, throwing your salary structure out of whack.

The temptation to be bold is enormous. But the downside to this strategy makes the approach foolhardy. This lack of patience leaves you vulnerable to unsound decisions and shoddy practices. For example, it might lead you to reduce your quality control or push your employees so hard they become fatigued and unproductive. You wind up running your enterprise in a fashion that is neither intelligent nor comfortable. Your firm becomes vulnerable instead of sound.

If you're in the midst of a revitalization process instead of a complete overhaul of an enterprise, you obviously don't need to be quite as methodical in your employment of the Stepping Stones. You may lack only one more quality leader, need only a few adjustments in your marketing plan, or require a better-designed advertisement in the yellow pages to push you to a point where you feel the worst is over. In that situation, the home-run approach might work, but don't swing recklessly.

If want to reduce the turmoil created by change, you need to quickly identify and maintain a core of veteran leadership below management level. These people have experience in your company and now have become part of the growth process. They're the stabilizing elements in an otherwise unstable situation.

These core leaders give your business a sense of continuity. When I read about a company eliminating a huge percentage of its employees in a cost-cutting move, I have an image in my mind of people flopping around in the ocean, reaching out desperately, wondering what will become of their lives. If that firm doesn't maintain some sort of continuity by retaining a core leadership group, the entire organization likewise will flounder as it attempts to stabilize the chaos.

The fact we had strong core leaders contributed greatly to the Packers' ability to make an unexpected impact on the league from 1992–94. From the start, we wanted eight or so players to become spokes on a wheel. They would be the leaders. Then we could mold the rest of the roster within the wheel. We wanted 20 more players to attach themselves to the spokes. They're the rest of your best performers. The remainder of the roster would lay in between the spokes. They can be replaced. Any organization should be structured in this manner. The spokes form the pillars of stability. They provide strength even when the rest of the wheel is changing. Instead of floundering, employees within this type of structure can grab on to something solid.

For our team to keep improving, leadership had to develop within the locker room. The addition of Reggie White in 1993 was huge because he's a natural leader whose voice became a strong influence. Linebacker Johnny Holland and safety LeRoy Butler were undeniable spokesmen for the defensive unit. Tackle Ken Ruettgers, because of his seniority, and Sterling Sharpe, because of the quality of his play, helped on offense. Fortunately for us, Brett Favre is a natural leader, and it was only a matter of time before he took over the locker room. These were the guys we depended on to hold things together on the players' level. Over time the core group grew, and the wheel evolved as we had hoped.

We were particularly fortunate that Brett emerged as a primary leader off the field as well as on. Ideally, you always want your quarterback to fill this leadership role because he's such a valuable part of your team. Sometimes the quarterback's personality inhibits his ability to become the force you'd like, but that wasn't a problem with Brett.

He's so outgoing, natural, and funny that it's impossible to resist his charm. He doesn't act like an elite player. He doesn't expect special treatment or limit his mingling with teammates. Instead, when there's a prank in the locker room, the first guy you blame is Brett. He's like a big kid who has never grown up. Consider the way he dresses year-round, no matter how bad the weather—he wears flip-flops, shorts, and a T-shirt. He can never be accused of flaunting his wealth or his stature. Steve Mariucci, who was our quarterback coach and now is the 49ers' head coach, tells this great story about Brett. They were neighbors in Green Bay. Even during the worst snowstorms, Brett would never bother cleaning off his car before leaving for practice. Instead, Steve would watch Brett drive away with his head stuck out the side window, trying to see where he was headed. It's a wonder he arrived safely at work. No question, his teammates were drawn to this special charisma.

Employees always look to their peers for support and advice, and they react to their body language. If a respected employee holds up well despite all the organizational changes, it tends to influence the behavior of everyone else. I couldn't tell LeRoy Butler, "Look, you must be a leader for us, so please tell your teammates we're on the right track." His role, as well as every informal leader's role, had to evolve. A manager can help out by quickly identifying these key employees and ensuring they're included in the information loop. If you demonstrate respect for them, it will facilitate their ability to buy into what you want done. If you explain your goals well enough, they become an extension of the message you want to dispense within your firm.

Mike went so far as to form a players' committee comprised of these leaders. He would meet with them, seek their advice, and ask their opinions on rules and methods, such as the way practices were conducted. It created a sense of ownership within the team. The players didn't feel quite as isolated from the decision-making progress. Instead, they felt—rightfully so—that management wanted to hear their voice. Mike demonstrated his respect for these leaders by incorporating many of their suggestions into his system.

All businesses would be well-advised to form a workers' committee that meets regularly with upper management. The committee's input should be heard directly by key bosses rather than being filtered through intermediate steps. Management also must be committed to this arrangement by demonstrating its desire to *sincerely* listen to and act on those ideas that will make a difference in the conduct of the firm. If you communicate with your employees for "show" purposes only—I meet with them all the time, so how can they say we don't talk?—but never intend to treat their concerns seriously, you'll destroy morale.

These internal leaders also help spread the good word about what you're accomplishing to people outside the organization. During those early years, we were trying to sell the Packers to players from the rest of the league, so they would consider signing with us later as free agents. The guys who had been here before Mike and could see the positive changes he was making became great spokesmen for us. If a LeRoy Butler or a Ken Ruettgers told a player from another team that it was exciting to be a Packer, that became a better endorsement than anything I could ever say. Your hope is that employees will be so enthusiastic and so energized by the revitalization process that it makes your recruiting of new personnel that much easier.

I know that if I was considering a job with another firm, particularly one with a so-so track record, I certainly would contact current employees to obtain an accurate picture of this potential company. If we had the Butlers and the Ruettgers telling their friends the Packers were the pits, we would have a tremendous handicap to overcome. Fortunately, they couldn't have been more pleased with what was transpiring.

Credibility becomes such a huge part of all this. You demonstrate a sign of progress, such as our 9–7 record in 1992, and it creates a buzz. You aren't looking for sudden miracles—I didn't expect to be swamped with phone calls from players wanting to be a Packer—but you utilize every positive you can to help alter your image. In our situation, I found that agents suddenly were much more receptive to our inquiries. When I first arrived in Green Bay, some agents never would have considered the Packers. But after 1992, the players' underground, which we discussed in Stepping Stone Four, started spewing out better news about us. That, in turn, influenced agents to view us more favorably.

Tootie Robbins started at tackle for us in 1992 and then signed with New Orleans during the next off-season. Once he got to the Saints' training camp, he realized he had made a mistake. He went for the money and not the organization. He began calling our players and telling them how he had messed up. He was very popular in our locker room, so his words had an impact on current Packers. Eventually, the Saints cut Tootie, and we brought him back to play for us in 1993 before an injury ended his career. I knew his positive reinforcement also would filter through the players' underground. No question, our improved atmosphere figured into our signing of veteran guard Harry Galbreath, who joined us prior to the 1993 season. He wasn't a marquee name, but he was a significant Stepping Stone in our development, supplying us both with upgraded talent and sorely needed leadership.

I remember talking once to linebacker Tony Bennett, who was one of our star players in 1992 and 1993. We were coming off the field after losing to Dallas in a 1993 play-off game, and I said to him, "See, this is what it's all about. Do you understand that? This is what all the work and everything that we're doing is all about." I don't think he got it, but to me, playing Dallas in a play-off game represented an opportunity to move to the next level. Two years previously, we had had no games that served as a potential step-up for our organization. Yet if we had beaten Dallas, it would have been a significant accomplishment. Even though we lost, the game remained a positive step in our progress, and our employees needed to understand that.

You must identify, isolate, and utilize similar developmental achievements in your firm. Never hesitate to be bold and vocal about good news. Brag about yourself as much as you can because you can't rely on anyone else to do it for you. Just like us, your goal should be to take any opening created by your company's progress and turn it into a wide gap that could lead to anything from a new account to more receptive investors to a more favorable word on the street.

This cultivation of credibility accelerates the internal efficiency of your system. It transforms rules and goals that could be perceived by employees as unachievable ideals into living, functioning requirements that work. People listen closer, believe more, and work harder. It's easier to solve problems once you have credibility. The mentality of employees becomes . . . he told us we would improve and we have, so maybe he knows what he's doing and maybe if he says in the future that this is the way we need to correct an error, we'll believe him more readily.

Your internal credibility is tested by the way you handle personnel decisions. Even though we won from the start, stringing together three straight 9–7 seasons and two play-off appearances, it still wasn't easy being a Packer during this time. I'm sure the players came in every day wondering if the locker next to them would be empty—or how secure their job was. As I said previously, I don't believe in management by fear. Still, change inevitably generates degrees of fear, which translates into uneasiness. Important energy is drained off by these concerns, so it's imperative you reassure your employees as much as possible that your aim isn't to clean house but to retain and reward those who produce. Then once you make this promise, you must be consistent in its enforcement.

LeRoy Butler, our all-pro strong safety, understood our aim.

He told fans that our approach to performance was, in his words, based on "What have you done for me lately? If you're not doing the job, they're going to get somebody in here who will. We have a guy in Wolf who doesn't take any junk. Some teams have a pushover. But Ron is very hard-nosed. He wants to win. He comes from a winner. Why not win again? He just does what it takes to win."

Don't kid yourself. Employees are better judges of who's a quality worker and who isn't than you are. It should be your goal as a manager to develop the same feel they have about the performances of their peers. You can't overestimate the damage you cause when you promote a non-achiever, or when you don't replace a manager who's failing at his job. You can't allow yourself to be so isolated from the daily functioning of the office that you ignore personnel situations. You must devote the time and energy necessary to make the proper evaluations. For example, you can't expect a level of dedication from your employees that includes extended work hours when one of your top managers leaves exactly on time every day. Look around the office. Do you know what's happening from hour to hour with your employees and what influence your leaders have on the daily routine?

During these early seasons, I was constantly examining the roster and making what I considered honest evaluations of our players' abilities. It served no purpose to overstate their talents, even if it meant executing still more changes. I understand that continuous change can be such an exhausting process for everyone that you reach a point where you wonder if enough is enough. You can't let that happen. I was as anxious as anyone to limit the upheaval and allow ourselves to grow without all this disruption. But it's a mistake to pull back prematurely from the churning of the organization because you're concerned about morale. Unless you're relentless in your quest for success, you'll never achieve your goals.

To make the Packer Way work, Mike and I had to communicate on a consistently honest level. Very early in our relationship, we agreed we would always strive to make decisions that were best for the Packers, and not decisions that best served our individual agendas. That's a huge hurdle to overcome for any organization. Because everyone is so protective of his own turf, it becomes an enormous challenge to convince each person to put the company's benefit ahead of guarding his particular domain.

For example, you're discussing production deadlines with your staff. The person in charge of the assembly line wants as much lead time as possible to fill the orders. The salesperson wants less time spent in production and more output. The human services director is concerned about the effect extra work will have on people's attitude. The accountant is fretting about possible overtime costs and how they'll strain the budget.

All these concerns are valid, yet you must educate employees well enough so they can see a bigger picture. What's the solution that will produce a winner for our firm? You arrive at that point through communication that never compromises the organization-first goal. Those who can't deal with that reality have no future in a leadership position. Selfishness is an impediment to success. If Mike came into personnel meetings determined to retain some of his veterans because he felt more comfortable around them and I came in determined to protect all my young draft choices because I wanted my drafts to look good, we would constantly butt heads.

Fortunately, we both wanted to win so desperately that we limited these turf wars. Roster decisions would be based on one overriding standard: if you produce, you stay, and if you don't, you're gone. It kept arguing to a minimum because the measuring stick was consistent. If I made a bad personnel evaluation, I would not let it fester. We cut the player. I wasn't concerned about saving face and forcing Mike to continue training someone who obviously had no talent.

Besides, if I messed up, I didn't want to keep the mistake around as a reminder of my error. Otherwise, I'd be compounding my initial failure in two ways. First, by retaining an unproductive employee, I would prevent a more talented replacement from joining the staff, and that would hurt our ability to improve. Second, by keeping that person around, I'm sending a terrible message to the rest of the workforce, which already knows the employee in question is a weak link. I'd be saying it's okay to be mediocre, when just the opposite is true. Mike agreed with me on these points. To his credit, he also decided he would rather put up with the strains of constant roster turnover than accept a less tumultuous situation that would result in mediocrity.

We wanted to avoid anyone being able to point to a player and say, "That's Ron Wolf's guy, that's the only reason he's still a Packer," or, "If he wasn't Holmgren's favorite, he would have been cut long ago." I can't overstate how this type of understanding enhanced our ability to revitalize the franchise. That's why, no matter what your business, you must base personnel decisions on production. It reduces, if not eliminates, second-guessing and supposed biases.

At the same time, you must temper these personnel decisions with enough patience to allow new employees a chance to perform. You're always walking a fine line with these assessments. How much time is enough? This is where you must rely on your instincts instead of some "scientific" measure. You need to develop the kind of feel for your organization that enables you to recognize when an employee has become a burden, not an asset—and then you have to replace that person before he becomes a drain on the organization. The worst mistake you can make in this situation is to procrastinate in hopes things will change. They won't.

The pressures associated with time become even more exaggerated when you're in a rebuilding process. You're naturally in a rush, and your haste can lead to mistakes in your personnel evaluations. Keith Traylor is a perfect example. He was the Broncos' third-round choice in 1991, but was released. After the Raiders also cut him, we signed him during the summer of 1993. That season, he was active for five games as a linebacker. Even though he had ability, he struggled at that position. We should have been smart enough to move him to the defensive line and give him time to find himself as a player and a person. Instead, we became frustrated with his lack of improvement and we cut him prematurely. Unfortunately for us, he eventually developed into a really good player, first with the Chiefs and now with the Broncos. We were in a hurry, and our judgment concerning Traylor suffered.

As long as leaders show fairness in their employee relationships, your organization has a better chance of absorbing constant personnel shifts. Mike gained the players' respect because of his ability to be completely fair in his dealings with them. That's because he has unquestioned integrity. The players don't think he's devious. Even when they disagree with his decisions, they know he's doing what he thinks is best for the Packers. He's a sterling example of what makes leadership work.

In our early seasons, we were executing 40 to 50 roster changes per year, an enormous number for the NFL. Even though most of these involved players at the lower end of our roster, it still seemed like we had turned training camp into a season-long event. Once camp ends, many teams opt for roster stability. We couldn't afford that luxury. If a player was cut from another franchise, and we thought he had ability to help us, we would bring him in. We were trying to upgrade our special teams and our backup positions and, we hoped, also find some young athletes who could develop into starters. Often these new players were prospects we had liked in the draft but were unable to pick. Despite the fact another club may have given up on them, we relied on our original evaluation of them from college as a basis to at least try them out. It's the same as when you attempt to hire a promising college graduate, only to fail. I'd keep track of that person's whereabouts; perhaps sometime later, you could gain his services.

Inevitably, our personnel evaluations were going to affect veteran players who were heroes in the Green Bay area. We weren't oblivious to the effect our decisions might have on the world outside our office, yet the bottom line had to be applied to every-one, hero or not. Safety Chuck Cecil, for example, was revered in Green Bay. He had been a Pro Bowl player and had earned a deserved reputation for being tough and hard-nosed. He also missed too many tackles, which became painfully obvious to us during the 1992 season. If Chuck remained a starter, we couldn't improve. He was a free agent and we chose not to re-sign him, much to the chagrin of the media and fans.

It was the first of many occasions in Green Bay in which our decisions were called to task by outside sources. It's the same as when you sell off a segment of your company, or close a store, or reduce the payroll, or reshuffle the internal responsibilities of your managers, or fire a star employee. Externally, stockholders and analysts could react negatively, questioning the long-term implications of your moves. Internally, employees could be won-dering what the heck is happening. It creates an enormous pres-sure on you to be right—and the possibility you could be wrong often persuades people to back off from making the truly correct choices for their enterprise. Mike and I had to remain firm in these situations, just like you must. You have a plan and given time, patience, and hard work, your goals will be met. You've got to develop the courage to know you're right, and the forti-tude to hold up under pressure.

Ideally, I wanted a team that eventually would have a veteran starter at every position and a younger player backing him up rather than a situation where we had two veterans or two young-sters in the same spot. This was our Stepping Stone approach. It encourages a form of mentoring, but in our case, the teacher could very well instruct his way out of a job. We wanted the younger guys to learn by watching and listening to the veterans. Even if the older player wasn't very cooperative, just the way he went about performing his duties would be a beneficial example.

In your business, it's essential to also have an efficient mix of experience levels. Veteran employees can fill the same mentor roles as my veteran players did. They can become role models for their inexperienced peers, who can follow daily examples of how best to execute their jobs. They can offer advice and they can be used as a sounding board to bounce off ideas and problems.

Many of our veterans weren't good enough to make us champions, but they could at least buy us the time we needed to infuse our roster with higher-quality talent. Having one full season behind us was incredibly helpful. Even after watching all that film during the winter of 1991–92, I still needed to see the Packers in action, working in Mike's system, to obtain a truly complete picture of our talents. After a year with the organization, I thought we were much better situated to make correct personnel decisions.

We also could begin utilizing unfettered free agency, which was introduced in place of Plan B following the 1992 season. The timing couldn't have been better for us. It gave us an incredibly important additional tool that we could use to secure frontline, veteran players. Plan B was limited free agency involving players at the bottom of team rosters. The new free-agency system indirectly established a way to disperse talent throughout the league and prevent the best clubs from keeping all their top players. With a salary cap in place, franchises could no longer afford to pay all their stars, freeing some to sign with other teams. For a franchise like the Packers, this new source for acquiring personnel was a welcomed gift. It certainly helped speed up our rebuilding process, particularly when we signed Reggie White in the initial months of free agency. Free agency helped push the NFL into the real world of business, where employees have freedom to move to new jobs and the market drives salaries and expenses.

From the start, we decided to be as aggressive as possible in this new arena. We all had to learn how to best utilize the system; I certainly made some decisions I wouldn't repeat. We brought in players we thought would give us a year or two as a Stepping Stone, only to find out they were past their prime. Eventually, we learned, as did most teams, that it's far wiser to retain your own potential free agents instead of constantly adding outside players. As we improved, we felt less urgency to load up with a quantity of free agents. We could become more selective. We could use free agency to shore up the one or two most glaring needs on an otherwise solid team. That has become the ideal role for this new method.

Still, I would always advocate aggressive experimentation with business innovations in lieu of adopting a wait-and-see attitude. To hang back until these innovations are tested thoroughly always guarantees you won't be in the forefront of your industry. If I sense any opportunity to improve our organization, it's difficult for me to remain conservative. I'd rather institute the change, see if we can make it work, and then determine if we should implement the innovation permanently.

I'm a lot more hesitant about employing another method of improvement, the instant fix. That's the approach which says, "We'll try this way for now until we can come up with a better way of handling the problem." Early in our rebuilding process, we attempted too many instant fixes, usually by gambling with a veteran free agent who, as it turned out, already was on the downside of his career. You get into trouble two ways with this approach. If the instant fix turns out to be a dud, you have wasted time and money and likely stalled your growth process. If the instant fix turns out to be decent, you then fight the tendency to think the temporary solution actually can be permanent. That's a mistake.

In our situation, if we brought in a player as a stop-gap starter for a two-year period, we couldn't mistakenly push him to play for another season. It was up to us to have a better player ready to step in after two years, or it would interfere with our Stepping Stone philosophy. When you're forced to employ instant fixes in your business, it's essential to establish a target date by which you'll replace the stop-gap with a stronger, more permanent solution. Otherwise, you leave your organization vulnerable to a Band-Aid approach of management, with too many quick fixes and not enough solutions with staying power.

For example, after the 1992 season, we needed to strengthen

both the running back and receiver positions. Instead of developing young starters, we went after quick fixes. We signed Mark Clayton, the Miami Dolphins' star receiver, as a free agent, and we traded with the New England Patriots for running back John Stephens, a former 1,000-yard rusher. If they had lived up to our expectations, we might have won the 1993 division title. But both were no longer very good, and they didn't help us. We should have used their roster spots in a much wiser fashion.

This stage of the Stepping Stone process calls for patience and tunnel vision. Many fans were so happy with even one winning season that they were appalled by our ongoing roster shuffling. One member of the team's Board of Directors came up to me at a meeting and warned me, "Don't get too greedy." He was telling me it would be wiser to settle for what we had accomplished rather than risk the collapse of this unexpected improvement with additional moves that could backfire. I got angry. I wanted to be as greedy as possible for the Packers. If you allow yourself to become content, you can't achieve your goals. Instead, you should wake up every morning fearing that you aren't accomplishing enough to make your organization a success.

I was doing what I thought necessary to keep us moving forward. During those early years, the worst mistake I could have made was to sit back and enjoy our small achievements. As soon as you relax, you lose your edge as a businessman. I couldn't permit myself to be satisfied with one or two winning seasons. You've got to develop an internal accelerator that drives you forward—and you better always have the pedal to the floor.

By backing off, I guess I would have eased the pressure on all of us for a while. But I was more interested in becoming a Super Bowl champion than in reducing the stress. I took our early success as a challenge to see how methodically we could build upon that foundation and move higher in the standings.

Besides, I don't view most of what I do as risky. The decisions we make are generated intelligently from constant study, observation, and hard work. We don't just blast away without thought. When you're dealing with the unknown, you're always taking a risk. But we reduce the odds of failure by sticking with our system. Just because you might have enjoyed a record quarter for profits, or had your best month of car sales, or attracted the most customers of any week in the history of the business doesn't mean you've finished your work. Instead, these achievements should serve as indicators of what can be done if you can improve the quality of your organization even more.

In 1993, we finished with another 9–7 record and qualified for the play-offs for the first time since 1982. We then beat the Lions in a wild-card play-off game before losing in Dallas to the Cowboys. The Packers hadn't put together back-to-back winning records like this since 1966–67. We had shown our 1992 accomplishments were no fluke. It gave us increased credibility within the league and among players. It also bought us more time. To avoid the temptation of too many quick fixes, a business in flux needs a steady stream of success. Setbacks only serve to increase the potential of panic and heighten the chances of reaching hasty, poorly designed decisions that attempt to reverse unfavorable trends. We didn't win the division title in 1993, but making the play-offs helped offset this failure.

Now that you've stoked a high level of intensity within your firm, you can help it grow by making sure everyone understands what changes are needed to accomplish the next steps. In our staff meetings during the 1993–94 period, we constantly emphasized our strengths and worked to shore up our weaknesses. That's why it's so crucial to hire key employees who've been tested by adversity and have the necessary experience to cope with the kind of fluctuations in progress we encountered. This isn't a task for the weak of heart. You need to surround yourself with sophisticated leaders who can handle the bad times as well as the good. Anyone can get on the bandwagon. You need to have managers who don't bail out when the wagon stalls. Our leadership was mature enough to temper our natural impatience to win championships quickly with a realization that time was on our side.

At this juncture it's imperative that you successfully sort through the options of misleading optimism, extreme negativism, and reality. You would be wrong to present only good news—misleading optimism—while ignoring the bad. I believe in honest disclosure. If we have some troubles, let's get them in the open and let's explain what we'll do to eliminate them.

However, if you constantly dwell on the bad—extreme negativism—until your employees feel nothing they do is right, you can severely damage morale. This negative approach leads to a sense of inferiority that blocks aggressive thinking. We purposely avoid creating an atmosphere where faults are analyzed to an extreme and strengths are ignored. If you spend too much time as a company beating yourself up, you'll pull down the entire firm with you. The key is to honestly critique your efforts—reality—and implement necessary adjustments, then make sure everyone understands if we stay the course, we'll wind up on top.

This became especially important for us to remember after the 1994 season, when we produced our third straight 9–7 record. We were good enough to earn another play-off spot, beating the Lions again in a wild-card game before losing, again, in Dallas to the Cowboys, who clearly were a level above us in quality. From the outside it appeared we had stalled in our attempts to turn the Packers into champions. Although three straight winning seasons and two straight play-off appearances were a milestone for an organization that had known so much losing since the Lombardi years, our fans' wish list had changed. At first they had been content with dumping the losing image of the 1970s and 1980s. Now, though, they were restless.

The promise of 1992 wasn't evolving as they had hoped. It was nice to win again, but how about a division title or a more competitive showing against the Cowboys? I compare their unhappiness to the dismay of stockholders who write angry letters to corporate executives about stock prices. A few years earlier, their shares had jumped ahead, but since then they stalled at the same level for too long. They had made a profit, which kept them happy for a while, but now they wanted additional growth.

I understand this impatience. No one wanted to accelerate our improvement more than I did. Yet I also knew that we were much better than the 1992 team. Our Stepping Stone approach was working, and that's the message I was preaching to our organization and to our fans. People were viewing our glass as being half empty; I thought it was more than half full.

The change in the team's makeup had been remarkable. Many of the veterans who had kept us competitive were either gone or on the verge of being replaced by young players. Quarterback Brett Favre now was the established starter with almost three seasons of experience. Two youngsters, Mark Brunell, who was a fifth-round 1993 draft choice, and Ty Detmer, who was a 1992 ninth-round selection, were his backups. They would go on to become starters for the Jacksonville Jaguars and Philadelphia Eagles, respectively. Edgar Bennett, a 1992 fourth-round pick, had developed into a starting running back with star ability. Dorsey Levens, a 1994 fifth-round choice, was pushing for expanded playing time at fullback. Veteran Sterling Sharpe had become an elite receiver, and we were complementing his skills by adding young receivers, including gifted Robert Brooks, a 1992 third-round selection.

The offensive line still was in flux. Veteran Ken Ruettgers remained at left tackle and Frank Winters had surprised us by emerging as our starting center. We had moved up in the first round of the 1994 draft to select guard Aaron Taylor. But he wrecked his knee in the off-season, which had delayed his development. He now seemed ready to replace veteran Guy McIntyre, a former free agent who had been a stop-gap signing for us in 1994. Veteran guard Harry Galbreath, who was a 1993 free-agent acquisition, had become a major Stepping Stone, buying us time until a younger player emerged. Earl Dotson, a 1993 third-round pick, was ready to replace right tackle Joe Sims, a former street free agent. Mark Chmura, a sixth-round

1992 choice, had nudged aside veteran Ed West at tight end in the final weeks of the 1994 season.

On defense, draft selections such as cornerback Doug Evans (sixth round, 1993), safety George Teague (first round, 1993), linebacker Wayne Simmons (first round, 1993), end Gabe Wilkins (fourth round, 1994), and linebacker George Koonce, a 1992 free agent from the World League, were either already starting or about to become starters. They complemented core veterans Reggie White, LeRoy Butler, linebacker Fred Strickland, and defensive end Sean Jones. Both Jones and Strickland were 1994 free-agent signings.

The addition of Sean Jones had become even more important than I had anticipated. After the 1993 season, defensive coordinator Ray Rhodes was hired by the 49ers as their defensive coordinator, and we brought in veteran Fritz Shurmur as his replacement. Fritz changed our defensive scheme from a 3–4, where you start three linemen and four linebackers, to a 4–3, where you start four linemen and three linebackers. This meant we needed to improve the quality of our defensive front. It also meant a different role for our outside linebackers. Instead of concentrating almost exclusively on rushing the passer, they now also had to become involved in pass coverage.

During the months following the 1993 season, Tony Bennett, who had been a standout outside linebacker in our 3–4 setup, signed as a free agent with the Colts. He was a talented athlete, and his departure was controversial. But the principles behind our operating system determined Tony's future with us. We're convinced you shouldn't ask a person to undertake duties for which they're not qualified. Tony was a pass-rushing linebacker. He wasn't ideally suited to play either defensive end or outside linebacker in a 4–3 scheme. To ask him to function out of position would have been bad for him and for us.

The decision about Tony's future represented a good test of our management philosophy. On one hand, we would set him up for failure by moving him into a situation where he couldn't excel. On the other hand, Tony was talented and popular, and letting him go represented a risk. We could have made an exception with Tony, and anyone outside the organization wouldn't have blinked. But that's the easy way out for a company. You must be willing to execute the difficult choices; they ultimately enhance your chances of succeeding.

As it turned out, Sean Jones was a better defensive end than Bennett could ever have become, and he also supplied stabilizing leadership in the locker room. He was smart and vocal, and he was willing to become a player spokesman, relieving the burden of some of our younger athletes who were uncomfortable in that position. Plus, he had impeccable work habits. He was always studying film and preparing himself diligently for a game, and that set a great example for our inexperienced players. We got similar benefits from another free agent, guard Guy McIntyre. He had played with the 49ers, so he immediately had credibility in our locker room. Beyond that, he was a guy who scratched and clawed for everything he could achieve, a real battler who never gave an inch. Even when he was injured, he still wouldn't back off. He was a terrific positive influence on our players.

The presence of Jones and McIntyre reminded me that, no matter how long your tenure with the firm and no matter how much progress you've made, you can't stop striving to add leaders to your organization. You can never have too many of these rare employees. You also should never feel threatened that surrounding yourself with gifted associates could mean you're unintentionally grooming a replacement. If you shy away from adding topflight talent because of fears about your own job security, you're making a shortsighted, selfish decision that could harm your firm's future.

By the end of the 1994 season, we had a much faster, more athletic, more talented, and younger club compared to the 1992 squad. Through solid drafts and key free-agent decisions, we had methodically upgraded the roster. Since the beginning of the Stepping Stone process in 1992, we had made the transition from old to new at a significant number of positions. I also thought we had a fair amount of quality reserves, although not enough to satisfy me. The balance between older leaders and younger stars was improving. I felt we were ready to challenge the league's elite franchises.

Yet my optimism about 1995 was hardly universally shared outside the Packer complex. In addition to losing Bennett to free agency after the 1993 season, we now had to absorb the well-publicized departures during the 1994 off-season of two stars, linebacker Bryce Paup to Buffalo and tight end Jackie Harris to Tampa Bay. I didn't think Paup's skills were suited to playing linebacker in our 4–3 scheme, and we didn't offer him enough money to keep him. We made a mistake. He was a better player than I thought, and we should have done more to keep him in Green Bay. Harris had impressive pass-catching talents, but Tampa's contract offer was larger than we were willing to match. Most telling, we were also informed that Sterling Sharpe had to retire because of a neck problem. Doctors told him he risked paralysis if he continued playing.

These developments generated incredible public dismay. We had lost four established stars within a year, and, according to the prevailing opinion, they hadn't been adequately replaced. As a result, we weren't being viewed in the same favorable light that had surrounded us during our first three years in Green Bay. No question, the unexpected loss of Sharpe, who had caught 314 passes the previous three seasons, was a potentially damaging event. Still, I didn't share the general pessimism. I was confident our Stepping Stone system had been in place long enough to not only give us sufficient depth to absorb personnel losses, but also to produce new stars who, in many cases, would be better than the people they replaced. This is the strength of the Stepping Stone approach. It's geared toward developing a broad personnel base that represents both quality and quantity, with consistency at all levels of the organization.

People who thought our progress had stalled mistakenly concentrated their analysis on the stars we lost and ignored our supporting cast. They saw name players leaving; I saw all our young talent. I knew how good these players had become; they were ready to assume major roles. We would have more depth and balance than we had in the previous three years. Our personnel system had functioned beautifully. We used 16 trades during our first four drafts to increase our choices, which helped accelerate the quantity and quality of players we selected. Those drafts kept producing the bulk of the players the Packers needed, and we were able to utilize free agency and other trades just well enough to fill in whatever other voids we had.

Successful businesses must strive to mold a balanced organization. They can't be content to have a talented upper-management group while neglecting to also have solid ability spread throughout their support staff. Firms that have an uneven distribution of skills will produce an uneven quality flow. It's a mistake to rush through lower-echelon hirings and concentrate almost exclusively on filling upper-level vacancies. No question, you must have stars to win. Without them, you have no chance. That's why scouts call players like Brett Favre "difference makers." These employees have the special talent to handle the prestige accounts, do the key negotiating, sign up the finest new clients, write the top stories. But they also can't function at their best without quality support. We spent our first three years developing both stars and a supporting cast, so we wouldn't have any appreciable weaknesses. Examine your enterprise with a critical eye. Do you have enough balance to finish first? Do you spend enough time building the proper depth that a top-rate organization requires?

In the days before our 1995 training camp, even some of our players began questioning the status of the team. After reporting to camp, they changed their minds. They quickly saw that the club we had assembled was becoming special. Wayne Simmons showed he was prepared to replace Bryce Paup at linebacker. Aaron Taylor finally was healthy enough to start at guard. Dorsey Levens moved into fullback, and Edgar Bennett switched to running back. Gilbert Brown, whom we had picked up on waivers in 1993 after he was cut by the Vikings, was promoted to starting defensive tackle. He replaced Steve McMichael, the former Chicago Bears star, who hadn't played well after signing with us in 1994 as a free agent. Craig Newsome, our No. 1 pick in the 1995 draft, looked good enough in training camp to claim Terrell Buckley's starting cornerback spot. The players realized we had answered most of their doubts about our team.

Our feelings about 1995 turned out to be correct. After a slow start, the Packers streaked to an 11–5 record, our best since 1966. We won our first division title since 1972. Edgar Bennett became the first Packer to rush for at least 1,000 yards in 27 years. Robert Brooks replaced Sterling Sharpe and caught 102 passes, 44 more than in 1994. Brett Favre had his breakthrough season. He threw for more than 4,000 yards and registered 38 touchdown passes. He was named the league's most valuable player. He played through crippling injuries as did Reggie White, who was scheduled to undergo December surgery for a torn hamstring. Instead, four days after being proclaimed out for the season, he played in a game. Tight end Mark Chmura joined White and Favre in the Pro Bowl. The only sad note to the season was how it ended. After winning two play-off contests, we met Dallas in the NFC championship game. We lost to the Cowboys once more, costing us a trip to the Super Bowl.

Entering the 1995 off-season, we were one step from the goal that we established when we came to Green Bay in November of 1991. If we could figure out a way to beat the Cowboys, we had an excellent chance to emerge as the NFC's best team and make it to the Super Bowl. We were growing stronger all the time. The 1995 draft had increased our depth, producing an immediate starter in cornerback Craig Newsome and adding linebacker Brian Williams, receiver Antonio Freeman, and running back William Henderson to our list of potential future starters. But we weren't satisfied with our frontline players. George Teague, who had been our free safety for three years, wasn't ideally suited for the style of play being taught by defensive coordinator Fritz Shurmur. Fritz wanted a physical, hard-hitting safety who could support our run defense. George was more suited to be the true free safety that Ray Rhodes preferred. Our system dictated our decision. We needed the correct person in the correct spot. Teague moved to the Falcons, and we traded with Seattle for Eugene Robinson, who fit Fritz's demands perfectly.

We also decided to replace tackle John Jurkovic. He had enjoyed a fine career with the Packers, but if our team was going to take the next step, we needed to upgrade his position. Jurkovic had helped us as much as he could. As an organization, we had to recognize that and make a change, even though we knew he was very popular and his departure would be controversial.

It would have been easy to stay with Jurkovic. He was perceived as a quality player, he was extremely well liked by the media, and he still had ability. A fan approached me one day while I was standing in a grocery checkout line. The fan had read that John, who was a free agent, was visiting other teams. "He's in Jacksonville today, you know," the fan told me. He had a sense of urgency in his voice. If you don't do something, he was telling me, you'll lose John. A comfort zone surrounded the fans and Jurkovic, who appeared in a bunch of popular local television commercials. I could have embraced that comfort zone too and eliminated controversy. I could have overlooked John's shortcomings and rationalized that by retaining Jurkovic, I wasn't messing with the team's chemistry. But that wouldn't have made the Packers better.

When you're executing difficult decisions during difficult time, you have to fall back on your instincts. You know you're doing the right thing for the organization, so you can't back down. Teague was not a good fit anymore, so we had to move him. Jurkovic wasn't as good as we needed, so we had to replace him. If we didn't make these moves, I thought it would prevent us from improving as much as we must to challenge the Cowboys. We were so close to where we wanted to be. This wasn't the time to grow timid.

All the while, I kept thinking of that Board of Directors member who had warned me about becoming too greedy. His scolding became an inspiration. The Stepping Stone approach had worked well so far, but for the philosophy to mature completely, I had to remain greedy. I had to keep executing the steps necessary to complete the process. We had identified two weaknesses on an otherwise solid roster. We had to step up in those two areas and become better. If we hadn't made the changes, we probably would have finished with another good record in 1996. By executing the moves, however, we had a chance to become champions.

When you're almost as good as you want to be, you need to prod yourself to do even more than you already have. You need to become even more aggressive, more decisive, more ambitious. Otherwise, you'll get too wrapped up worrying about continuity, chemistry, and patience. None of those factors are more important than being the best. So do what you must to be No. 1.

The decision about Jurkovic reinforced my belief you can't fear change. We replaced Jurkovic with Santana Dotson, a free agent who has developed into our most complete defensive lineman. He wasn't considered an elite player for Tampa Bay—critics thought we made a bad decision signing him—but we thought he gave us added strength with his ability to play the run and rush the passer. He was a significant improvement over Jurkovic, just as Robinson was an upgrade over Teague.

They helped make our 1996 team strong enough to win Super Bowl XXXI. That squad was the culmination of a five-year remaking of the roster. We had no major holes in our lineup, we had depth everywhere, and we had a core of stars that we could depend upon to perform under pressure. We matured and peaked at the right time. We also now were structured so we could compete efficiently against our elite opponents. We had examined other good teams, particularly the Cowboys, and adjusted our squad to give us a better chance of winning any time we played these foes. I'm sure it could be argued we became obsessed with beating Dallas, but if you aren't driven to overcome your competition, you'll never be a winner.

Previously, we couldn't handle the Cowboys up the middle of

our defense. They simply had been too physically strong. So we made adjustments. Gilbert Brown stayed healthy enough to become a run stopper at defensive tackle. Santana Dotson proved a fine complement at the other tackle. We moved George Koonce from the outside to middle linebacker. Eugene Robinson's tackling ability at safety immediately elevated our performance against the run. As it turned out, we didn't meet the Cowboys in the play-offs—they lost in an early round—but we felt we were ready to defeat them if we did.

It makes good business sense to constantly analyze the competition and make internal adjustments that will enable you to compete more successfully. If you're consistently losing business because a competitor can manufacture a product faster, produce a presentation quicker, or entice clients with more perks, you've got to figure out why and execute the necessary adjustments or you'll always be trailing. I'm always playing what I call the "matchup" game in my head. I match our personnel, position by position, against personnel from a division opponent or a conference team, so I can see how we fare and where we might need to improve. You can do the same thing with your organization. Instead of personnel, you can match resources, business approaches, or sales pitches with your rivals. It's an effective method of dragging your thought process into the real world of competition.

I want to be aggressive in my approach to competitors. I want them to react to what we're doing, and never place my firm in a position where we're constantly adjusting to what someone else has done. In this race, I always want to be ahead and force everyone else to catch me.

We won our final eight games of the 1996 season, including three in the play-offs. Brett Favre again was the league's MVP. Our running attack, behind Edgar Bennett and Dorsey Levens, became incredibly productive in December and January. Mark Chmura and Keith Jackson gave us the best tight-end combination in the league. Our offense could beat you in so many ways. On defense, safeties LeRoy Butler and Eugene Robinson were outstanding, and our front line became dominant. Our defense finished ranked No. 1 in both total yards and fewest points surrendered; it was capable of pitching shutouts, which is essential to becoming a champion. Desmond Howard, who was signed late in training camp as a street free agent, emerged as the NFL's best kick returner and had a dazzling series of play-off performances, culminated by a kickoff return for a touchdown in the Super Bowl. Five 1995 draft choices—Antonio Freeman, Adam Timmerman, Craig Newsome, William Henderson, and Brian Williams—became starters, continuing our Stepping Stone process.

Our Super Bowl roster included just two players who were Packers before I was hired, LeRoy Butler and kicker Chris Jacke. The rest of the squad was comprised of 22 of our draft choices, 4 players who arrived through trades, 6 unrestricted free agents, 1 Plan B player, 5 players claimed off waivers, and 13 street free agents. We had made a league-high 49 trades in five years. Our success evolved in much the way we had envisioned during the initial days of our revitalization program.

And just like we had hoped back then, Lambeau Field and the environment had become huge pluses for the Packers. Opponents now feared playing us on our home field—and we relished the bad weather. Our team reflected the hearty characters and tough personalities you need to win in harsh conditions. Just like we had hoped, the history of the franchise flowed over; the story of the Packer rebirth and the city that so loves its team became the subject of countless articles and television pieces. Players no longer avoided Green Bay. This no longer was considered the outskirts of the league. Instead, America cultivated a love affair with the region. We became sentimental favorites—the smallest city in the league now boasting the most powerful team. The players knew they were good; they developed a swagger that only champions display.

It had been a dramatic and powerful turnaround. If someone had told me that, after my fifth full season with the franchise, we'd be in the Super Bowl, I would have told him he was nuts.

Yet, by never limiting our expectations nor being content with interim accomplishments, we were able to climb to the top of the league faster than anyone could have envisioned.

As wonderful as it felt that night in New Orleans, when we gave Green Bay its first NFL title since 1967 by beating New England in the Super Bowl, I'll never forget the ecstasy that enveloped me after we defeated Carolina for the NFC championship. It was an incredible and overwhelming rush. It also served as a release. I just wanted to yell and say to everybody, see, we did it, and you can do it too. I kind of went berserk during the trophy presentation. I kept pumping my arms and shouting to the players, "You believed, you believed, you believed." It was a special time because it meant so much to the guys who did it, who enabled us to reach this moment, who came and joined us and did, in fact, believe in the program we were selling. We had asked an organization to accept new concepts, absorb tumultuous change, and buy into the idea that dedication, devotion, and a profound work ethic would produce unprecedented results. These Packers had given a storied franchise a renewed reason to be proud—and every person who had contributed to the newfound success a reason to be incredibly happy. It filled all of us with a great sense of satisfaction.

Yet there were times along the way when I wondered if the Packers would ever be champions again. How we deal with setbacks and disappointments—and how you should likewise overcome bad news—is the subject of the eighth Stepping Stone: Handling the Unexpected. But first, here are the prominent points you should remember from Stepping Stone No. 7—Keeping It Going:

• How an organization handles the trauma created by a systematic plan aimed at change and improvement determines to a large extent the firm's long-term ability to win.

• To reach major goals, you must have the commitment to see the process through. You can't allow short-term obstacles and shortcut solutions to obscure your focus. You must be able to transmit to your employees the happiness you derive from even the smallest of positive signs that things are improving. You must resist the temptation to doubt yourself or your system, even when critics do. You must set the attitude of the organization by downplaying dark moments and presenting a consistently optimistic face to your employees.

• The cultivation of credibility accelerates the internal efficiency of your system. Success transforms rules and goals into living, functioning items that work. People listen closer, believe more, work harder. It's easier to solve problems once you have credibility. Employees see you are right on an issue, so in the future, they are more receptive to your suggestions.

• Maintain a high level of intensity and drive within your firm by ensuring everyone understands what changes are needed to accomplish the next steps.

• Maintain an environment in which employees are given adequate time to mature. Protect them from hasty, poorly conceived personnel decisions.

• To keep continuity within your organization and bring about stability, you need to maintain a core group of leaders below management level.

• Don't allow stress to drain an organization to a point where, once some progress is realized, everyone is tempted to relax and horde the advances instead of pushing to make them even greater.

• Cultivate an atmosphere in which your key leaders place the good of the company ahead of their own individual areas of expertise.

• Resist the temptation to short-change a well-conceived growth plan by trying to hit a "home run" designed to prematurely push the process over the top.

• Successful businesses have a proper balance of strength throughout the firm. Organizations with quality leaders and a weak support staff are likely to perform at less-than-peak efficiency.

• Be aggressive in your desire to integrate new technologies within your business. It's wiser to try something new and fail than hold back and never become an industry leader.

• Maintain your greed when striving for improvement and progress within your company.

• It's critical that you make the difficult decisions and resist the temptation to overlook exceptions or allow a bad situation to continue just to avoid controversy both inside and outside the organization.

CHAPTER EIGHT

Handling the Unexpected

The Packers opened the 1997 season on Monday night against our longtime rival, the Chicago Bears. It was a time of great joy for the team and for the sellout crowd in Lambeau Field. This was our first game since winning Super Bowl XXXI, and the franchise and its fans still were in a festive mood. The organization certainly felt good about itself, and with ample reason. We were sitting atop the National Football League, relishing a view we hadn't enjoyed in 30 years. The expectations about this new season were enormous, but not surprising. After all, we believed we were still the NFL's elite franchise.

It didn't take long for excitement to be tempered. On the Bears' first play from scrimmage, on a play so much like so many others you'll see in every contest, one of our starting cornerbacks, Craig Newsome, turned his knee the wrong way and crumbled to the ground. I was sitting in my usual spot, in a private box with Bob Harlan and Mike Reinfeldt. I expected Newsome, a physical player with an incredibly bright future, to bounce up and return to the huddle. Instead, he went to the sidelines. Our trainer soon gave us startling news. Craig had badly injured his knee and wouldn't return. Indeed, he could be out for the season.

It was a devastating blow. In just his third year, Craig was developing into one of our best players, so his loss would weaken our defense. His injury also deflated the mood in our box. The game was continuing, but reality had sent us reeling. If Newsome couldn't return for the rest of 1997, we had to replace his spot on the roster immediately. While we were churning those thoughts, tight end Mark Chmura also went down, and the initial report on his knee was not encouraging. We found ourselves combating a sinking feeling that embraced all three of us in that box.

Why us? Why now?

I call it the Woe-Is-Me Disease. It can strike an organization at any moment, whether the business is trying to improve or trying to remain successful. A big deal falls through. A top salesperson quits. A crucial machine breaks down, stopping production. A third-quarter report falls short of expectations. A part on back order is delayed even more. A rival store opens down the street, threatening customer flow. A stock falls just as you're contemplating selling it. An unexpected home repair ruins a vacation. You can plan for the expected, that's easy. But how you deal with the eighth Stepping Stone—Handling the Unexpected—will contribute greatly to the ability of your enterprise to continue steady growth instead of suffering damaging, if not permanent, setbacks.

You have two options when confronted with the unexpected. You can either feel sorry for yourself and do nothing, which unfortunately is the course followed far too often by businesses and individuals. You get angry, you sulk, you swear, you convince yourself it's not fair, that the whole world is against you. I feel all those things. But I don't stop there. I move on to the second option: you forge ahead and try to deal with the problem at hand.

It's difficult to avoid catching the Woe-Is-Me Disease. After all, no one ever believes they deserve a negative blow, particularly if you're working hard and sticking with your business plan. Your first instincts are to immediately turn inward. You become bogged down with the "What Ifs?" What if this hadn't happened—look how much better we would be. You spend so much time dealing with What Ifs, which you can't control, that you neglect what you can influence. This negative reaction has some telling ramifications. It potentially can paralyze everything and everyone linked to your situation. Instead of the setback being kept in context, it becomes an enormous burden, halting decision making and affecting morale. It diverts attention away from normal activities and impedes progress.

You find yourself slipping into a defensive, crisis-management mode. Everyone gets uptight, the mood of the organization turns sour, and instead of funneling your thought process toward pushing for improvements, you're confronted with the challenge of stopping the relapse. Employees sense your depression, and it affects not only their attitude but also the spirit of your business.

It doesn't have to be that way. It takes strength to cure yourself of the Woe-Is-Me Disease, but it can be done. It's all a matter of planning. Instead of ignoring the possibility that something bad will happen, you anticipate the worst-case scenarios and have an action plan in place to handle the setbacks. Preparation eliminates the Woe-Is-Me Disease because everyone in the organization understands that when a crisis occurs, we're ready to deal with it, correct it, and keep going, hopefully without missing a step. You counter the negative with an immediate and decisive positive that stops the backtracking and gets things on course.

Let me use the Newsome injury to illustrate what I mean. When I received an indication the problem could be serious, I felt a momentary twinge of anxiety about how his absence would affect the team. You've worked so hard as an organization to climb to the top, and you'd like to feel you should be rewarded for your efforts—yet losing Newsome hardly was a reward. It was as if someone decided we had celebrated long enough, and now it was time for a reality check. I wanted to make sure we were good enough to meet this test.

We felt we had a competent replacement for Newsome already on our roster. Tyrone Williams, a second-year player from Nebraska who had been a reserve on our Super Bowl team, had developed nicely. Now he would be asked to step up and assume a bigger role than he had anticipated. We were confident that our system had prepared him for this promotion. He had received excellent coaching geared toward making sure a reserve is groomed enough to become a starter when needed. Williams may not have been as experienced as Newsome, but the whole basis of the Stepping Stone theory is to give your organization the depth it requires to absorb these unexpected personnel blows. If one of your best employees suddenly isn't available, have you trained the next layer of workers well enough that one of them can move in as a competent replacement?

Once Williams became a starter and Newsome was placed on injured reserve, we had a hole to fill on our roster. We needed to add another cornerback to the active squad, in case of more injuries and to help our special teams. The other problem concerned the salary cap. Salaries of injured players continue to count under the cap, so the fact Newsome could be sidelined indefinitely did not free up any money. Mike Reinfeldt, who handles our cap calculations, immediately figured out how much we could spend on a new player.

The next step was to consult our ready list, which contains the name of every available street free agent whom we think is good enough to make an NFL roster. We have these players broken down by position, and each has a grade. This list is compiled to help us deal with a Newsome-like emergency. It's updated constantly as part of our ongoing personnel responsibilities. As the Bears game continued, we reviewed the ready list and discussed potential replacements. By halftime, we decided we should promote cornerback Randy Kinder, who currently was under contract on our practice squad. The NFL allows you to keep up to five players on the practice squad, which serves as a developmental arm for your team. We also identified a player we would add to the practice squad to take Kinder's place, fullback Steve Lee, who was a free agent. We then talked to the agents for both players to inform them of our plans and verify their interest. All this had been accomplished in less than 90 minutes because we were prepared—we had the ready list, we had up-to-the-minute salary cap information, we had agent phone numbers. We didn't scramble. Instead, we properly executed a plan that was in place to cover an event of this kind.

Once the game ended—we had beaten the Bears, 38–24—I went to the locker room and talked to Mike Holmgren and Fritz Shurmur, our defensive coordinator. We discussed the situation, and I explained my thinking concerning the roster changes. They agreed with me about Kinder and Lee, but Chmura would be sidelined for about six weeks, and Mike wanted another tight end on the active roster. That meant opening up a second slot. Kicker Brett Conway, our third-round 1997 choice, had been injured, but I wanted to keep him active so if he healed, we could use him. Now, that no longer was an option. We decided to put him on injured reserve and sign free agent tight end Reggie Johnson, another player from our ready list, in his place. We executed the necessary personnel moves, including sending Newsome to the injured reserve list. He would need surgery and doctors said he would not heal fast enough to play the rest of the season.

Our changes didn't make up for the fact that we had lost a quality player. None of us were attempting to soft-pedal the loss to ourselves, to the team, or to the fans. It was obvious we weren't as good without Newsome. Still, we had faith in Williams's ability to give us a quality performance, which he did. Indeed, he missed only one play during the rest of the season. And, by moving quickly and decisively, we demonstrated that our organization wouldn't become paralyzed by traumatic events. That's the reason we're constantly updating the ready list and why we put so much time into the scouting and grading of players. The last thing we needed at this point was to give any indication we were flustered by the injury, or thrown into chaos, with no clue what to do.

We could have increased the severity of the situation by feeling sorry for ourselves and complaining, both internally and to the media. But the reality was, Newsome was hurt and there was absolutely nothing we could do to change that. It was imperative that I put his injury behind me as soon as possible. That doesn't mean a lack of empathy for him, or for anyone affected by setbacks. Instead, it's an acknowledgment of the realities of business. You can be sympathetic while also pushing ahead as hard as possible to make up for the reversal.

Every business should have a ready list that's activated in case of emergencies. What if a key employee suddenly dies or is incapacitated in an accident? You should know now how you would handle these situations—whom you would promote, whom you would hire? No one wants to think about any of these scenarios—why dwell on potential bad news?—but experience tells us they'll happen. What if you're running a magazine and the subject of your cover story resigns from office or dies? Do you have a backup idea to drop in place at the last moment?

At the same time, I don't waste energy worrying about things I can't control. This is another aspect of the What If mentality. For example, if I didn't have enough money to pay a valuable employee to stay with my firm and his loss has hindered our development, I may not be happy about it. But I also can't fret needlessly about the implications. I accept our financial limitations, and then I turn my focus to filling the position with a more talented replacement. What good does it do to constantly conjure up past injustices and inequities and wail about them— except to waste valuable energy that could be used much more positively?

Through the years, I've developed an ability to remain calm amid the emotion and hubbub caused by an unexpected event. The noisier and more tumultuous it gets, the better I seem to function. I've convinced myself that it's during these emergencies that my employer needs my expertise and experience the most, so I have an obligation not to let him down.

Mike Holmgren is particularly good at dealing with the Woe-Is-Me Disease. That's because he acknowledges something that seems so simple but escapes so many people: the game still has to be played. Substitute "game" for your situation—the business still has to continue, the customer still has to be served, the sales call still has to be made, the product still has to be produced, the part still has to be replaced. He wants no part of any "skyis-falling" talk. His focus becomes, how do we fulfill this revised goal?

That emerges as Mike's consuming mission every time there's a setback. He wants to win so badly that he won't allow a misstep to thwart him. Maybe for an upcoming game, he has only one healthy running back. So he'll turn more to one back and three receivers. Or maybe his receivers are limping, so his game plan will put more emphasis on our running attack. He'll juggle and maneuver and create temporary solutions, anything to give us a chance instead of just hanging on. He never allows any of his internal feelings to affect his dealings with the players. He never makes or uses excuses. Excuses aren't allowed to become a crutch. His message is always positive and upbeat. Hey, if we want to win badly enough, we'll find a way to do it. Someone hurt? We'll bring in a replacement, coach him well, and he'll do the job.

Instead of viewing the unexpected as a cruel impediment, look at it as a stimulating challenge. When the whole world seems to be crumbling around you, I understand that viewing anything as a "test" can be extremely difficult. But without embracing reversals as opportunities to prove your worth, they'll grab you and toss you to the sidelines, where you become a spectator instead of a participant. You need to adopt a mind-set based on aggressiveness—just as everything else in our Stepping Stone philosophies stems from an aggressive approach. I never want to retreat, I never want to give in, I never want to feel I'm letting circumstances dictate my course of action. I want to be the pace-setter, I want to be the one who establishes the agenda, I want to demonstrate the energy and positive thinking that will over-come any obstacle. I'm not afraid to stick out my chin and let people take their best shots.

Imagine how we felt when the doctors told us after the 1994 season that Sterling Sharpe should retire rather than risk paralysis from contact. Sterling had developed a condition in his neck that left him vulnerable to crippling injury. At the time, he was one of the elite receivers in the league, and people viewed his loss as being insurmountable for our organization. With the arrival of Mike Holmgren and the emergence of Brett Favre, he had flourished, putting together consecutive seasons of 108, 112, and 94 catches. He was the go-to receiver in an offense that depended, more than anything else, on its passing schemes. He had become a consistent, durable, tough player who loved the thrill of competing. He was as good as anyone in the game at his craft, including Jerry Rice. He wasn't an explosive touchdown maker like Rice, but he was the player I would want in crucial situations. He trained so diligently that he appeared indestructible. I couldn't comprehend he could be hurt so badly.

He also was our best player, the equivalent of the top producer in your firm, the leading salesman, the most efficient worker, the most reliable customer service representative. Considering we were in the middle stages of our development program, his loss came at a particularly difficult time. We were just beginning to produce depth at the receiver position, but it was an ongoing process. Without Sharpe, we were left with an enormous void and the possibility that our growth would be stalled. It was a pivotal moment in our revitalization efforts. How we overcame this blow would tell a lot about the strength of our organization and about the quality of its leadership, starting from the top.

It was at this juncture that I allowed myself to think that maybe we would never accomplish our ultimate goals. Maybe somebody was telling us the mountain was too high to climb, and we had better reassess our situation. I kept envisioning a greasy pole. We'd inch our way toward the top, and we'd reach out to grab the flag, only to hit more grease and slide backward. I couldn't accept that this actually was happening to us. You feel like rolling up in the fetal position and shutting out the rest of the world.

Our system and the leaders under me bailed us out. Robert Brooks, who was our third pick in the 1992 draft, had caught 58 passes in 1994 starting as the receiver opposite Sharpe. In 1995, without Sharpe, he stepped up big-time. We thought he was a quality player when we drafted him, but we never envisioned what he became in 1995. He caught 102 passes for a team-record 1,497 yards. He and Sharpe are the only players in franchise history to have 100 receptions in a season. He also had nine 100-yard receiving games, breaking another record held by Sharpe. In his fourth year under the coaching of Mike Holmgren and his staff, he had developed into one of the league's best. The fact that he didn't have to start as a rookie, and could spend time learning from veterans and refining his skills, enabled him to gain the knowledge of the scheme that he needed to excel. He is a prime example of the Stepping Stone approach at work.

Even with Sharpe gone, Holmgren and his coaches never backed off a bit from their determination to make things work. Mike didn't use the Sharpe injury as an excuse, nor did he allow his players to let down because of Sterling's absence. This strong, positive leadership amid a major crisis kept everyone focused. The message became: we won't let this stop us from growing.

What we couldn't anticipate was how our offense actually benefited in some ways from Sharpe's retirement. Brett Favre had become so dependent on him that other receivers weren't as involved in the offense as they probably should have been. Now, Brett had no choice but to look to other targets. He no longer had one player yapping in his ear, demanding passes be thrown his way. We began spreading out the ball more, involving more receivers and making us much more difficult to defend. We not only survived Sterling's loss, but grew stronger. We produced an 11–5 record, our best since 1972. By season's end, no one was talking anymore about whether we could survive without Sharpe.

The Sharpe episode taught me a great lesson that should be remembered by every businessman. Sometimes, when things seem the bleakest, organizations built on solid principles and filled with self-starters and great leaders on every level have a way of turning bad moments into something very good. It takes faith in your method of operation and a belief that your company is capable of overcoming any obstacle, but the end result can be a stronger enterprise. Sharpe's retirement forced us to find another way to maintain our quality and challenged us to keep getting better, and we were up to the task. His absence gave other employees a chance to flourish. They capitalized on the opportunity to succeed, but it also was an indication that we hadn't ignored the supporting cast while upgrading our elite personnel.

That's why you can't allow setbacks to become permanent obstacles. That's why you can't allow employees to whine and why you can't allow unexpected developments to send morale spiraling. I don't care if you have to put on a big act—you must never let others see you depressed. As soon as you feel sorry for yourself in public, you have risked irreparable harm to your plans. I'm convinced you can overcome virtually anything if you can avoid the sulks and demonstrate enough intelligence, gumption, and patience.

Even though we made it to the Super Bowl within five years, we might have arrived even faster if everything had unfolded without any glitches. Including Sharpe, we had a series of career-ending injuries that eliminated vital Stepping Stones and slowed our progress. I'm certain, for example, that linebacker Mark D'Onofrio, our 1992 second-round choice, would have been a perennial Pro Bowl pick. But during his rookie season, he tore a hamstring so badly that it eventually forced him to retire in 1993. The doctors told me it was a fluke, something they'd never seen before. The hamstring had ripped completely off the bone. Johnny Holland, another gifted linebacker, had six straight 100-tackle seasons before a neck injury forced him to retire in 1994 at the peak of his career. He was our defensive signal caller, a natural leader and a solid citizen, so his departure was particularly difficult. Linebacker Brian Noble hurt a knee so badly that he also retired in 1994.

It would have been difficult enough to lose one linebacker, but for three to have their careers ended prematurely really crippled our defense. We also thought we had solid Stepping Stones in center James Campen and defensive back Roland Mitchell, but physical problems forced them into early retirement.

In 1994, I traded up in the first round to draft Notre Dame guard Aaron Taylor, whom we thought had Pro Bowl potential. We envisioned him as a stabilizing force at guard. He hurt each knee before the end of his second season, and he'll never be the player we projected. He started on both of our Super Bowl teams and then signed with the San Diego Chargers in the early months of 1998.

Every NFL team has injury problems. But most of the time, they're temporary and the player returns to finish out his career. It didn't seem to work that way for us, so it took us longer, particularly on defense, to build a unit good enough to compete for a Super Bowl. We kept plugging away, finding alternatives to make up for these losses, until we won the championship.

Even if your competitors don't seem to be absorbing the same amount of negative blows as you, don't be deterred from your goals. It all comes down to confidence and willpower. You must feel good enough about your system to believe you'll succeed. And you must be able to get off the mat every time and keep fighting, no matter how many knockdowns you suffer. Your competitors have to know you'll always be a factor, no matter how difficult the dilemma.

The Woe-Is-Me Disease also occurs when you and your organization make mistakes because of poor judgment. You simply mess up something that has consequences for your firm, whether it's a bad hire, an unnecessary purchase, an investment that flops, or a new product line that fails to take off. Unlike the unexpected setbacks, these are moves that you carefully planned and approved, only to have them turn out to be mistakes. Depending on the severity of the error, they could do major harm to your situation, perhaps even severely stalling your growth plans.

I've found that many executives have difficulty dealing with their internal mistakes. So often, it comes down to ego and pride. If I acknowledge I messed up, then my employees and my peers might view me differently. They may not respect me as much, or they might consider me weak, or they may not want to deal with me as readily. They might lose faith in my ability to succeed. So rather than exorcise the mistake, I'll either allow the mistake to fester—the policy I instituted isn't working but instead of changing it, I keep it in force—or I'll attempt to remedy my error through misguided corrective actions.

The problem is, many times mistakes can't be fixed. Take a poor hiring decision. You might think you can turn it around by giving the individual more training or putting him in a different position. Most times, though, a bad hire is a bad hire, and the only solution is to terminate the individual. Keeping him around bogs down the organization, reducing production.

I won't tell you I'm immune to the fallout from mistakes. Quite the contrary. They hurt me deeply. I wonder why I can't be smarter and avoid making the errors that I commit. Sometimes the weaknesses in my decisions are so obvious, but I become blinded and forge ahead anyway. Ego is too heavily involved. Hey, I'm the boss, I know best, so this is the way it's going to be. Forget the advice of my staff, which weighs against my choice. Forget my vow never to allow emotion or stubbornness to become part of the decision-making process. All that's tossed aside, just so I can prove I'm smarter than anyone else.

That's one way mistakes occur. Another is to ignore, deviate from, or cut off the decision-making process you've instituted within your organization. Errors happen when you don't allow the process to reach a conclusion. Instead, you make a hasty choice, perhaps fearing that if you wait, you'll miss out on a particularly qualified candidate, or won't land a juicy order or will lose out to another bidder. By stepping away from the formal procedure, you're shortchanging the thoroughness and analysis necessary to make correct decisions. You have established these steps because you *know* they lead to proper evaluations and reduce the chance of error. So you can't relent to pressure or temptation. Every time you do, you risk making poor moves.

The best managers deal with their mistakes quickly and decisively. I'm not afraid to acknowledge my errors. If anything, I think the honesty is appreciated by employees, who understand I'm not trying to mislead them. No one wants to mess up, but it's going to happen. I think that once you admit to yourself you're not infallible and that, no matter how hard you try, you'll mess up, it enables you to deal better with errors; that, in turn, helps you execute your duties more effectively. The key, to me, is to eradicate the mistake as soon as possible. I can't understand why anyone would want the error hanging around, reminding them of their lapse. It's bad enough I have to look at myself in the mirror everyday. I don't need further reinforcement when I arrive in the office.

I make many of my mistakes in public, on draft day. Drafting players is an inexact science, and anyone who says otherwise is kidding himself. Yet each April, we close the doors to our draft room and spend two days hoping months of hard work have given us the insight we need to select players who can improve our team. Since none of them have ever played a down in the NFL, we have no real way to guarantee their success. We can look at our information and rely on our instincts and years of experience to help narrow the margin for error. But we can't eliminate the foul-ups, just as you can't erase the likelihood that any step you take will backfire, particularly when it involves another human being. Until that person actually is working with you and is tested through on-the-job pressures, you'll never really know if he's capable of fulfilling your expectations.

I'm considered good at what I do, yet I look at my Green Bay drafts and sometimes wonder what the heck I was thinking when we made some of our choices. I've found it very helpful to painstakingly analyze all my drafts, selection by selection. I want to understand why we made our picks. Why did some work? Why did others fail? What could we have done differently to avoid the mistakes? What positives can we draw from the successes to help us become more effective next year? I'm constantly reviewing everything I do, not to second-guess myself but to learn from my own actions. You come away sure you'll do better next time. That knowledge gives you confidence to push on.

I'd recommend the same reflective process for your business—but do it yourself. Don't appoint a study committee or bring in a consultant. It's your responsibility to determine why errors were made, not someone else's. It's the only way you can really understand all the nuances involved. Sometimes it's depressing to relive the bad moments, but I'm convinced history is, indeed, the best teacher. You can profit from your mistakes as long as you're willing to readily admit you messed up—and as long as you maintain an open mind about what went wrong.

If I was a product manager with a company and my new line flopped, I wouldn't rely solely on company research to explain why. I'd be in the stores myself, asking customers what they didn't like. I would be comparing my product with our rival's, trying to figure out what we missed in our decision-making process. The challenge wouldn't be to see how long I could sulk, but to make adjustments that, next time, would be successful.

I didn't wait long to take my first misstep with the Packers. On the first pick of our very first draft in 1992, I chose cornerback Terrell Buckley. I knew better. I wanted big, physical cornerbacks with long arms, yet Terrell was only 5–9 and not very strong. He was an exception, but I became enamored with what I perceived as his big-play ability. Every business should be searching for these difference makers—those individuals who give you an edge. They have the knack of performing under pressure, of producing when needed, of never backing off at the most difficult times. If you have enough of these special performers in your organization, you'll win.

It is the same with a football team. You want the quarterback who'll complete the pressure pass or the runner who'll pick up the key first down or the cornerback who'll defend the pivotal third-down pass. I convinced myself that Buckley, despite falling outside our physical requirements, was capable of not only stopping receivers but also turning interceptions into touchdowns. I saw him as an offensive playmaker playing defense. I reached for something that probably wasn't there because of our needs, and in the process, I violated one of the key rules governing our selection of personnel: don't pick exceptions. If I had stuck with my principles, I never would have chosen Buckley.

If I wanted a cornerback, I should have taken Troy Vincent. Troy became a starter with the Miami Dolphins, then signed as a free agent with the Philadelphia Eagles. He was bigger, stronger, and more durable than Terrell. I really yearned to pick tackle Bob Whitfield, even though cornerback was a bigger need in 1992. I thought Whitfield was one of the elite players available in the draft. He since has gone on to become a solid starter for the Atlanta Falcons. Yet, as an organization, we entered the draft hoping to choose Desmond Howard, the Heisman Trophy winner from Michigan who was a talented receiver and kick returner. Again, we were dazzled by Howard's playmaking powers and his ability to fill two of our major needs. He had the speed to turn small runs into large gains, and that's what every team wants. He also was small—too small for our system. He was another exception, but we were prepared to ignore that red flag. As it turned out, the Redskins jumped ahead of us in the draft and grabbed Howard, who later went from Washington to the Jacksonville Jaguars and then was cut. We wound up signing him as a street free agent before the 1996 season, and he became a stellar return man for our Super Bowl team.

Once Howard was taken in the draft, we switched to Buckley, not Whitfield or Vincent. Terrell started three years for us, then went to Miami where he started immediately for the Dolphins. He's had a fine pro career. Yet, as the fifth player chosen in a draft, he hasn't been the special athlete you're seeking when you pick that high. I thought he was finally coming around during his last season with us, then I realized I was misleading myself. Early on, he got caught up trying to be another Deion Sanders, but he lacked Deion's talents and charisma. He also thought he could play baseball, just as Deion was doing, and he spent a summer in the minor leagues instead of working to be a better football player. His head wasn't where it needed to be. It was best for the team to move on without him, and that's the decision we made. Even though he's no longer a Packer, I know he'll always be held up as one of my most damaging mistakes.

If I could redo the pick, I wouldn't have taken Buckley. I'm not going to stubbornly insist I was right, or make excuses. What good would that do? I was on a radio talk show in Milwaukee, and the host thought he could really get to me. He was proud of himself because he had all the facts about Terrell Buckley and he said to me, "Ron Wolf, what would you say if the fans in the state of Wisconsin said that Terrell Buckley isn't good enough to play?"

I paused and replied, "I'd say they're right." And stopped. Everything went dead for at least ten seconds. He didn't know what to say. He wanted to start an argument, but there was nothing to dispute. He finally wound up praising me for my honesty. I'm not sure what honesty has to do with it. It was a bad pick, and I would be stupid to defend it. Instead, I want to learn from it. I reviewed the 1992 draft and saw how I was tempted by exceptions with both Buckley and Howard. Since neither has developed into a star, it only confirms my belief that you need to stay within your system and function according to your rules. Our rule says, don't draft exceptions—and I shouldn't make any exceptions to that mandate.

It was a great lesson about discipline—a lesson every company should heed. Stay with what you know is right, no matter the temptation. Besides, what's the sense of lying to yourself or others about errors? It's a lot easier to be straightforward and move on. If you keep manufacturing excuses for your mistakes, you eventually forget what you have said and what you haven't, and you get caught in the web. It's so easy to avoid the trap. Just be true to yourself.

We won't allow mistakes to hinder the progress of the Packers, either on the field or in the front office. Production becomes the judge that keeps us straight. If the person can't produce, no matter his pedigree, he's gone. Being a high-round pick, or a high-salaried employee, won't save anyone. Obviously, if we make too many errors, we'll never reach our expectations, but you've got to acknowledge to yourself that you won't be perfect either, whatever your position.

Actually, the worst mistake you can make is to be afraid . . . to make mistakes. If you get gun-shy and pull back and begin procrastinating over your decision making for fear you'll be wrong, you will become passive. The aggressiveness you need to excel will give way to insecurity. Doing nothing in pursuit of the right goals is a thousand times worse than being wrong. We draft the players we think will improve our chances of winning. We never select them because we like their parents or they're handsome. As long as we make our choices believing the players in question will upgrade our talent level, I know I have the best intentions of the organization in mind.

I'm going to keep reloading and firing away. We brought in Eric Dickerson, the NFL's No. 2 all-time rusher, hoping he had something left. He didn't, but it was worth the try. We signed Reggie Cobb from Tampa Bay as a free agent in 1994, thinking he was the answer at running back. He didn't fit into our system, and we had to let him go, but it was worth the try. I still regret not being as aggressive as I should have been when Marcus Allen, another great running back, was a free agent. He would have been a wonderful addition to our team, but I didn't think he would play much longer. Instead, he didn't retire until after the 1997 season. Sometimes you just outsmart yourself; it's something you need to watch. If it feels good and looks good, do it.

At the same time, it's healthy for everyone in your organization to identify plans, ideas, or personnel moves that, for some reason, you weren't able to execute—and now you're glad you didn't. It's a way of making sure you always remember good fortune—okay, pure luck—is a constant factor that influences developments far more than we want to acknowledge. In our case, we made big runs at two free agents, receiver Andre Rison and linebacker Cornelius Bennett. We wanted Rison to replace

Sterling Sharpe after Sharpe had retired. And we wanted Bennett to bolster our linebacking situation, which had been weakened by injuries. We were outbid for both of them, and I've been thankful ever since. If we had signed them, it would have maxed out our salary cap and ruined our flexibility regarding future personnel moves. And neither would have been the player we had envisioned. Ironically, we eventually claimed Andre on waivers during the middle of the 1996 season after Robert Brooks was hurt, and he became a pivotal performer on our Super Bowl team. But we still would have overpaid if we had signed him to take over for Sharpe.

I learned an important lesson from the Bennett-Rison situations: you may already have people in your organization that, given the opportunity, can perform just as well, if not better, than these "big-name" people you want to import. It was a reminder that production, not résumés, is what counts—and that too often, we become so dazzled by the reputation of people from other organizations that we fail to recognize the talents of our own personnel. If you've trained your own people properly, you should have able replacements already on the payroll. But how many times do we see companies hire someone at a higher salary than a current employee at the same level—and discover that the new person isn't as good as the established worker? When that happens in football, you wind up with unhappy players and demands to have contracts renegotiated—and more headaches than the situation is worth.

As much as possible, I try to have a fallback plan that will help alleviate, if not reverse, any mistakes, particularly involving personnel. If I give up a draft choice, I already have a strategy in mind to get that pick back with another trade. Or, during the ensuing months, I'll strive to work a deal that will recover the selection. I'm never functioning in a vacuum. Just because you make one move doesn't mean you shouldn't be contemplating another and another and another. It's an ongoing process that works only if you aren't restrained by any tendencies to be timid.

Once you hesitate, you cut into the aggressive attitude you must maintain to work through the mistakes.

If you fill a position, that doesn't mean you're automatically successful. So don't dump the names of other potential candidates. If the new employee doesn't work out, you should already have decided on your next choice. If you have a yearly plan in place, you also should have alternative possibilities in mind that you can substitute if you see your original ideas aren't working. Why prolong a bad trend out of stubbornness or lack of alternatives?

You can't justify a mistake by convincing yourself that, as disappointing as the error might be, at least the person or policy or product now is a known commodity, so why mess with it? You talk yourself into believing that if you go in another direction, you might wind up with something just as bad, if not worse. So you do nothing. That's the worst kind of convoluted thinking. I have enough faith in our ability as an organization and in the system we have devised to believe that given a second chance, we'll most definitely improve on the mistake. So the sales manager didn't work out. I'll find a better one. So the sales pitch didn't work. I'll devise a better one. So the new product didn't sell. I'll invent a better one. Cut your losses, renew the analysis, and enjoy more success next time.

I'll give you an example of how determination pays off. In 1996, we picked tackle John Michels in the first round. We needed to groom a left tackle to replace veteran Ken Ruettgers, who had been battling injury problems and was nearing the end of his career. In the same draft, I also liked linebacker Ray Lewis and defensive end Tony Brackens. But Lewis was chosen by the Baltimore Ravens before our turn in the first round, and I convinced myself to lay off Brackens because he had a history of injuries that I was afraid would shorten his career. Considering our history of losing players because of injuries, I didn't want to run that risk with another athlete. I didn't think Michels was ready to start, but I also thought we had time to train him.

Then, on the first day of training camp, Ruettgers told us he was retiring. I was upset he waited so long because it severely hindered our chances of obtaining a veteran to replace him. We had to turn to Michels, who lacked experience and strength. He did the best he could under the circumstances, but we ultimately had to replace him with veteran Bruce Wilkinson, one of the unsung heroes on our Super Bowl roster.

In the 1997 pre-draft scouting process, we identified tackle Ross Verba as an elite prospect. We wanted to pick him. We probably could have looked at the potential selection of Verba in two ways: one, if we chose him, it would be an admission Michels was a mistake, which would reflect badly on the organization, or, two, if we chose him, it would hinder Michels's development, since we still felt John could be an effective NFL player. I think both lines of thinking are bogus. I didn't care if people saw Verba as an attempt to make up for Michels. I wasn't about to shy away from another left tackle because I feared his selection would be viewed as an admission we made a mistake the previous season. Verba was too good to pass up, and if I let my ego interfere, I would be hurting the team. Nor could I become gun-shy. Just because one left tackle prospect struggled was no reason to think the next one would, too. And if Michels wasn't good enough to compete with Verba, we could live with that. It's our job to either teach him to play another position or to turn him into a competent reserve who can start when necessary. Either way, the Packers would benefit. So we chose Verba.

He was an immediate hit. He moved into the starting left tackle position and, despite being a rookie, fared well during the 1997 season. He is tough and physical and plays with an aggressive attitude that filtered through the rest of his teammates and made us a more pugnacious line. Verba was the right choice—and it happened because our prospect-evaluation system worked. We didn't allow the Michels episode to weaken our resolve. We never lost confidence that we could judge the talent of prospects and make proper selections. Verba reinforced our belief that, if we stay with what we know is right, we'll have more hits than misses. If we hadn't, we would have passed up a talented player.

Your ability to handle mistakes and setbacks properly depends so much on how well you maintain an upbeat attitude. You have to develop the ability to remember all the positives that have happened in the past to you and use those pluses as a reminder every time you become depressed over errors. This becomes your internal reassurance guide. It's so easy to knock yourself down and think you're inadequate, particularly when your missteps are the subject of either internal or external debate, or both. At those times, keep reassuring yourself that you know what you're doing and that you can work through the down times. For example, I look back at our drafts and see lots of very successful choices, even in the later rounds, where we took players who have become starters and, in some cases, stars in the NFL. Other clubs had a chance to pick these athletes, but instead, we got them. So for every first-round pick like Terrell Buckley or George Teague, who didn't turn out as well as we had hoped, we have countered with the likes of Mark Chmura (sixth round), Robert Brooks (third round), Dorsey Levens (fifth round), Brian Williams (third round), Edgar Bennett (fourth round), and Adam Timmerman (seventh round).

You've reached a position of influence and authority because of your intelligence, experience, and talents. Don't allow anything to negate your instincts. Remain confident that you know what's right for your organization and that you understand how to achieve success. You've got to develop this kind of tunnel vision because, even when you have become No. 1, as the Packers did at the end of the 1996 season, the obstacles that could knock you from the top won't disappear. How you deal with those situations is the essence of the ninth Stepping Stone: Staying on Top. But first, here are the prominent points you should remember from Stepping Stone No. 8—Handling the Unexpected:

• When unexpected setbacks occur, fight the Woe-Is-Me Disease, the mentality that convinces you the world is against you and that you don't deserve this punishment. You need to resist the temptation to feel sorry for yourself, and instead, you must confront the unexpected and take positive actions to counter it.

• Proper planning is the most effective and quickest way to counter unexpected developments. Have a ready list prepared that outlines how you'll respond to emergencies.

• Don't spend time worrying about what you can't control and What Ifs. Concentrate your energy on things you can influence and change.

• Instead of viewing the unexpected as a setback, consider it a test of your organization's ability to overcome challenges.

• Mistakes in judgment can be paralyzing if you attempt to fix the errors instead of exorcising them.

• Organizations built on solid principles and filled with self-starters and great leaders on every level have a way of turning bleak moments into something good. It takes faith in your methods of operation and a belief that your company is capable of overcoming any obstacle, but the end result can be a stronger organization.

• Errors happen when you don't allow the decision-making process to reach a conclusion. Instead, you make a hasty choice. By stepping away from the formal process, you're shortchanging the analysis necessary to make correct decisions. You have established these steps because you *know* they lead to proper evaluations and reduce the chance of error. So you can't bow to pressure or temptation.

• The best managers deal with their mistakes decisively and quickly. Don't be afraid to acknowledge your errors. Employees appreciate this honesty.

• Carefully analyze your mistakes. Do the analysis yourself. Don't appoint a study committee or bring in a consultant. You can profit from your errors as long as you're willing to readily admit you messed up and as long as you maintain an open mind about what went wrong.

• The worst mistake you can make is to be afraid . . . to make mistakes. If you get gun-shy and pull back and begin procrastinating over your decision making for fear you'll be wrong, you'll become passive. Doing nothing in pursuit of the right goals is a thousand times worse than making a mistake.

• Don't prolong a mistake by convincing yourself that, as disappointing as the error might be, at least the person or policy or product now is a known commodity, so why mess with it? Have enough faith in your ability as an organization and in the system you have devised to believe that given a second chance, you'll most definitely improve on the mistake.

• Handling setbacks and mistakes properly depends on how well you maintain an upbeat attitude. You have to develop the ability to remember all the positives that have happened to your enterprise in the past and use those pluses as a reminder every time you want to become depressed over errors.

• Always have a fallback plan when you make decisions, so if your first choice doesn't work, you already have alternatives that can be quickly implemented. The goal is to cut your losses as soon as possible and not let the mistakes linger.

CHAPTER NINE

STEPPING STONE NO. 9

Staying on Top

Some days, when I find myself worrying too much about the ever-changing landscape of pro football and fretting too much about the myriad of challenges confronting the Packers, I think back to my first years in Green Bay. I think about how we couldn't get agents to return calls and how players didn't want to join the team. I think about how everyone thought 9–7 seasons were terrific. I think about how we desperately wanted to improve so we could become NFL champions.

I think about all that, and it serves as a wake-up call. No matter how frustrating it has become at times dealing with problems of success, I never again want to go through what we experienced in the early 1990s. I want to do everything I can to keep the Packers at the forefront of the NFL, where we are the lead dog, not one of the followers. Once you've enjoyed the satisfaction of reaching the top and being No. 1, there's no other feeling that can replace it. Once you've been there, trust me, you spend every minute figuring out a way to always be better than everyone else.

After we lost to the Denver Broncos in Super Bowl XXXII, I went into a funk. I forgot about all our accomplishments over the previous five years. I forgot that we're still regarded as one of the two or three elite franchises in the league. I forgot we retain the talent and leadership to challenge for many future championships. All I could think about was that game and how we let what would have been a second straight title slip away.

It took the Winter Olympics to clear my mind. I don't watch a lot of television, but I do tune in to the cable network sports news programs. During the Olympics, those shows telecast plenty of highlights, including clips of both winners and losers. I took particular note of how the losers dealt so graciously with their setbacks. Here were these young people, some no older than 18 or 19. They had trained so intensely and so long for a few moments of glory, and then they lost. Yet they were able to quickly regain their composure and maturely handle what had to be a crushing feeling.

I told myself if they could absorb defeat with so much poise, what was wrong with me? I supposedly was mature and experienced. Yet I sure wasn't demonstrating either trait. Besides, I wasn't being very realistic. We had lost a game I was convinced we would win, and I'll always remain frustrated that we were unsuccessful. But that defeat didn't suddenly turn everything we'd achieved into failure. There were 28 other franchises that gladly would have traded places with us that Super Bowl Sunday, so we should never forget the magnitude of what we've accomplished since 1991. I know one thing for sure. If anyone else wants to represent the NFC in ensuing Super Bowls, they're going to have to deal with us first, and I believe we'll continue to be a formidable obstacle.

Nothing has changed within our system or within our structure that would deter us from continued success. What was solid before the Bronco game continues to be solid. We have a staff of gifted employees, a great head coach, and a core group of stars who will keep us competitive. Yet the results of Super Bowl XXXII demonstrate the pressures and complexities associated with our last Stepping Stone: Staying on Top. It's always difficult to remain No. 1, and if you falter even slightly, the insecurity that's generated presents as big a challenge to your enterprise as anything you've faced climbing to the top. Your organization suddenly is dealing with a vastly different set of obstacles and issues. How you work your way through these new hurdles determines your ability to remain a winner.

More than anything else, you have to *want* to stay the best. Organizations that have tasted success often fall into a trap.

Everyone will give you lip service about wanting to remain No. 1, but the test is whether the lust to stay in front is sufficient. Quite the opposite often happens. Everyone starts believing all the press clippings. They're being told how great they are and, sure enough, they buy into the praise. They believe they can put things on cruise control and still be dominant. They either forget or neglect what made them successful in the first place, the four C's (certain devotion, certain dedication, certain work ethic, and certain results).

I see it all the time with players. Their efforts are rewarded by a new, lucrative contract. They say financial security won't alter their performance, that they'll remain just as determined and dedicated as they've always been. But something inside them changes. They've lost the hunger that pushed them to become the best. They don't work out as much, they don't practice as hard. The changes don't have to be significant. Just enough for them to lose their edge. Competition is so keen that it only takes a slight slippage in ability to bring them back to the rest of the field. Frequently, they get entangled with the trappings of success. The luxury cars, the big houses, the fancy vacations. The show becomes more important than the substance. They no longer play at a star level.

Elite businesses aren't immune to these problems. They move into fancy buildings. They pay exorbitant salaries. They travel lavishly. They add more layers of bureaucracy and, in the process, impede communications and decision making. They expand too rapidly, take on too much debt. Their priorities change, even if they maintain nothing is different. If you fall into this trap, both you and your company lose the drive that has carried you to the top. Your stomach is full; you don't hunger anymore. And you tumble.

Decisions that once seemed routine now become potential bombshells. Here's an example of what I mean. Every team that wins the Super Bowl buys expensive rings for its players and staff. They present these rings at an elaborate private celebration where they can toast the triumph. Plus, it has also become tradition to visit the White House and be honored by the President. In planning for these events, Mike and I had to decide what to do about three players—Andre Rison, Desmond Howard, and Chris Jacke—who no longer were Packers. In our experience with the 49ers and Raiders after their championships, players who weren't affiliated anymore with the team weren't invited to these festivities. So we didn't include Rison, Howard, and Jacke.

Some of those players thought they should be invited—and a lot of fans and people in the media agreed. It became very controversial. I'm not sure why anyone who had left the team would want to participate in these events, but they did. The Packers finally changed their minds and included them. I didn't agree and still don't, but we absorbed the incident without any long-term damage. Still, this is the kind of situation produced by success that can cut into your firm's effectiveness.

That's why companies and athletes who become No. 1 and stay there are truly remarkable. You can never underestimate the willpower of Bill Russell, Michael Jordan, Ray Nitschke, Terry Bradshaw, or Otto Graham. The more they won, the more determined they became. Something inside them wouldn't allow them to settle for anything but a prolonged residency in the front of the pack. I see that fire in Brett Favre. Even though he's one of the NFL's highest-paid players, he still desperately thirsts for victory.

I'm sure every Packer player wanted to win Super Bowl XXXII, but I'm not sure if all of them were as dedicated on that one day as they needed to be. They might have convinced themselves they were better than the Broncos, and they didn't push themselves as hard as they should have. In the months since the loss, people have come up to me and have told me if we played Denver ten times, we would win seven. I know they're offering me some consolation, but the point is, this wasn't a best-of-ten series. It was a one-game championship, and we didn't want to win badly enough. The edge we needed wasn't there, not like it was the previous year. We felt we were superior, and as a result, we didn't respect our opposition enough. That's the kind of elitist thinking you can develop once you are the best, and we showed how it can hinder your performance.

Too often, success breeds the wrong priorities. Petty issues become major battles. People expect to be treated differently; they expect special favors. They fight over the closest parking spaces, the biggest office, the most perks. They adopt a selfish attitude: hey, look at me, I'm Johnny Big Shot, aren't you going to do something for me today? Shouldn't I be able to go to the front of the line? Shouldn't I get a free car or free meals? You begin hearing complaints about issues that weren't that important to anyone when you were struggling.

If companies want to stay on top, they have to quash these tendencies before they damage production. As a leader, you especially have to resist the temptations of success and keep a tight rein on your ego—after all, how can you expect your employees not to change if you do?—while continuing to run your business in the same manner that reaped rewards in the first place. You have to maintain the same priorities that got your firm in front. If people resist, you either straighten them out or terminate them. You can't afford to have anyone lose his focus and put himself ahead of what's right for the organization.

I frequently ask myself why I continue to travel as much as I do, fulfilling my scouting requirements. I'd like to pull back, but I can't. I've seen other guys fail after they backed off, and it's been a great lesson for me. Now that we're successful, I refuse to do anything differently. I don't want to chance having my selfishness hurt the organization. You've got to constantly guard against allowing a change in your priorities or the priorities of those around you to put your company at risk.

I become very angry when people's thinking falls out of whack. Soon after our Super Bowl victory, an employee came to me complaining about his bonus. It wasn't large enough, and he was offended. So I told him, "Then, just give it back and you won't be offended anymore. Then we'll make sure you don't get another bonus. That way, we won't risk offending you again." Of course, that's not what he wanted to hear. He wasn't about to give back the money. Maybe because I know what it's like to work for $60 a week or pick potatoes for next to nothing, I have an appreciation for what has happened to my life and to the Packers. People who think winning the Super Bowl entitles them to special favors, that suddenly they're owed something by the rest of the world, rub me the wrong way. I look at them as cancers that need to be eliminated.

Since we've become good, we've had complaints about everything from the cost of sodas in the soda machine—"why aren't they free?"—to who should receive Super Bowl rings to the failure of some players to buy donuts when they were scheduled. Dealing with these annoying complaints drains energy and distracts an organization from its most important tasks. To end the pettiness, you must make it clear to everyone that such nonsense won't be tolerated.

Maybe it gets to a point where the loyalty and adherence to company priorities that you expect just aren't possible anymore. Maybe there's a point where you just don't feel your voice is being heard anymore. I don't know when that happens, maybe somewhere between 10 and 15 years or so with one business. Maybe that's when it's good for everyone—you, the employees, the firm—to make a switch.

To stay on top, you have to overcome potentially damaging employee turnover in your organization. The good news about winning is that your employees are viewed with an increased respect within their industry. The bad news, at least to your firm, is that they also become more attractive to rivals, who will court them and hire them. It's almost certain that your staff will be reshuffled and that you'll suffer some major leadership hits. Your ability to remain among the best will be determined in part by how you deal with this talent drain and the looming detrimental effect it could have on your enterprise.

You'll have a better chance of absorbing the turmoil if you come to terms with two key inevitabilities created by success:

you won't be able to afford everyone, and you won't be able to accommodate everyone's employment goals.

To stay within your budget and to exhibit proper fiscal responsibility, it's impossible to become entangled in a bidding war for each employee who is enticed by another firm. You must set some priorities. Which employees will you attempt to retain through raises and added benefits? Who will you let go? The ones you want to keep should be accommodated long before any suitors come calling. When your firm achieves success, reward these employees quickly and well. Your objective to is to keep as many of your key people as possible, particularly your core leadership group. But you can't do it by procrastinating. You need to take preemptive action.

For example, we had to make a decision—do we tie up Brett Favre with a long-term contract or risk losing him to free agency so we could afford to pay a bunch of other players? We believe our future will be bright as long as Favre is our quarterback. So that's the choice we made. As our younger players improved and became more attractive to other teams, we simply didn't have enough resources to satisfy everyone else's salary demands.

The more your business is held in esteem, the more pressure you'll feel regarding personnel. It makes sense. If you have a company striving to improve, why not look to the best for great employees? For Super Bowl winners, the worst period comes during the second off-season after their victory. It happened to the Dallas Cowboys and it happened to us during the months following the 1997 season. We survived the 1996 off-season pretty well—the only free agent we attempted to keep, Desmond Howard, signed a contract with the Oakland Raiders that we decided was higher than we were willing to pay—but salary cap restraints prevented us from retaining all our post-1997 free agents. So we had to prioritize our needs.

We decided to try to re-sign receivers Robert Brooks and Antonio Freeman, linebacker Brian Williams, safety LeRoy Butler, and running back Dorsey Levens. That meant we couldn't afford new agreements for running back Edgar Bennett, cornerback Doug Evans, safety Eugene Robinson, defensive end Gabe Wilkins, and punter Craig Hentrich. To make up for those substantial losses, I've had to utilize the same tools that helped us become good in the first place: promote young players already on the roster to starting spots; draft potential starters, and rely on free agency to fill in remaining holes. Despite our personnel losses, we believe we still have enough elite players, including younger athletes who have matured under our Stepping Stone approach, to compete for a championship.

Your firm can't use a draft to improve. But as you become more successful, you should increase your recruiting efforts, putting more time and manpower into this endeavor to make sure you're consistently feeding your organization with new blood to offset the defections. You need to look ahead constantly, projecting whom you want to retain and whom you might lose. That way, you can make sure you're recruiting for the positions you'll likely need to fill in the future.

At the same time, you also must develop an ability to anticipate the market regarding potential changes in salary and benefit demands. What you think you can afford today may not be the case tomorrow, and you can't be caught off guard by shifting trends. Instead, you must stay a step ahead on these matters.

This is one of the most difficult tasks for any manager, particularly when you're within a quickly shifting marketplace that's affected by dramatic economic upturns. In these situations, when your company is churning out huge profits and your industry is growing rapidly, you can find yourself entangled in a time warp. What you once considered exceptional compensation packages for employees suddenly are just average—and the change tests your value system. Can you adapt to a situation in which you now must pay a top manager $150,000 when you once thought his position worth no more than $100,000? If you fight these trends too much, you risk having your company fall behind in the battle to retain elite employees, and that, in turn, will threaten the long-term success of your enterprise.

Everyone in the NFL is struggling with this economic tug-of-war. Increased television revenue has sent our salary cap sky-rocketing. So players are demanding more money. So you no longer can be just a talent evaluator. Instead, you need to forecast the game's financial future. If I pay Player A a huge, new contract, I have to be convinced Player A will be worth that money over the course of his agreement. Two years from now, he can't suddenly drop off. Otherwise, we're stuck with paying him even though he's no longer good enough. I especially can't allow the Packers to hand out exorbitant salaries for average players, like major league baseball does. I can't allow us to fall into a trap where, because we might need a player to fill a position, we overpay just to say, "See, we took care of that void. We did our job." Doesn't matter if the guy isn't very good or doesn't upgrade us, we did something, so that becomes enough. You see that sort of rationale in baseball all the time, and it's a way to ruin our sport.

I don't want to overpay for what I call a "slappy," a mediocre athlete who happens to be in the right place at the right time. If you add too many slappies to your firm, you'll stop winning. I've challenged myself that I can recruit the right players to maintain our status as a top franchise without settling for slappies. I see that as my responsibility to the Packers. Yet I have to weigh that quest against my charge to keep our team competitive. It violates every standard I embrace when a so-so player receives a contract worth far more than his actual value, but I can't allow the revulsion I feel over this issue to cloud my thinking to the point that I have become a detriment to the team's future.

It's a dilemma every responsible manager faces, and it becomes even more exaggerated when both the economy and your industry are healthy. You don't want to get stuck with a lot of overpaid employees with large salaries who don't live up to your expectations. Production will be threatened, and the turmoil and financial upheaval that results from correcting this nightmare stretches your budget and undermines the drive you've instilled within your firm.

The other inevitable change involving employees and success is your inability to satisfy ambition. I want my employees to grow to the point where they want, and warrant, increased responsibility and authority. The problem is, your organization can satisfy these quests for only so long. Let's say you have an employee who has become proficient enough to handle the duties of a key manager. But your current managers are entrenched, and you can't create additional top-level positions. The employee in question is not showing any disloyalty by craving someone else's job. He's just reflecting the drive you have fostered within your firm.

It's only natural that employees in this situation might look elsewhere to satisfy their professional ambitions. I won't impede their chances by refusing to let them out of their contracts. I also won't participate in a bidding war for their services. By refusing to make a counteroffer, I'm not demonstrating unhappiness with the parties in question. Rather, it reflects an acknowledgment of human nature. I don't care how well I satisfy your fiscal requirements. If you feel unfulfilled because you don't have the job title or the authority you want, you'll remain unhappy. So it's better for you to move on.

The Packers face this dilemma with Mike Holmgren. Mike has expressed an interest in becoming both coach and general manager of an organization. There's no questioning his coaching ability, and he's demonstrated a great understanding of personnel since he's been with the Packers. So I'm sure he can handle the general manager's duties. But as long as I'm at Green Bay, Mike won't run the football operation here. That's my job. So if he feels coaching no longer completely satisfies him and he wants to expand his responsibilities, he'll have to go elsewhere.

During the days leading up to Super Bowl XXXII, we had to deal with rumors that the Seattle Seahawks wanted him to be both coach and director of their football operations. Mike never had to decide whether he wanted to leave because Seattle never asked Bob Harlan for formal permission to talk to him. So it really was a nonstory.

As an organization, we had to prevent this situation from becoming an ongoing distraction. After the 1997 season, Mike had two years left on his contract, and NFL commissioner Paul Tagliabue has made it very clear he expects individuals to honor those agreements. But we chose to add a clause to Mike's contract that allows him to leave after the 1998 season as long as he accepts an offer from another team that names him both coach and general manager. In turn, the Packers will receive compensation for losing him. It makes perfect sense to me. We're recognizing the sanctity of a contract, but we're also acknowledging Mike's professional goals. We want him happy, and we want the organization happy.

I have enough confidence in my abilities that if we lose Mike, I can find a competent replacement. You can't allow your organization to become so dependent on any one individual that his departure will hamstring your ability to stay on top. Obviously, this kind of change would present difficulties. You've got a great leader, everyone is in a groove, you've developed a comfort zone, and now all that is disrupted. But I have to keep reminding myself of when I was younger. If I had a chance to better myself and someone had not helped me, I would have been furious.

I haven't been immune to the rewards of success. I was flattered by the fact the Seahawks called Bob Harlan and asked for permission around Super Bowl XXXII to talk to me about running their football operations. I thought about their request and told Bob I wasn't interested. At no time did the Seahawks make me an offer; it never got that far.

I was aware of reports that Seattle was willing to pay me substantially more than I'm presently earning. I had a problem with the image I would have presented if I interviewed and accepted the position. It would have seemed as if my services could be bought. Considering how I feel about today's player contracts and how athletes sometimes have sacrificed loyalty for a few extra bucks, I would have come off as a phony by going to Seattle. I would have allowed money to influence me. People talk about loyalty, dedication, and job opportunities, and here I am in what really and truly is the best place in football, the one situation where anyone with a sense of football history would want to be, doing my job without any interference and for a handsome compensation, and I would throw that away just for more money? The concept made me very uncomfortable.

At the same time, I'm not saying I will always be in Green Bay. I can't envision a scenario where I would leave, but it would be foolish for anyone to say never. That's the reality of the business world we all must deal with every day. The landscape changes, particularly when you're enjoying success, and you have to remain flexible enough to accommodate the new challenges that result.

To stay on top, you have to *resist* the doubters. They're out there, all right, ready to spring as soon as you show a weakness. Before Super Bowl XXXII, I had a number of flattering articles written about the Packers and me. When we lost, everything changed. The Broncos now had the right answers. We were being pressed about how we'd keep things from falling apart. One game shouldn't change everything that much, but being No. 1 is a fragile state. You can't allow yourself much celebration or enjoyment—unless you relish losing your spot quickly.

People will doubt you can be good again. You feel pressure from outside the organization—from stockholders, from commentators, from disgruntled customers. You feel pressure from inside the organization—from your leaders, from the staff. They raise issues, they pose questions, they say things that indicate they aren't sure what we're doing is quite right anymore. I refuse to be influenced by the doubters. It annoys me to read and hear criticism, but I won't allowed it to alter my thinking. Whenever you do anything as a manager, you fight doubt. When you hire a new employee, approve a large expenditure, or ratify a new agreement, you always wonder, could I be wrong? You've got to fight through the hesitation: do what you believe is right and don't give in to the skeptics.

Once you've reached the top, people will take shots at what you're doing. But you can't allow these attacks to shake your ability to make decisions. If your company suffers some erosion, whether it's because you've lost employees, failed to land some orders, or witnessed an increase in competition, you must revert to the wisdom you displayed when you were building success. Now that you're the best, you haven't suddenly lost your acumen to make the right choices. So believe in yourself more than you ever have.

Our society has evolved to a point today where it seems everyone wants the most successful people and businesses to suffer a reversal of fortune. I remember how I felt when we first started with the Packers, and no one outside the organization did anything to help us succeed. Interestingly, that attitude doesn't change once you reach the top. If anything, it gets worse. To remain the best, you can't expect any favors from anyone. People will jump on the bandwagon, hoping to benefit from your triumphs. But they aren't adding strength to your position; they just want to gain from it.

The doubters test the very foundation of everything you have worked so hard to build. When doubts arise, you can get a good read about the continuing impact of your organizational message. When life's wonderful, it's easy for employees to be loyal. But when you're challenged to stay No. 1, does their faith waiver?

After losing a number of quality free agents to free agency following the 1997 season, we know our ability to challenge again for the Super Bowl is in doubt. Doubters look at our defections; I look at our strengths. We still have the most dangerous offense in the NFL and the best quarterback. Our coaches not only can exploit that superiority in games but our organization can also use this positive situation to build up staff morale. How many defenses can successfully stop us? I daresay, not many. Plus, on defense, we have a very talented group of linebackers, two young and exciting starting cornerbacks, and one of the best safeties in the game, LeRoy Butler.

When the doubters appear, you must ensure your employees understand the reality of your situation. I'm not about to sugar-coat any problems, but this isn't the time to dwell on the negative and forget about the things we should relish. Constant internal bashing serves no useful purpose, other than killing morale and fostering a Woe-Is-Me attitude. An organization didn't become proficient by accident. Instead, it gained superiority through a relentless quest for quality. When things don't go as well as planned, that's the time to do more than fall back on your strengths. It's time to brag about them.

I view the challenges of doubters as a test, to make sure we never settle for the status quo. Just as the player with a new contract can develop a comfort zone, topflight businesses also can stop pushing themselves to improve. The organizational thinking becomes, you've reached your goal, so why disturb the chemistry and structure that got you there? Even if the Packers weren't subjected to free-agent raids, I wouldn't be content with our situation. Anytime you decide to tread water, you fall behind. You need to constantly infuse your enterprise with new looks. Despite what you might think, you're never as good as you think. If you fall prey to such self-absorption, your tumble from the top will be swift.

Even when I'm on vacation, I never stop thinking about how I can improve the Packers. I have an obligation to not only keep the organization competitive, but also to make the Packers harder to beat. Once you ease off, you'll be passed by. You're finished as an effective manager. I enjoyed our Super Bowl triumph, but not for long. I never want to develop such a sense of satisfaction that I lose the burning desire to be No. 1. In my case, just knowing people doubt my abilities to maintain excellence keeps pushing me forward.

To stay on top, you have to *master* the problem of employee loyalty vs. production. On your climb to the top, your organization has cultivated enough stability that you likely now have a number of long-term employees who have made outstanding contributions. But that doesn't automatically guarantee them a lifetime job. It's more important than ever to make sure production, and nothing else, is used as a measure of success. If sentimentality is allowed to figure too prominently into the equation, you can cut into the effectiveness of your organization.

Bill Walsh, the great former 49er coach, strove to identify those players who were nearing the end of their careers. He wanted to release them a year before it became obvious that they should retire. The better your situation becomes, the more crucial it is for you to recognize those employees who no longer can help the enterprise succeed. Then you must replace them.

The problem is, you also have to deal with the attachment that has formed between the company and the employee. Our coaches inevitably develop a fondness for certain players. These usually are the athletes who have the most impressive work habits or have persevered through the most difficult times. Even when the team's performance suffers because of these players, most coaches have difficulty cutting them. Mike Holmgren and I realize we eventually have to determine the future of our athletes. So we've tried to remain detached from them. It's harder for him because he's around them a lot more than I am, just as a division manager is a lot closer than the company president to his staff. The immediate supervisor has helped train the employee and has watched the person grow. They might even have become friends. All these factors combine to make firing difficult. Besides, if he's released, there's an unknown factor involved. Maybe his replacement won't be an improvement, so what's the point of making the change? The best interests of your company are damaged by this kind of cautious, counterproductive thinking.

I'm not immune to having special feelings for some Packers. Take Bruce Wilkerson, our veteran offensive tackle. He's just a name in the program to most people. Oh yeah, that guy from Tennessee, old what's his name. But he's a reason our game is so great. He keeps his mouth shut, he fulfills his assignments, he performs with great pride and dedication, and he does it all exceptionally well. He's the consummate pro in a sport that needs more of his kind. And what can we do for him? Well, before free agency, we could reward loyalty by keeping a guy an extra year, paying him his full salary, and allowing him to prepare for life after football. But, because of salary cap restrictions, we now pay him the minimum—and we can't afford to give him an extra year. That's his reward. It's a darn shame, but that's the way the system is constructed. During my time in Green Bay, he's one of the guys that I'm proud to have known.

Loyalty can't and shouldn't be ignored. I'm saddened to see the deterioration of loyalty between organizations and players. Free agency has destroyed this link. Kids growing up no longer can feel comfortable rooting for a player from their favorite team; odds are, he'll move to another club or two before his career is over. That eliminates one of the great attractions sports has had for all of us. We don't have the opportunity we once did to cultivate our athletic heroes. We root for franchises as a whole, but we never know what uniform this year's stars will wear next season. This player movement takes something away from our game.

I can't blame players for wanting to excel financially. My argument with them starts when an athlete switches to a lesser team for a small raise. It seems to me this is when loyalty should play a larger role in his thinking than it does.

At the same time, you can't allow sentimentality to outweigh production. I see it all the time in sports. Great teams that don't constantly churn their roster, adding and deleting as warranted, fall from the top quickly. It takes courage to make the hard personnel decisions, no matter your business, but you have to do it. In our case, if a guy can't play, it's done. He's gone. He may be able to play for someone else, but not for us. Sometimes, as was the case with safety Eugene Robinson following the 1997 season, we want the player to take on a reduced role as a backup. That proposal didn't appeal to Eugene, who eventually signed as a free agent with the Atlanta Falcons.

It's much easier to make the tough personnel decision while your company is growing rather than once you've reached your goals. Yet the moment you start procrastinating or become too influenced by sentiments that aren't directly related to production, you begin to introduce the wrong priorities into your system. If you try to win a popularity contest instead of doing what's right for your organization, you're severely hindering your chances of staying strong.

During the months following our Super Bowl victory, we decided we needed to make a change with our kicker, Chris Jacke. He was the leading scorer on our championship squad, and he had enjoyed productive years for the Packers. But we were convinced as an organization that his best years had passed. In 1996, his accuracy percentage was in the lower third of league kickers, and that wasn't good enough. If we kept him around, we felt our ability to win would suffer. So we didn't bring him back for 1997. I saw a way to improve our team, and I had to make sure I judged Jacke on his recent performance, not on his longtime status as a Packer. I used production as my guide, and he hadn't produced.

His departure shocked our fans, who considered him untouchable, and it created a storm of controversy that didn't die down all season. Some of the debate was fanned by the fact rookie Brett Conway, our 1997 third-round pick, hurt his leg in training camp and couldn't kick. But his replacement, a rookie street free agent named Ryan Longwell, had a fine season, exceeding what we thought Jacke would produce. So we upgraded that position. Jacke became a Pittsburgh Steeler, then was hurt and got cut. Even after he healed, he remained unsigned until the last weeks of the season, when he was picked up by the Redskins, then released. Obviously, the rest of the league didn't think much of his abilities either. As an organization, we made a difficult, unpopular decision that worked. And that's all that matters.

If these choices eliminate complacency, so much the better. It's worth risking some internal unhappiness to keep everyone alert. Your company will benefit because you reduced the chances of employees resting on their accomplishments and curtailing production. After the Jacke episode, I would think very few Packers felt completely secure. And that's fine.

To stay on top, you have to *raise* your standards. What was good enough to propel you to the front isn't good enough anymore to keep you there. We learned that lesson all too well in Super Bowl XXXII. We came into the game as the hottest team in football and played decently. But it wasn't sufficient. We know now that, if we hope to prevail when faced with a similar challenge in the future, we have to raise our performance to a higher level.

No matter if you think you're already demanding enough of yourself and your organization, there's room for improvement. You must ask for additional dedication and production. What sufficed in years past no longer can be used as today's measurement—or tomorrow's. Instead, you must set new goals to refocus priorities. Raise the bar and push everyone to upgrade their performances.

Here's an example. I once thought if we could hit .200 every year as far as adding new talent to our roster, we'd be doing a good job. That meant for every ten new players we viewed as potential additions, two had to make the roster. Not anymore. Now, we had better hit .300 or higher if we want to stay competitive. Our needs have changed, so our standards have been changed. Same with the draft. Before free agency, you could pick the best available athletes and not be as concerned about immediate roster problems. Now, if we have the normal seven selections, I feel we have to come away from every draft with at least three, if not four, potential starters—and they need to move into the lineup within a couple of years, if not sooner. We can't wait anymore for them to develop over four or five years. Without enough good young players, we're cutting into the Stepping Stone approach. We won't have new faces ready to replace veteran players as they are phased out or sign with another team.

Previously, you also could take shots with the draft. By that,

I mean you could gamble a bit and make some risky picks. In the late rounds, you could choose a track guy or a basketball player or some athlete with hardly any experience who had a glimmer of potential. Do that now and you're wasting a valuable selection. The risky choices have become street free agents. We've had to adapt. But it's the only way to remain No. 1.

Managers who want to stay on top have an obligation to their organization to *implement* innovations in their industry. Otherwise, they weaken the chances of the firm to remain among the elite. This means networking takes on even more importance. You absolutely have to cultivate trustworthy sources both inside and outside your field. They serve as your sounding board and your warning system. You also have to read a lot. Every day I scan newspaper clippings about every team in the league. I want to know everything I can about the football business and what people in my industry are thinking, whether they're players or executives. I need this information so I'm not surprised by developments.

I also must be willing to implement whatever it takes to make sure my organization is a leader, whether that means embracing new technological trends or making adjustments in the way we spend money or how we recruit personnel. One of my most difficult challenges is to refrain from using these words: "That's the way we've always done it, and it has worked." What worked yesterday may not work anymore, and you have to be open-minded enough to understand that. When you've seen certain procedures create success, you rightfully develop a deep attachment and loyalty to them. After all, you made your company into a winner applying these principles. But if the landscape around you calls for different approaches and you either can't see the changes or refuse to adapt them, your enterprise can't continue to excel.

For years, I've struggled with the increasing specialization in football. When I first became a scout, the game was far less complicated. There weren't a lot of substitutions, and players prided themselves on their durability. Gradually, all that has evolved. Rosters have increased from 33 players to 45 on game day. Coaches have developed specialists—third-down receivers, third-down runners, third-down linebackers, different secondary packages according to down and distance. Teams now have one player who snaps on punts and field goals and does little else. Another only returns kicks. For a long time, I was convinced that if a franchise could develop as many players as possible who didn't need to be replaced by specialists it would have a decided advantage. And that was my aim with the Packers.

By studying the league, I've now seen that specialization works better than I thought, particularly with the kicking game. If we want to stay competitive, I have to refine my thinking. It doesn't matter one iota if I believe these changes aren't necessarily good for the sport. The only thing that matters is that the Packers don't fall behind. If we must have one person who snaps and another specialist who holds and a third who return kicks, we'll do it. In your business, you need to make sure you don't allow your personal biases to interfere with the evolution of changes within your industry. Otherwise, it will impede your progress.

To stay on top, you must *communicate* more openly within your organization than ever before. To become the best, you have to develop excellent internal communications. To maintain your elite status, it's essential to encourage even better discussions. You want to cultivate new ideas, helpful innovations, and great notions that will keep you ahead of the pack. As a manager, you need to do even more to nourish an open give-and-take, so everyone feels they're part of the ongoing process to improve the firm's effectiveness. All the petty stuff I mentioned earlier can shut down communication, kill morale, and create little fiefdoms within an organization, where turf battles become more important than production. To prevent these negative situations from happening, you have to keep the discussion process flowing.

Mike Holmgren and I have worked hard to keep our lines of communication open. We understand each other better now than ever. We're smart enough to know that, no matter the success we've enjoyed, neither of us can do this alone. That's the feeling of unity and togetherness that you must continue to foster within your enterprise. Once you're on top, you must guard against allowing this company-wide feeling of cooperation to diminish into selfish compartments. You've heard the complaint: Joe over there in the corner office isn't nearly as accessible as he used to be, now that we're flourishing as a firm and he's had a promotion and a salary increase. I intentionally keep our organization lean. I don't want layers of bureaucracy to bog down communication and make it more difficult for top management to understand what's happening throughout the company. I don't care if other quality organizations in the NFL have larger front-office staffs. I'm in this to win, not to match expenditures with my peers.

In all our years together, I've only insisted that Mike keep one player, which I think is pretty remarkable, considering the huge number of athletes we've discussed. But that incident has bothered me ever since because it violated how I should conduct business with Mike. Yet, despite that episode, we continue to agree on a philosophy regarding player cuts, and that's helped the Packers maintain our excellence. We still have one overriding criterion regarding our roster: if the player makes us better, he stays—and if he doesn't, he goes. Neither one of us has become more protective of our own area. The Packers, more than the individual, are what's important to us.

Good communication also includes a willingness to analyze your actions. Any organization that has become successful has done an excellent job of reviewing its decisions, learning from them, and then improving. Once you've become the best, you must guard against shutting down this quest to examine yourself and learn from everything, regardless of its outcome. Just because you're good, you can never think you know all the answers. I've been amazed by how much smarter some people within our organization have become since we won Super Bowl XXXI. Their knowledge has increased tenfold, and you wonder how it happens. Winning can do that to people. Obviously, employees of companies that have achieved success should consider themselves talented. The firm couldn't have grown without their contributions. But no one has magic answers to any of this. There's no substitution for hard work, determination, and constant self-examination.

Coaches and players are quoted all the time saying they never watch tapes of a big game that they didn't win or of an important play that they botched. I know it hurts to review bad moments, but when things are most difficult, you must ignore the temptation to back off from an intelligent, methodical, internal evaluation. Everyone has to be willing to improve; you can't allow anyone to develop a "know-it-all" attitude or have anyone dismiss a setback as merely an aberration, and not an indication of a company's weakness. Analyze what went wrong first before you reach any conclusions.

I made myself watch a tape of Super Bowl XXXII. I wanted to satisfy my curiosity about why we lost, about what I could have done differently to help us win, about why we didn't play as well as we had hoped. It's easy to blame a specific player or a specific play, but that's not what I'm after. What I want are the answers that can make us more formidable next year—and make us unbeatable the next time we're involved in a big game.

Any successful business that suffers a similar major reversal has to follow this kind of approach. If a key client pulls his business or you fail to land a substantial order or you fall short of budget because of internal production breakdowns, you've got to work your way through the immediate reactions, whether they be anger, self-pity, or depression—and then do whatever study is necessary to help prevent a repeat of the failure.

After completing my analysis of Super Bowl XXXII, I certainly don't think the loss means we've become a less competent organization. Until proven otherwise, we remain one of the two best teams in the NFL. The loss is not a refutation of our methods, nor an indication we don't have the answers anymore. What I can't allow—and what you can't allow when your organization stumbles and confidence is shaken—is for this crushing disappointment to turn into a long-term funk. If a manager fails to find ways to help his business shake off these tumultuous events, he'll never be able to maintain the firm's elite status.

I expanded my analysis of the 1997 Packers to also include our 1996 team. I thought our 1997 squad could compensate for the loss of tight end Keith Jackson and defensive end Sean Jones, both of whom retired following our Super Bowl triumph. But we never replaced their talents or their leadership. That's a major reason why I think our 1996 team was better, even though both clubs finished with the same 13–3 record. Plus, we never compensated for the absence of Desmond Howard; our return game in 1997 was poor compared to 1996. I wanted a return man who could play another position; I was wrong and I've learned. Now, I'll be more apt to carry someone who only returns kicks. I also could have worked harder to bolster our defensive line depth. But my study convinced me we don't have fundamental flaws in our organization or in our team that will keep us from competing again at a high level. And that's a relief to our entire operation.

You always hear that the biggest burden of being No. 1 is the pressure this role generates. Certainly, the 1997 season—and the Super Bowl loss—taught us that what you hear is right. Everyone wants to knock you off, so you must perform at your best all the time. You can't let up. If you do, you risk losing your position. Your margin of error has been reduced and, to a large extent, the carefree, let-it-all-hang-out attitude that carried you as a pretender is replaced by a more pressurized, more demanding atmosphere. As an organization, you have to understand how your world has changed and make the necessary adjustments.

Once you're on top, you also realize others are studying your methods, copying them, and finding ways to execute them even better. You always must remember that no one is ever content to let you stay No. 1. Their every moment is spent figuring out how to unseat you—just as you once were scratching to become the best. I never want to put us in a position where we have to react instead of dictate. To accomplish this goal, you must remain flexible and bold.

For example, if the personnel strengths of future Packer teams indicate we need to change schemes, then we have to be open enough to accept that reality. If we don't have enough defensive linemen to play a 4–3 scheme that calls for four linemen and three linebackers, but have enough linebackers to play a 3–4, with four linebackers and three linemen, then that's what we should do, even if we used the 4–3 in two Super Bowls. Opponents are counting on your predictability, so be as unpredictable and feisty as possible.

I look back with great satisfaction at the effort and sacrifices so many people made over the years to allow the Packer Way to work. We've proven that if you follow the first eight Stepping Stones, your organization can become a winner. Now we're determined to utilize the lessons I've outlined throughout the ninth Stepping Stone—Staying on Top—to ultimately win another Super Bowl.

That's become the marching orders of this organization, just as it should be the challenge of any business that won't settle for anything less than the best. Our mission statement from now on is this: we want to meet our challenge head on and show we're smart enough and talented enough and experienced enough to once again be on top.

Like I said, I hate to lose. And I always will.

Here are the prominent points you should remember from Stepping Stone No. 9—Staying on Top:

• As your organization achieves success, you're presented with a new set of challenges and issues that must be solved to remain among the elite.

• More than anything else, you have to *want* to stay the best. Successful organizations that believe they're as good as everyone says they are either forget or neglect what made them successful in the first place, the four C's (certain devotion, certain dedication, certain work ethic, and certain results).

• Too often, success breeds the wrong priorities. Petty issues become major battles. If companies want to stay on top, they have to prevent these negatives from damaging morale or the decision-making process.

• As a leader, you have to resist the temptations of success and keep a rein on your ego. You can't afford to have anyone lose their focus and put themselves ahead of what's right for the organization.

• To offset the personnel losses that usually accompany success, you must increase your recruiting efforts, putting more time and manpower into this endeavor to make sure you're consistently feeding your organization with new blood to make up for the defections.

• Execute whatever financial steps you must to retain your key personnel, becoming proactive in this area instead of reacting when another company begins courting their services. To be proactive financially, you must develop an ability to anticipate the market regarding potential changes in salary and benefit demands.

• Don't impede the ambitions of your best employees by refusing to let them out of their contracts when other companies want to hire them, or by becoming involved in a bidding war for their services.

• You can't allow your organization to become so dependent on any one individual that his loss will hamstring your ability to be the best.

• Regard the challenges of doubters as a test, to make sure you never settle for the status quo.

• Just as the player with the new contract can develop a comfort zone, topflight businesses can also stop pushing themselves to improve. Anytime you decide to tread water, you fall behind.

• When you're successful, it's more important than ever to base personnel decisions on production, and not on sentimentality or loyalty.

• To stay on top, raise your standards. What was good enough to propel you to the front isn't good enough anymore to keep you there.

• If changing business trends call for different approaches and you either can't recognize the changes or refuse to adapt to them, your company can't continue to excel.

• Communicate within your organization more openly than ever before. You want to cultivate new ideas, helpful innovations, and great notions that will keep you ahead of the pack.

• Continue to analyze your decisions. Once you're the best, you need to guard against shutting down this quest to learn from both your successes and failures.

Epilogue

I've worked thirty-six years in pro football, trying to figure out guidelines that will bring stability and consistency to my job. I ultimately settled on the Nine Stepping Stones that I've outlined in the previous chapters. Now those Stepping Stones will be put to a challenging test as the Packers embark on a new journey without Mike Holmgren.

Whenever continuity is disrupted, your organization's ability not only to survive but also to advance is based strictly on the strength that you have established with your management style. . . . People's lives have been disrupted. Changes have been made. New faces now occupy familiar offices. Leaders have left; others have arrived to take their places. The comfort zone that surrounds all successful organizations— and the Packers have proven to be a successful organization—is punctured. There are questions that need answering, roles that have to be filled, voids that must be occupied. Those under you look to you for information, for constancy, for rock-solid demonstrations that we are still striving to get better, not just hoping to hold our own.

This is when leadership counts the most. Anyone can lead when things are rolling along fine, when productivity is high, and the cash flow is exceeding expectations and raises are abundant, and the competition is viewing you from behind. You need only to keep nudging things along, making sure everything and everyone stays on the right track. It is like putting your business on cruise control and sitting back and reaping the benefits.

But it is when your endeavor suddenly is not as successful as it has been that your leadership skills are tested thoroughly. You look at yourself and you ask, have I lost my edge? Do I still have what it takes to make this business work? Can I help us regain our dominant position? Can I bring back normalcy and the feel-good atmosphere that surrounds any ultrasuccessful enterprise? Can I get us back to where we were—and where we want to be?

That is why the Nine Stepping Stones have taken on even more importance for the Green Bay Packers. I don't have to spend my time trying to devise ways of getting us back on track as a franchise. Those paths are already in place. They've been tested, refined, and proven. Now, we just have to follow them and make them work again.

Losing Mike after last season was not a surprise. Although he never once said he did not want to coach the Packers, he made it clear he would welcome the challenge of a more complex job that included control over personnel. It was obvious to me that, after the 1998 season, if he was offered control of a team's football organization, he would jump at the opportunity. We had already acknowledged that possibility by specifying a clause in his original contract with the Packers, which allowed him to leave for this kind of position in exchange for a second-round draft choice. As last season unfolded, I reconciled myself to the fact that he was leaving. He never backed off his statement about being intrigued by more responsibility, and it was obvious to me that no matter how much we paid him, we couldn't satisfy his new job quest.

I guess I could have left or changed to a new position within the organization. If I had done either, he might have stayed. But I never considered those options, nor did anyone within the Packers ever suggest these alternatives. I want to stay in football. I remain challenged by what I am doing and energized by the potential that I see within our organization to reaffirm the Packers' status as the best team and franchise in football.

Of course, not having Mike would be a significant loss. Besides trading for Brett Favre, hiring Mike was the most telling addition I made to the Packers in my first months in charge of the football operations. He had never been a head coach before, but it was soon obvious he was a natural for the position. We quickly meshed as a team, and I am proud to say we never had an argument over personnel matters.

More than anything, he was a brilliant coach. A masterful offensive strategist and strong leader, he brought discipline and toughness to the team. As we upgraded the talent, he accelerated our progress and soon turned us into contenders. His work with Brett Favre will rank as one of the finest coaching jobs in league history. He took a raw talent, demanded excellence, and wound up with a player I think eventually could be viewed as one of the best ever to play that position. Of course, the culmination of all of our efforts came when we won Super Bowl XXXI.

But despite Mike's importance to the team, I was determined to prevent his departure to the Seattle Seahawks from becoming a watershed moment in the history of the Packers. No question, he was an integral part of our success. But an organization has to be strong enough, and deep enough, to absorb even the loss of one of its elite leaders. You either must have capable replacements waiting within the organization, or you must already have identified worthy candidates from the outside who can step in and keep your business running smoothly.

I understood that if Mike left we also might see the departure of others from our organization. We employ very talented people and it would be only natural that Mike would want to take some of them to Seattle. And that is what he did. Along with the bulk of his coaching staff, joining Mike with the Seahawks were Mike Reinfeldt, our vice president of administration and primary contract negotiator, and John Dorsey, our director of college scouting. Although both Reinfeldt and Dorsey excel at what they do, I was comfortable we could replace them quickly. And we did.

As I discussed at length in Chapter Two, Hire the Best—Before Anyone Else Does, the smart executive has a ready list prepared, filled with names of people he feels are qualified to replace departed leaders. It is far too late to be compiling this kind of list when you discover someone is leaving. That is when you have to deal with too much turmoil and emotion to make wise decisions. When things are calmer, you are much more able to sort through potential candidates, explore their backgrounds, and become familiar with those who are most appealing.

I followed my own advice with Holmgren's replacement. Once the 1998 season started, it took me about a month to come to terms with the fact this would be Mike's last year in Green Bay. He hadn't said it would be, and he obviously had not conducted any discussions with other teams. But my gut told me it was over. We would do what any organization should do with a talented executive like Mike—we would make him an offer we hoped he wouldn't refuse—but I also recognized I could never negotiate against the kind of job opportunity Mike was seeking. So instead of holding out hollow hope that something would change and he would return, I began work figuring out who would succeed him as coach.

I immediately started increasing my game observations. By that, I mean I paid more attention during games than I usually do to how other coaches worked, how they approached their job, how their players seemed to respond. Of course, I couldn't have contact with anyone, and didn't, but that doesn't prevent you from filing away information that you can check later when you are making final decisions.

I also spent more time in my office than I normally would, preparing myself for this coaching change. Instead of following my normal scouting routine during the season, I decided it was more important to curtail my travel and focus on what would be an enormously important decision for the future of the franchise. It was a wise choice. During my scouting excursions, I found myself becoming an instant evaluator. Instead of thoroughly scouting a prospect, I was thinking too much about the coaching situation and not enough about my other duties. I was short-changing the scouting process and making hasty judgments. And that isn't desirable.

It becomes a matter of priorities. You need to figure out, given all the tugs on your time, what items demand, and deserve, the most attention. I would rather concentrate on a few vital areas and delegate other responsibilities to my associates. It would be harmful to the Packers, and to my personal mental well-being, to spread myself so thin that nothing was done as thoroughly or effectively as I felt necessary.

So coaching became my focus. When I hired Mike, I had studied the league and determined that we had a better chance for success if we brought in an offensive-minded coach. It was a trend that had worked pretty successfully through the rest of the league, and Mike's record as coach was a validation of this trend. But in the seven years since he came to Green Bay, our situation had changed.

As a manager, I have an obligation to my organization to analyze our current needs and not get caught in the past. If you aren't constantly analyzing your situation, and figuring out strengths and weaknesses and needs, you can easily find yourself confronted with problems you could have avoided with due diligence. Both your internal situation and the world around you are constantly changing. You can never rest on your laurels; you can never believe you know all the answers; you can never accept the fact that you have outsmarted the opposition. If you fall prey to any or all of these potential traps, you and your business will suffer.

In my analysis of our situation and our needs, I became convinced that we required a coach with head-coaching experience. We had a veteran team capable of great things, so this was not the time or place to bring in someone without experience and conduct on-the-job training. We had to have someone who understood the role of a head coach, had managed the time demands, had been through the organization of training camps and practice schedules, who understood squad composition and player cuts, who had dealt with media demands. The job is incredibly time consuming and has many more distractions than people probably realize. You can learn how to be a head coach, but that takes time, and that is one thing I felt we couldn't afford to waste.

I believe sincerely that there are right people for particular situations. My study of the Civil War, particularly of the generals who led both armies, has convinced me of that. You can win wars, and football games and business battles, by making the right leadership choices. Sometimes, you need a gentle, guiding hand, someone who can develop an enterprise and teach the inexperienced and bring stability and calmness to the situation. Other times, you need a more experienced touch, a motivator, a no-nonsense personality who can push and shove and produce performances beyond anticipation.

We needed a motivator and a prodder, with extensive experience. That narrowed my list considerably. I was aware that Ray Rhodes, who had been Mike's first defensive coordinator in Green Bay, was under fire as the Eagles head coach last season. I also knew that unless the Eagles let him go, I would not approach him about our job. Yet, if he came free, he automatically would climb to the top of my list. Rhodes is a tough, tough guy who can motivate and get players to play very hard for him. He also was in his fourth year as a head coach, so he had plenty of experience.

I realized it would be a potentially controversial hire. After being named 1995 Coach of the Year with the Eagles, his teams had struggled the last few seasons. I knew there would be questions about his ability to produce a winner, but I don't believe that a great leader suddenly loses the ability to lead. Maybe the situation around him was not conducive to winning; maybe we could give him better support in Green Bay, including better players. With us, he could coach, and we would handle the personnel aspect, with his input. This would allow him to focus on coaching, which, I'm convinced, is what he does best.

Still, as long as Ray was employed by the Eagles, I had to make sure I had alternatives. But I never had to talk to anyone else. Once the season ended, his relationship with Philadelphia was terminated. As soon as it became apparent that our head coaching position was vacant, I called him immediately and flew to meet with him. We talked for maybe five hours. The fact that I knew him—he had been with the Packers for two years before leaving to join the 49ers staff—helped. But that wasn't enough to get him the job.

We went through all types of scenarios. We brought up all the pertinent issues, all the touchy subjects, the fact that he hadn't been a successful head coach the last two seasons, the fact that some members of his family hadn't been happy in Green Bay. We brought up all these issues to make sure we could work them out and to see if we were compatible. You aren't doing your job, or protecting your company, if you avoid the tough subjects. Nor are you being fair to the prospective employee. You need to know his answers to these tough questions, and you need to know how he will deal with any subsequent discussion of these topics, particularly if he is in the public realm. You want no surprises with any hire, particularly one so important as a leader.

Ray, to his credit, didn't duck responsibility about what happened in Philadelphia. He outlined the various problems he had, and I found his answers acceptable. But past problems were not the main topic of our discussion. The interview was about finding someone who had the ability to be a very successful head coach—if given the proper tools to work with. And I am not sure he had those in Philadelphia. But he would in Green Bay.

I came away from our meeting feeling we would be compatible. I felt he could win. That is the key thing. And I felt he could move the team in the direction we wanted to go.

I told Ray we have to get back to playing the type of football we are capable of playing, considering the quality of the players we have. We have a lot of good players filling a lot of positions, and it is up to our coach and his staff to make them perform up to their capabilities. We have to recapture our toughness and swagger, which we kind of lost last year.

I define toughness in this fashion: It is the plain ability to stand up and play, stand up and be accountable and be accounted for. There were some times last year when teams were giving us stuff and we weren't capable of taking it. That is lack of toughness. We were a better team last year than we showed, despite the injuries and everything else that happened. We underachieved and that annoys me, because you don't get many opportunities to take advantage of greatness, and we wasted one.

We should have gone further. Although a lot of franchises would have been satisfied with an 11–5 record and a playoff spot, that is not good enough for us anymore. We need to find a way to play better, to get everything out of the talent we have and return to the top. That is the challenge facing Ray Rhodes.

It will be different without Mike, no question. Over a seven-year period, you grow accustomed to someone's personality and style. He made a huge impact on this franchise and on this team. But Ray brings a different feel, a new perspective. Ray can be earthy and funny and forceful. Much more than Mike, he will walk into the locker room and mingle with his players, maybe even sit down to play dominoes with them. Not that Mike's approach didn't work; it's just that each person has a different style. Your own organization has to be broad enough and intelligent enough to accommodate such differences, as long as they produce results.

I don't feel pressure to win without Mike, and I certainly hope Ray doesn't feel an extra burden either. I know people will look at this period as the post-Holmgren years, and they will wonder how his departure will affect us. Quite frankly, I am not sure I agree that there should be added scrutiny just because Mike left. Our organization has to be strong enough to absorb departures and still be able to excel.

In Chapter Nine, I discussed the methods of Staying on Top. That task has proved more daunting than I anticipated. No matter how many times people tell you that once you are No. 1, others will begin to strip away your talent, deplete your depth, and weaken your chances of remaining the best, you really don't believe them. You have the self-confidence to convince yourself that it won't happen, that you are smart enough and experienced enough to overcome the obstacles and the raids and remain the frontrunner.

But it is a difficult, difficult challenge. "To strip away your talent" doesn't just refer to the loss of players; it also means being forced into personnel moves that you may not want to make but have to in order to keep a roster pieced together.

For example, after the 1997 season, we lost cornerback Doug Evans to free agency. He signed with the Carolina Panthers. We thought that through the draft and our own free agency moves, we could still enter the 1998 season with four quality cornerbacks. We knew our starting corner situation, with Craig Newsome and Tyrone Williams, would be solid. But in this era of football, you need four corners to neutralize multi-receiver formations. As long as our starters stayed healthy, we were okay. But as soon as one went down, we quickly realized we didn't have a top-notch third corner. Instead, we had to move over free safety Darren Sharper, who was in his first year as a starter. His switch weakened the safety position and prevented him from settling into his new position, which, in turn, hindered his development.

Our attempts to add depth at corner just didn't work out. We didn't get any help through the draft, as we had hoped, and the veteran free agents we brought in never played as well as we wanted. So we had a giant hole, brought on by the stripping of talent. When we played teams like the Vikings, with their depth at receiver, we had trouble matching up correctly, particularly if we went into the game with injuries in the secondary.

We also didn't handle the loss to Denver in Super Bowl XXXII as well as we should have, either from a player or from a team standpoint. I thought we could absorb the loss, learn from it, and move on. But the moving on became difficult. I saw too many quotes from players talking about how we had lost some of the magic that we had during the 1996 season. My feeling is, you wouldn't be saying that if you got over the loss quickly. It was the same with the organization. The shock and hurt lingered and lingered and affected how we handled things the next two years.

I'm disappointed by how we have dealt with the last two years.

When you win the Super Bowl, you don't expect that within two seasons, you can't win your division. And that is what happened to us in 1998 when the Vikings took the NFC Central title. I look at our team, and I see the talent we still have, and I want better. I would have expected to have won more than one Super Bowl, and that saddens me. It reinforces the lesson I tell everyone around here, a lesson you hear all the time in sports and in business—a lesson that the naïve pay no attention to: When you have a chance to be the best, you'd better do everything it takes to get there because you may not have the opportunity again.

If I had gone into the locker room after we beat the Patriots to win Super Bowl XXXI and told the players that within two years, Mike would be gone and we wouldn't even be the best team in our division, they would have laughed me out of the place. When you are giddy with victory, it is tough to seriously contemplate the downside of success. But you must.

That's why, when you have a chance to complete business deals that are sound, even if it means stretching your resources and taking a calculated risk, you have to pull the trigger. You can't sit there and say, I'll pass on this one and maybe next time I'll like my opportunity better. There may never be a next time, so you'd better jump when you have the chance.

At the same time, you must learn from all these experiences. Otherwise, you aren't attempting to grow as a manager. I have two alternatives when confronted with disappointment: I can sulk and not learn, or I can analyze and improve. I think we have done the latter. Our goal is to get things flowing again and not commit the same mistakes twice.

Here's what I mean. After the 1997 season, we decided not to re-sign Eugene Robinson, our veteran free safety. We had Darren Sharper ready to step in as starter, and it seemed like the right time to make the change. We just didn't think Robinson could play effectively at our level anymore. We thought he was done as a player. We were wrong.

Maybe if we hadn't had the cornerback injuries and Darren

didn't have to move so much from one position to another, the secondary would have been more settled. But the reality is, he did have to keep jumping, and it left things unsteady. If we had retained Robinson, even in a back-up role, he would have been available to take over for Sharper and our secondary would have maintained some steadiness.

We also missed his leadership, particularly in the locker room. You should never underestimate the importance of these role players among their peers, whether it is with a sports team or in an office environment. What Eugene brought to the table as a leader wasn't adequately replaced in 1998, and we could have used it.

The important lesson I learned as a manager from the Robinson episode is: When you consider terminating a veteran employee, you must ask yourself, "Do we have him adequately replaced?" Others in the organization assured me we did. But next time, I will be more diligent in my pursuit of that answer. If I'm unconvinced, then I won't be in as much of a hurry to get rid of him. You drag your feet more and work to put yourself in a better situation to make the move that you know eventually will have to come.

At the same time, you have to acknowledge to yourself that you aren't perfect. If you were, this wouldn't be any fun. Management consists of a series of ongoing choices, and making the right selections from among all those choices determines your success. It's not supposed to be easy. Still, you can never allow yourself to become gun shy. You have to be resolute in your decision-making and not pull back because of past mistakes. If you become hesitant, then suddenly you never can make a decision. Instead, you go with the flow, you worry about what outsiders are going to say and nothing happens to help your endeavor. You can't operate that way.

The great thing about business, particularly mine, is that if you are able to stay in it long enough, you can benefit from your past mistakes. You become emotional about your players, about games, about plays. You get attached to the players who helped make you successful. You have to be careful to remain objective enough to make clear decisions. And you have to continue to work hard; you can never stop plugging away. And you have to watch that those under you don't stop either. Maybe success has spoiled them, maybe they aren't working as diligently as they once did, even though they think they are. Maybe they now have less patience and want to hire folks who understand things quicker or better, rather than wanting to spend the time teaching and training. You can never allow this to happen. Never.

Nor can you feel sorry for yourself. In 1998, five players broke their legs, including running back Dorsey Levens, one of the keys to any success we anticipated. Our running backs were wiped out by these leg injuries. I told Mike Holmgren that he could coach for another twenty years and never duplicate this type of injury problem. Did these injuries contribute to the fact that we lost the division title to the Vikings and then our playoff game to the 49ers? Undoubtedly. But if we allow ourselves to use these excuses to explain away our failure to achieve our goal, which is to win a Super Bowl, we become soft. Maybe it wasn't fair to have so many broken legs, but you can't exist in a world of what ifs and could haves and would have beens.

Entering last season, I thought we had done a pretty good job of setting up the team for a title run. Coming off the 1997 season, which ended with the Super Bowl loss to Denver, we knew we had to strengthen our defensive line. We also were hoping that Reggie White, who was contemplating retirement, would play another season. He finally decided to do just that, and we used the draft and free agency to complement him with more line quality and depth.

Our most significant move was made in the April 1998 draft. We entered that draft with the twenty-ninth pick in the first round. I didn't think we could help ourselves on defense with that choice, and worrying about it kept me from sleeping very well the night before the draft. I got to the office early on draft morning and was sitting at my desk when the phone rang. It was ESPN commentator Chris Mortensen, who was in Miami.

He told me Dolphin coach Jimmy Johnson already was in his office too. So I decided to call Jimmy. I asked him if he wanted to do any dealing. He said he wouldn't mind. He would trade his nineteenth pick in the first round for our twenty-ninth if we tossed in a second-round choice. I told him I would call back in five minutes.

I walked the halls, looking for someone to talk to. I found Bob Harlan, our president, and explained the deal to him, and he said it was okay with him. I called Jimmy and we agreed. By then, Mike Holmgren had arrived, and he also signed off on the trade. Now I thought we could get a defensive back, Shaun Williams, at nineteen. But as the first round unfolded, defensive end Vonnie Holliday from North Carolina kept dropping. I was surprised. I thought he was a top-ten prospect. He was still left at nineteen, and we never hesitated to take him. He wound up as the second-best rookie last season, right behind Randy Moss. It was as if we had received a gift from the football gods.

A lot of general managers won't trade in the draft. But that is counter to my philosophy. When the game is over—whether it is the draft or on Sunday afternoon—I want all twelve cartridges used up. I don't want six left to be fired. I want to come after people, whether it means moving up in the first round or going after quarterbacks on defense. I believe football is an aggressive game and you have to knock the other person down. No guts, no glory. It is that simple.

But it is becoming harder than ever to persuade teams to trade. I understood that fact even more clearly following the 1999 draft. We had the twenty-fifth pick in the first round, and I would have loved to have moved up much higher, so we could have chosen receiver David Boston. But I didn't want to give up future draft selections, so I didn't have enough ammunition to maneuver. We wound up staying put and got a quality player, cornerback Antuan Edwards of Clemson. I went into that draft determined to strengthen our secondary, so we would not face a repeat of our 1998 season problems in the defensive backfield. We wound up picking four defensive backs, and I feel comfortable that we have gone a long way toward neutralizing our deficiencies.

I remain confident that we will improve upon our performance of last season. We have a formidable team, built around an offense that features the best quarterback in football, Brett Favre. Dorsey Levens should be healthy, and I am excited about our offensive line and about what Ray Rhodes and his defensive coordinator, Emmitt Thomas, will do with our defense. Our new offensive coordinator, Sherm Lewis, will have a chance to call plays full-time, and it will be exciting to watch how he attacks defenses.

I am also confident that the Stepping Stones that we have established within the organization will allow us to flourish. We have absorbed the changes of the past months very well and are functioning at an efficient, productive level. Ray Rhodes and his staff have settled in and quickly gotten a good handle on the players they inherited and the team they will direct.

I will never be satisfied until we win another Super Bowl. I see no reason why we can't make a serious run at the championship. That's our desire and our goal, and none of us will ever work for anything less. You, too, should want to be the best. Believe me, there is nothing else like it in the world.